MW00335618

Aztec and Maya Apocalypses

Aztec
and
Maya Apocalypses

*Old World Tales of Doom
in a New World Setting*

Mark Z. Christensen

UNIVERSITY OF OKLAHOMA PRESS : NORMAN

Publication of this book is make possible through the generosity of Edith Kinney Gaylord.

Portions of chapter 3 and 5 were previously published in Mark Z. Christensen, *The Teabo Manuscript: Maya Christian Copybooks, Chilam Balams, and Native Text Production in Yucatán* (Austin: University of Texas Press, 2016).

Library of Congress Cataloging-in-Publication Data

Names: Christensen, Mark Z., author.
Title: Aztec and Maya apocalypses : old world tales of doom in a new world setting / Mark Z. Christensen.
Description: Norman : University of Oklahoma Press, 2022. | Includes bibliographical references and index. | Summary: "Analyzes Spanish Catholic priests' 'official' ecclesiastical texts and Indigenous authors' rendering of those texts from the sixteenth to the early nineteenth century in order to trace European and Indigenous influences, both stylistic and substantive, on beliefs in New Spain about the Second Coming of Christ, the resurrection of the dead, and the Final Judgment. Includes author's own translations of Spanish, Nahuatl, and Mayan Texts"—Provided by publisher.
Identifiers: LCCN 2022000602 | ISBN 978-0-8061-9035-8 (hardcover)
Subjects: LCSH: Apocalyptic literature. | Aztecs—Religion. | Mayas—Religion. | End of the world.
Classification: LCC BS646 .C47 2022 | DDC 220/.046—dc23/eng/20220527
LC record available at https://lccn.loc.gov/2022000602

The paper in this book meets the guidelines for permanence and durability of the Committee on Production Guidelines for Book Longevity of the Council on Library Resources, Inc. ∞

To Zack, my end and beginning

Contents

Acknowledgments

Like the Apocalypse, which is a culmination of many individual events, this book is the result of many individual moments of support, and I am grateful for each one. As always, Matthew Restall has proven both unfailing in his enthusiasm for this project and generous in his willingness to provide feedback. He was and continues to be a wonderful mentor. John F. Chuchiak likewise continues to be a wealth of support, and I am grateful for his generous sharing of insights and opinions on all things Maya. Louise Burkhart has inspired me from the beginning, and I will always be indebted to her support and advice. Moreover, Ben Leeming has benefited me with his friendship and his sharing of Fabián de Aquino with me, and I am grateful for our countless conversations on everything from Nahuatl and Maya texts to raising kids. I am also indebted to Fr. Roger Corriveau A.A., for his crucial assistance with the Latin passages and his doctrinal insights, and to David Bolles, who is always willing to share his expertise on the Yucatec Maya and offer advice on particularly difficult words and phrases.

This work would not have been possible without the scholars whose studies have provided the rich, existing scholarship on Old and New World eschatology. I am grateful to those who have gone before me and who inspired my scholarship with their own and enriched my understanding through the written word and myriad conversations and emails. I dare not attempt a complete list here, but my particular thanks to Berenice Alcántara Rojas, Victoria Bricker, Joe Campbell, María Castañeda de la Paz, Allen Christenson, Chris Hodson, Rebecca Horn, Kris Lane, Mark Lentz, Miriam Melton-Villanueva, Bernard McGinn, Michel Oudijk, John F. Schwaller, Amara Solari, Jonathan Truitt, and Stephanie Wood. Some of the Nahuatl translations likewise benefited from the collective expertise of the Northeastern Group of Nahuatl Scholars conference. Carlos Armando Mendoza Alonzo at the AHAY provided his valuable assistance, and my thanks also to Richard Perry for generously sharing his vast corpus of images of colonial churches with me. Likewise, my thanks to those who helped improve this book's final form, including Alessandra Tamulevich at the University of Oklahoma Press, Scott Johnson, my research assistants Molly Hansen and Travis Meyer, and the two anonymous readers, whose excellent comments enhanced the book's strength and depth. Also, this book benefited from a generous publication subvention from the College of Family, Home, and Social Sciences at Brigham Young University. Finally, I owe an unpayable debt to my wife and five young kids for making my arrival home at the end of each workday a joyful and renewing beginning.

Conventions of
Translation and Terminology

The analyses of the texts in this book benefit from techniques derived from the school of thought known as the "New Philology." Its late founder, James Lockhart, believed that a study of the philological makeup of a text reveals important details otherwise overlooked or unnoticed. Although linguists may, at times, find the philological analyses included here lacking in particularity, the nonspecialist reader should appreciate them and reap the benefits of insight they provide.

Nahuatl and Maya texts compose the backbone of this study, which also draws on Spanish and Latin sources. Fortunately, scholars have long since translated many of the Latin works into English, and for those lacking translations, I have enlisted the expertise of others far more proficient in Latin than me, particularly Fr. Roger Corriveau A.A. Moreover, the website vulgate.org provided the English translations of biblical passages from the Vulgate, altered at times for readability. All translations of Nahuatl, Maya, and Spanish are my own unless otherwise noted. The translation from the Teabo Manuscript in chapter 5 and part of the translation of the Maya Sermons text from chapter 3 appeared in my book *The Teabo Manuscript* and are used here with permission. The translations themselves often adopt a figurative rather than literal meaning to enhance their readability. Colonial authors rarely preoccupied themselves with punctuation or consistent spacing and paragraphing. Again, for ease of the reader, I have spaced and formatted the translations according to modern standards. Occasionally I use brackets to clarify intended meanings in the text; any additional comments on the translations appear in the notes. All biblical quotations are from the New American Bible (NAB) unless otherwise noted.

Many of the translated texts contain headings and subheadings in Latin and, to a lesser degree, Spanish. Moreover, authors often loosely quote the Vulgate in their texts, and such translations derive from the author's Latin, not the Vulgate itself. All such entries appear translated in italics, and as the texts themselves frequently omit a quote's citation, I have made every effort to locate the origin of such passages and include them in the notes.

Introduction

The Beginning of the End

HAMLET: What news?
ROSENCRANTZ: None, my lord, but [that] the world's grown honest.
HAMLET: Then is doomsday near.

William Shakespeare

The Apocalypse has come. It is everywhere, here and now. It inspires the abundant dystopian novels that cover the shelves of Barnes & Noble and films that fill the screens of movie theaters; it creates zombie-inspired television series that currently inundate the airwaves; and it even appears in our modern politics, where people believe that either Donald Trump is the Antichrist or global warming is a sign of the end of the world. To be sure, the media, always scrapping for viewer ratings, loves the Apocalypse. As a former resident of New England, I endured my fair share of apocalypses from the "Snowmageddon" of 2015 (*Boston Globe*) to the "Tick Apocalypse" of 2017 (*New York Post*). Currently, the United States is witnessing what major newspapers have deemed the "Restaurant Apocalypse," as large chains and independent owners alike fight to keep their doors open in light of the COVID-19 pandemic. Indeed, as I write, I do so in quarantine as the pandemic sweeps across the globe thus fulfilling, in the eyes of some, apocalyptic prophecy. The Apocalypse has come indeed.

In truth, Christianity could not exist without the Apocalypse. The Second Coming of Christ, the resurrection of the dead, and the accompanying Final Judgment are all central tenets of the Faith. So paramount is apocalyptic eschatology that it has been referred to as "the mother of Christianity."[1] Although the Church emphasized salvation through the sacraments early on, the Apocalypse continued to influence innumerable religious texts and images throughout the medieval and early modern periods as worldly events frequently provoked or assuaged apocalyptic thinking.[2] Yet whether believing the Final Judgment was coming in ten days or ten centuries, a belief in the event was always present in Christianity as was, nearly always, a curiosity concerning its timing.

The Christian Apocalypse has its roots in Second Temple Judaism (c. 300 b.c.–70 a.d.). Put simply, Jewish eschatology, as derived from texts from this period, revolved around an end of the world that results in justice for, and the exaltation of, Israel, or the Jewish people. When the early Christians adopted such ideas, they molded the Apocalypse to fit contemporary needs and events with sermons and images that were both moving and terrifying.[3] This evolution of the Apocalypse continued throughout Christianity's long history and continues today with myriad churches proclaiming, with equally moving sermons, somewhat similar but ultimately disparate beliefs on the Final Judgment evolved to accommodate their modern environment.

So it was when early modern ecclesiastics brought the Apocalypse to the Yucatec Maya and the Nahuatl-speaking peoples often referred to today as "Aztecs," but as "Nahuas" by historians and other scholars.[4] Eschatological sermons in Nahuatl and Maya were as moving and terrifying as those heard in Europe. Yet the Apocalypse and its eschatology had changed once again, this time to accommodate an Indigenous audience and the political and social atmosphere of New Spain. This book examines this stage in the evolution of apocalyptic and eschatological thought when ecclesiastics, Nahuas, and Mayas interpreted, reworked, and preserved perhaps the most fundamental aspect of Christianity—the Apocalypse.

Content and Context of the Book

Arguably more than any other doctrine, the Apocalypse is the most enduring and influential element of Christianity. Indeed, fingerprints of the

Apocalypse cover the colonial evidence remaining today. The Apocalypse was one of the greatest theological impetuses to early exploration and missionary efforts; it shaped religious and political policy; it contributed to the creation of some of the world's finest examples of Indigenous-language texts; it burned in the hearts of ecclesiastics, inspiring them to new theological aspirations; it saturated pedagogical texts; and it created a bridge connecting preexisting Indigenous and Christian worldviews.

Certainly the influence of the Apocalypse on Christianity and European society has not been overlooked by the historiography. Numerous monographs and edited volumes are dedicated to the topic, and the trend gives no indication of slowing.[5] Although lacking the same level of interest, scholars of New Spain have likewise acknowledged the Apocalypse. However, the topic typically is dressed in millenarian trappings and limited to the ideological beliefs of the early friars. Perhaps most influential and oft cited are the works of John Leddy Phelan, *The Millennial Kingdom of the Franciscans in the New World* (1970), and Georges Baudot, *Utopia and History in Mexico* (1995). The former connects the sixteenth-century Franciscan chronicler, Gerónimo de Mendieta, to Joachim of Fiore and a millennial outlook that supported a New World setting for the upcoming Millennial Kingdom; the latter argues the millenarianism of the early Franciscans and their efforts to bring about a utopia along a "Joachinist perspective."[6] Although subsequent articles and book chapters by various authors recounting early evangelization efforts at times reinforced and at others challenged Phelan and Baudot's works, all contributed to the dominant trend of viewing the Apocalypse in the New World primarily through the perspective of millenarianism, or lack thereof, of the early Franciscans.[7]

Those few works outside this trend commonly trace colonial apocalyptic and millenarian ideologies over the centuries to their present, somewhat altered forms. Frank Graziano's (1999) work on the New World in general and Martin Munro's (2015) examination of Haiti and the Caribbean provide apt examples, while Miguel López-Lozano (2008) examines various dystopian novels of Chicano and Mexican authors to argue a connection between the negative aspects of the building of a colonial utopia and those found in present-day modernization. More recent still is an anthology of apocalyptic poems, essays, and other works of Mexican activist and writer Homero Aridjis—who has written extensively on the subject—created as "the sounds

3

similar to the trumpets of the Apocalypse began to filter through the news on television, radio, and newspaper: a viral and terrible pandemic."[8]

The year 2012, unfortunately, did very little to change this paradigm. In fact, the year brought with it a slew of books and TV documentaries that crammed, bent, and broke archeological and colonial evidence to fit personal ideologies and agendas and to win viewers rather than provide an objective, informed history.[9] Notable exceptions did exist, including David Stuart's *The Order of Days* and Matthew Restall and Amara Solari's *2012 and the End of the World*. In the latter, Restall and Solari provided a pioneering examination of the impact Western eschatology had on colonial Maya society and how our ideas of an apocalyptic 2012 were simply that: our own, derived from a long history of European millenarianism.[10] For the most part, however, any discussion of the Apocalypse in New Spain seemed restricted to the millenarianism of the early friars and fanaticism of 2012.

Even more limited are studies examining the religious texts in Nahuatl and Maya that conveyed the Apocalypse to New World audiences. Studies on colonial religion should avoid two traps that position themselves on either end of an ideological spectrum. The first assumes that European religion transplanted itself with little or no alteration. The second—and the one seemingly with the loudest siren call today—takes for granted that Indigenous people altered everything and that each change was an intentionally subversive attempt to modify, even resist, Catholicism in order to preserve Indigenous culture. Yet perhaps the reality for most occurred somewhere between these two polarities at a place of acceptance and resistance where Old World doctrine met its New World audience to negotiate continually a livable version of the Faith.[11] After all, the vast majority of colonial Indigenous peoples were born into a world that included both Catholicism and ancient traditions that necessitated negotiation to form a personal, fluid, even breathable worldview. Often underappreciated—or unnoticed altogether—in this negotiation are the Old World roots of New World texts.[12] Missed, then, is the opportunity to illustrate both the continuation of texts and stories throughout the centuries on either side of the Atlantic and also how ecclesiastics and Indigenous people employed and tailored such discourses to local audiences in New Spain.

Overall, then, a study on the Indigenous-language texts that presented the Apocalypse to Nahuas and Mayas throughout the colonial period; a look at their Old and New World messages; and an examination of those who wrote, copied, and preserved them that looks beyond the millenarianism of the early friars is lacking. Although scholars have examined a few specific eschatological sermons or texts, particularly in Nahuatl, no work exists that truly explores the importance and transmission of the Apocalypse in the evangelization and colonial religion of the Nahua and Maya through Indigenous-language religious texts.[13] Nor, generally, have translations of such texts been made available to readers. This book begins to fill this historiographical gap by striving to achieve three goals.

The first concerns the use of Nahuatl and Maya religious texts from the sixteenth to the early nineteenth centuries to expose the instruction intended for the Nahua and Yucatec Maya on the Apocalypse and eschatological doctrine, and the importance of Doomsday in conveying and upholding Catholicism. The second goal endeavors to demonstrate in new and vibrant ways the importance of knowing both sides of the negotiation that is colonial religion. Texts composed in the early years of the Church and the medieval and early modern periods affected those created in Nahuatl and Maya. To illustrate this, each of the chapters highlights various eschatological themes tracing their Old World origins to their New World applications to illustrate better how ecclesiastics, Nahuas, and Mayas created, conveyed, and preserved the Apocalypse in both old and new, official and unofficial ways that produced culturally specific Nahua and Maya Catholicisms and Apocalypses. Admittedly, Indigenous writers derived from the elite, not the common masses, and although the apocalyptic messages they composed were designed for all, what the average Nahua or Maya heard (as literacy was restricted to the elite) or understood often lies beyond our reach. Such limitations notwithstanding, the following texts offer a clearer picture of the process of forming colonial religion, and how various ecclesiastics, Nahuas, and Mayas preached, and even understood, Catholicism.

The third and final goal is to seek out treatises written in Nahuatl and Yucatec Maya from a variety of religious texts and provide the reader with English translations. These translated texts provide the opportunity to see firsthand the negotiations made by ecclesiastics, Nahuas, and Mayas when composing their eschatological treatises. The Apocalypse formed an important part of ecclesiastics' sermons concerning the season of Advent, when discussing the seventh Articles of Faith, and in individual treatises dedicated to the topic.[14] Indigenous authors also betrayed the influence of the Apocalypse in their own, unofficial works. From personal compositions in Nahuatl to manuscript compilations composed and maintained in Maya towns, the Apocalypse appears as a Christian topic Indigenous people deemed important enough to preserve on their own. After all, eschatological texts appealed to the fatalism and cyclical worldviews held by many Nahuas and Mayas, thus making these stories a favorite among Indigenous audiences, and such texts certainly were relevant amid the apocalyptic population decline and calamities of the colonial period.[15] Too long have these important discourses lingered in general obscurity, known only to an interested few with the language capabilities to decipher their content. The ecclesiastics, Nahuas, and Mayas who spent countless hours on their eschatological compositions and those who preserved them in their private manuscripts—sometimes for centuries—certainly would have considered their general obscurity today a poignant loss and perhaps a portent of doom.

Together, this work uncovers the importance of the Old World Apocalypse and eschatology in that preached in the New World and its varied and negotiated message in Indigenous-language texts, while allowing readers to have access to the actual eschatological texts themselves. The book exposes how Nahuas, Mayas, and Spaniards carried on a tradition of apocalyptic and eschatological thought that began before the birth of Christianity. Indeed, in many ways the patterns and insights revealed here reflect those evident today as Christians, and society in general, attempt to predict and understand a cataclysmic end that could occur through terrorism, a new form of viral disease, global warming, or a dose of all the above.

Chapter 1 illustrates the malleability and relevancy of the Apocalypse and how it became an important lens through which to view the world, particularly in the minds of Spaniards as they conquered and reconquered souls for their God with an increasingly millenarian mindset—one that spread to New Spain to influence evangelization, only to become tempered by its realities. The remaining chapters move beyond millenarianism to begin the book's textual analysis. Following an eschatological timeline of sorts, the chapters illustrate how friars and Indigenous people instructed their fold on death's first judgment, limbo, and purgatory (chapter 2); the signs heralding the Apocalypse itself (chapter 3); the seventh Articles of Faith and their doctrines, particularly that of the resurrection (chapter 4); and heaven and hell (chapter 5).

Old and New World Worldviews

To better understand the context for the following texts, a general review of Catholic and Mesoamerican worldviews is necessary. It is important to understand from the outset that worldviews—whether Catholic, Nahua, or Maya—are not static and change according to the times. Who the deities are and their relationship to humankind and humankind's responsibility to the divine shift throughout the ages. The Catholic Church called numerous councils over the years to clarify and develop doctrine. For example, the fourth-century Council of Nicaea established that Christ and God are "one in being" and divine; the Council of Trent (1545–63) outlined early modern Catholicism's response to Protestant reformers and endorsed challenged beliefs including the cult of saints, the authority of the Church, indulgences, and the role of the bishop; and the Second Vatican Council in the 1960s authorized the performance of the liturgy in the vernacular, reasserted the importance of the family, and reshaped the Church's relationships with other faiths to promote a discourse of commonalities.[16] Most recently, Pope Francis has made unprecedented efforts to extend further this unity among God's children. In one instance he stated, "the Lord has redeemed all of us . . . even the atheists"—a statement that would have earned him the attention of the Spanish Inquisition and one that riled more than a few Church authorities today![17]

As will be seen throughout this book, the worldview of the Catholic Church evolved over the years from its Jewish and even pagan roots, and although its overall structure remained somewhat constant, its particulars were subject to change.[18] In this general structure, God created the earth and humankind over the space of six creative periods, or days, thus becoming the Heavenly Father and lord of the earth. On earth, God's children became susceptible to sin and corruption. God, then, assisted humankind to conquer sin by sacrificing himself in the flesh as Jesus Christ for their salvation. This sacrifice, if accepted by an individual, allows them to cleanse themselves of sin and return and live with God after death. In addition, God speaks his will through holy individuals (popes, bishops, priests, and so on) who serve as spiritual leaders and who help humankind receive God's blessings while on earth. To show appreciation for God's sacrifice and continual guidance and merit his assistance, humankind offers sacrifices of time and money in specific holy structures, or churches, and adheres to the rituals established by a religious calendar of feast and holy days.

Often, Catholics attending Mass recite the Nicene Creed stating that Christ will "come again in glory to judge the living and the dead," and indeed the Apocalypse and Final Judgment are the culminating climax of the Catholic worldview. Yet upon one's death, or personal apocalypse, many events occur prior to the soul's final judgment, the first of which is the "particular judgment" (chapter 2): if entirely pure, the soul enters heaven immediately; if purification is warranted then the soul departs to purgatory; if the soul contains mortal sin, it is damned in hell. Meanwhile, signs and portents (chapter 3) herald the approach of the impending global Apocalypse causing speculation and consternation, certainly, but also reminding the Christian to live in a state of readiness. Upon the Final Judgment, the souls reunite with their bodies in the resurrection and stand before Christ to account for their works on earth (chapter 4). According to the *Catechism of the Catholic Church*, "after the universal judgment, the righteous will reign forever with Christ, glorified in body and soul; the universe itself will be renewed."[19] With the kingdom of God on earth in its perfected and purified form, humankind will live in happiness in God's presence, which is the definition of heaven. The wicked will live apart from God, which is the definition of hell, where they experience its sufferings (chapter 5).[20] Finally, for the majority of Christianity's lifespan, knowledge of these important events, their outcomes, and the necessary rituals remained in the hands of a few literate educated individuals, often elite, thus empowering them. Although the power such knowledge gave priests as "stewards of the mysteries of God" supported socioreligious hierarchies, it also drew criticism including that of Martin Luther who decried that the "stewardship has now been developed into so great a pomp of power and so terrible a tyranny, that no heathen empire or earthly power can be compared with it."[21]

Like the Catholic Church, the worldviews of both the Nahua and Maya fluctuated over time and, certainly, space. Although both cultures shared features common to those of other Mesoamerican peoples, a single Nahua or Maya creation myth did not exist. Instead, as David Stuart observed for the Maya, Mesoamerican city-states typically possessed their own individual supernatural narrative of being and existence, with "each a center of the cosmos in its own way."[22] And such worldviews were vulnerable to change.

No single record exists detailing the precontact worldview of either the Nahua or Maya. Instead, a potpourri of sources combine to give a general scent of what once existed in common among the cultures of Mesoamerica and, in many cases, what still continues today. Most Mesoamerican cultures contain worldviews with progressive creation stories where deities—through a process of trial and error, creation, and destruction—created the world and humankind through their own labor and personal sacrifice, literally in some cases. The world and its creations are very much alive and follow a cyclical pattern of birth, death, and renewal. To show their appreciation and reinvigorate the earth's animistic essence, humankind performed various rituals that often included human blood as the supplier of such essence. As Stuart observes regarding Mesoamerican worldviews, "in a self-fulfilling cycle, sacrifice begets creation and creation begets sacrifice."[23] Educated religious specialists performed these rituals in sacred locations including temples and according to a religious calendar.

Various legends among both the Nahua and the Maya describe cyclical processes of creation and destruction of the world's inhabitants with each cycle becoming an "age" of sorts until the gods created a suitable human capable of properly venerating the divine. This emphasis of period beginnings and endings, then, allows for the possibility for a future destruction and recreation of the world's inhabitants. For the Nahua, they were in the fifth creation or age of the world; for the Maya, the fourth. Each of the previous ages varied in duration so there was no expectation of an "end date" to the current one—despite what the television and its 2012 programs claimed—only an understanding that it was a possibility in the future.[24]

Arguably, the most famous image depicting such a worldview is the Calendar Stone of the Mexica (see figure 0.1). Often mistakenly appearing on websites and television shows as the Maya calendar, the Calendar Stone greets the viewer with the open-mouthed face of what scholars believe to be either the Mexica sun or earth god. The stone contains the four dates of the four previous world-endings—4 Jaguar, 4 Wind, 4 Rain, 4 Water—with a date in the center relating to the ending of the fifth and current era

Figure 0.1 Aztec Calendar Stone. Instituto Nacional de Antropología e Historia, National Museum of Anthropology, Mexico City. Photograph by Gary Todd, 2012. Courtesy Wikimedia Commons.

on 4 Earthquake. As Restall and Solari argued, the stone was not apocalyptic, rather it intended to create a history that connected the ruling Mexica Empire with the world's ages and ascribed to them the power and responsibility for upholding and maintaining the current era.[25] Regardless, Mesoamerican worldviews never saw such periods of destruction as "ends," but as beginnings to a new age and a renewal of the earth. Knowledge of the calendars and period histories empowered trained religious specialists and validated their elevated role in society as those who can prognosticate and avoid catastrophe through necessary rituals.[26]

Interestingly, when compared side by side, both Catholic and Mesoamerican worldviews share a number of general similarities—in truth, the same could be said for most world religions. Both believed in a progressive creation of the cosmos; both view the sacrifice of deity/ies as necessary for humankind; in return, both view sacrifice performed by humankind as important in obtaining the favor of the divine and maintaining a social and cosmic order; both practice such ceremonies of sacrifice and worship according to sacred calendars and in sacred places such as churches and temples; both entrust trained, often elite individuals with the knowledge of such calendars, histories, and rituals, which validate and empower them as elevated members of society; and both believe that this era will eventually conclude with a disaster of some kind that will give birth to a new age and world.[27] This final similarity is important, and one that frequently goes overlooked, as it provided an excellent delivery device for the message of Christianity and its important role both now and in the world to come.

Such general similarities allowed for possibilities to incorporate the new into the old. After all, Mesoamerican peoples had long been accustomed to adopting and submitting to the gods of their victors, oftentimes including them into their own pantheon, and as we have seen, Catholicism itself was certainly no stranger to change. In the end and although different from the period endings of Mesoamerica, the Apocalypse would not be too foreign of a concept for most Nahua and Maya instructors and parishioners to accept. As one scholar put it, "suturing disparate cultural elements was a way of life for an indigenous individual negotiating a colonial present."[28] Moreover, knowledge of Doomsday, and Christianity in general, validated the elevated positions and authority of ecclesiastics and their Indigenous stewards in ways reminiscent of pre-contact religious specialists charged with maintaining a balance between the natural and supernatural. Ultimately, receiving influence from both Old and New Worlds, the Apocalypse evolved once again to become a topic frequently included in both the sermons of ecclesiastics and the personal compositions of Indigenous writers, all of which helped produce and reflect a variety of Nahua and Maya Apocalypses.

≡ 1 ≡

Old World Roots, New World Shoots

But the day of the Lord will come like a thief.

2 Peter 3:10

And this gospel of the kingdom will be preached throughout the world as a witness to all nations, and then the end will come.

Matthew 24:14

When will this prophecy be fulfilled? Would I not be worthy to see this conversion (of the New World), as we are already at the evening and end of our days and in the last age of the world?

Fray Martín de Valencia

In his second epistle to fellow Christians, Peter exhorts all to adhere to the Faith and wait for the Second Coming of Christ. He recounts how heaven and earth will be dissolved and melted by the purifying fire which accompanies the return of Christ. This frightful scene is coupled with a dose of uncertainty as Peter instructs his audience that no one knows the day of Christ's return, for as the quotation above testifies, his arrival will be as unexpected as a thief in the night.[1] Put simply, the Apocalypse was the ultimate pop quiz for all Christians who were instructed to live each day as if it were their last, prepared for the surprise Final Judgment of their lord.

The elements of fear and surprise often prove invaluable for those striving to encourage a particular belief or practice among others, and this certainly contributed to the resilience of apocalyptic eschatology in Christian belief. Yet such a resilience can also be attributed to the Apocalypse's ability to be seen in everyday life. Many of those who experienced droughts, famines, pestilence, discoveries, political shifts, and wars throughout history have done so through an apocalyptic lens. From the persecution of early Christians and the Black Death to the discovery of the New World and Martin Luther to the Maya calendar "ending" in 2012, all were seen as divine omens that the end was nigh.[2] Even now, websites explain how ISIS is the Antichrist, or at least the organization that will give rise to the villainous figure, or how the COVID-19 pandemic is the fourth seal of Revelation now broken.

The resilience of the Apocalypse through its ability to encourage Christian behavior and explain everyday events while justifying military and political events affords it an expansive history and scope that impacted both the Old and New Worlds. This chapter introduces the major themes and characters of the Apocalypse and pays particular attention to those of relevance to the evangelization of New Spain. Beginning with its Jewish origins and ending with its arrival and application in the New World, this chapter largely draws upon the vast scholarship on both the Old World Apocalypse and early missionary efforts in New Spain to convey the evolution of apocalyptic thought as it shifted to explain and justify various events and movements throughout the ages on both sides of the Atlantic. Certainly the chapter does not attempt a comprehensive history of the matter. Instead, the following presents an overview of main concepts and events to provide the necessary context with which to understand the subsequent examined texts, highlight the malleability of apocalyptic thought, and shed additional light on the Old World roots and New World shoots of the Apocalypse and its role in evangelization.

The Beginning of the End

Early Christian apocalyptic eschatology has its origins in Judaism. In fact, as Bernard McGinn notes, there is "considerable doubt about whether some late first- and early second-century apocalypses are to be labeled Jewish or

Christian."[3] By the first century A.D., Jewish eschatology included a resurrection, a peaceful messianic age, and a last judgment.[4] Regardless, the
various works in the New Testament including the Pauline epistles, the
Gospels, and of course, the book of Revelation, or Apocalypse, stand as witnesses to the impact the Apocalypse had on the early Church.[5] Indeed, the
majority of New Testament authors reference the Second Coming of Christ.

The early apocalyptic eschatology stressed the imminent danger and
impending doom of the any-day-now return of Christ. Yet as the decades
and centuries passed with no returning messiah, apocalyptic thought
expanded out of necessity to accommodate the delay. Works that employed
historical and present concerns to stress calamity and the welcome of an
apocalypse, which renews, restores, and rewards the just continued in popularity. However, apocalyptic texts relating visions and spiritual voyages
also began to appear including the Ascension of Isaiah and the Apocalypses
of Paul, Peter, and Thomas. Such works stressed a personal experience in
the afterlife—a personal apocalypse—either good or bad, and moved away
from preaching of imminent crisis. Furthermore, themes such as the Antichrist and concern with the duration of the earth and the millennium also
appeared in these early years.[6]

As Rome adopted Christianity in the fourth century and opposition
waned, apocalypticism prophesying imminent doom fell out of vogue.
The mixed reception of the book of Revelation demonstrates this shift in
apocalyptic eschatology and interpretation and the varied interpretations
and reception of apocalyptic messages. The book of Revelation is, perhaps,
the cornerstone to Christian apocalypticism. The book contains revelations
given to John on the Greek island of Patmos concerning advice given to
"seven churches which are in Asia" and the earth's existence.[7] The work is
highly metaphorical and symbolic, with beasts, dragons, archangels, horsemen, and portents of doom destined to herald the Second Coming of Christ.
A literal interpretation of the book's apocalyptic message made sense to
many second-century Christians who viewed the Second Coming as both
physical and spiritual salvation from Roman control. Others who viewed a
possible reconciliation with Rome, however, chose a more spiritual interpretation of the book. Differences in literal and spiritual interpretations of
Revelation continued among Christians in both the East and the West, with
the latter occasionally adhering to a more millenarian, literal belief.[8]

The beliefs and writings of Montanus and Saint Augustine regarding the New Jerusalem recorded in Revelation further illustrate such differences. The second-century visionary preacher, Montanus, lived in Turkey and not only prophesied the approaching return of Christ but also declared the site for the New Jerusalem to be the Phrygian town of Pepuza. The New Jerusalem is a reference to the prophecy, seen in various places throughout the Bible but especially in Revelation 21, for a celestial, glorified Jerusalem to reign during the messianic age. The new city is perhaps better understood as a piece of the restorative puzzle inherent in the Apocalypse narrative. Montanus, and many others then and now, chose to view the New Jerusalem in a physical, literal light. The Church ultimately proclaimed his teachings heretical, although the imagery lived on with a few Franciscans relating Mexico City to this prophetic New Jerusalem.[9]

A few centuries later, Saint Augustine argued a different, symbolic understanding. By the fifth century, some came to view Rome and the Church as divinely connected. That is, until the Visigoths invaded the city in 410 A.D. Writing his *City of God* in defense of Christians blamed for the sack of Rome and breaking the connection between Rome and God's city, Augustine declared that the New Jerusalem would reside in heaven where the righteous would dwell with God after the Final Judgment.[10] In short, the City of God and the New Jerusalem were not temporal, man-built metropolises of the earth, but a spiritual symbol of the Church, its followers, and the kingdom of heaven. Such disparate opinions concerning Revelation's apocalyptic messages—and even its validity in the biblical canon!—was and remains common. Indeed, Saint Jerome commented on the diverse meanings within Revelation stating, "the apocalypse of John has as many mysteries as words . . . manifold meanings lie hid in its every word."[11]

This varied interpretation of the Apocalypse also includes such topics as the millennium. Following a period of apocalyptic war, Revelation 20:1–6 refers to an age of peace where Christ will rule his kingdom for a period of one thousand years—a millennium. The conclusion of the period initiates the Final Judgment when all humankind, including the wicked, resurrect and stand before God to receive eternal glory or condemnation. This thousand-year period came to be called "the millennium" and what it was and when it would occur became the subject of much debate.[12] Today, the Catholic Church labels such belief as a deception of the Antichrist, believing instead that Christ already reigns upon this earth; his kingdom is but a seed that will eventually flourish into the fullness of the kingdom of God after his return.[13] Prior to this contemporary stance however, Christian theologians developed various theories defining the duration of the millennium and when it will occur.

As Grant Underwood noted, a literal belief in the millennium, or millenarianism, derived from Jewish apocalyptic belief, Zoroastrianism, and Babylonian astrology and found both supporters and opponents in the early Church.[14] Although Saint Jerome opposed millennial beliefs, Saint Augustine supported the idea initially. Eventually, however, Augustine related the millennium to the age of Christ's earthly Church, ending with his second coming and the Final Judgment. Moreover, the thousand years were simply metaphorical for a long period of time (similar to the use of *centzontli*, or four hundred, in Nahuatl). This non- or amillennial interpretation, which upholds the Apocalypse but dismisses the thousand-year reign of Christ on earth, held strong among many Western religious commentaries.[15] As Saint Jerome declared in the early fifth century, "The Saints will in no wise have an earthly kingdom, but only a celestial one; thus must cease the fable of one thousand years."[16]

Despite the popularity of a nonliteral belief in the millennium, the twelfth-century exposition on Revelation by Joachim of Fiore (c. 1132–1202) established another influential line of thought. Perhaps straddling both amillennial and millennial traditions, Joachim's ambiguous interpretation of the millennium could place it partially during the Church's domain on earth and partially during a future era.[17] Although Joachim agreed that Revelation's thousand years should not be understood literally, his nebulous interpretation of the millennium and historical interpretation of Revelation opened the door for subsequent followers to part fully with amillennialism and interpret everyday events as signs from Revelation heralding in a literal millennial age.[18]

Overall, then, the delay in Christ's return caused an important shift in apocalyptic eschatology to form a more symbolic, nonliteral interpretation of the Bible. The Church Fathers Jerome and Augustine both combated the idea of an imminent apocalypse and the tendency to link apocalyptic texts and passages to everyday events. Instead, they argued, apocalyptic discourse should be seen in the light of larger battle between good and evil.[19]

Although they and others would be successful in promoting an overall spiritual interpretation of Revelation and various eschatological prophecies, the uncertainties, challenges, and discoveries of everyday life allowed literal interpretations to remain close to the hearts of many.

For example, many saw the fifth-century Vandal invasions of Rome in an apocalyptic light; Otto I's soldiers interpreted an eclipse in 968 as a portent of doom; in the thirteenth century, Pope Innocent III and others would correlate Islam with the Antichrist; and the fall of Constantinople to Muslim forces in 1453 was seen as fulfillment of apocalyptic prophecy to herald in the end of times.[20] Natural disasters and phenomena that occurred frequently throughout the medieval and early modern period likewise encouraged apocalypticism. According to James Palmer, the French chronicler and monk Ralph Glaber recorded one example of many. Glaber reported that during the millennial anniversary of Christ's death in 1033 terrifying events occurred, including famine, "madness," and even cannibalism. Such events were seen as portents of apocalyptic doom.[21] To be sure, the Apocalypse, both imminent and symbolic, was alive throughout the Middle Ages and greatly impacted the formation and expansion of Christendom as it sought to spread the Gospel and claim its place atop a world order it aspired to govern in the name of Christ.[22]

Christians in the Middle Ages accessed the Apocalypse through various mediums. One came in the oral discourses common in the season of Advent which discuss the birth, or first coming of Christ (see chapter 2). Another was found in the copious readings and works of the various religious orders that focused on expositions on the book of Revelation, or the writings relating the visionary experiences of Saints Paul or Thomas, to name a few. Even if one were to miss the oral and written messages, the visual instruction on the Apocalypse through monuments and works of art, which decorated public spaces and, especially, church buildings spoke as loudly as the preachers.[23] Even the most casual medieval Christian, for example, surely was given pause when they walked through the doorway of the twelfth-century Chartres Cathedral in France only to be greeted by an elaborate depiction of the Final Judgment with Christ sitting in the center of Revelation's four apocalyptic beasts (see figure 1.1).

Indeed, the impact of the Apocalypse on medieval society was immense. As Richard Emmerson asserts, "the Apocalypse is ubiquitous, all pervasive

Figure 1.1 Chartres Cathedral, The Last Judgment. Photograph by Chris Hodson.

like the innumerable eyes on Chaucer's cosmic goddess Fame."[24] To be sure, the Apocalypse and its imagery transcended boundaries, borders, and class to appear in both secular and religious texts, among the elite of Castile and the commoners of Ireland. Doomsday-inspired themes appeared in works from Dante to Chaucer and, eventually, Shakespeare. Poems, plays, and religious treatises all promulgated its themes.[25]

As will be seen throughout this book, some of these mediums even made their way across the Atlantic. For the moment, one brief example will suffice. The third-century Apocalypse of Paul is, essentially, an explanation of what occurred to Paul while he was "caught up to the third heaven."[26] The tale recounts the spiritual journey of Paul as he visits heaven and hell to witness both their beauty and horror. For example, while he witnessed the bejeweled righteous sit upon golden thrones in heaven, he likewise viewed those who hurt the widows and poor be punished by having their hands and feet cut off before being trapped naked in ice and snow to be eaten by worms in hell. The Apocalypse of Paul enjoyed immense popularity and is likely the same work Dante references when, in regard to his own unworthiness for a glimpse into the afterlife, states, "I am not Paul."[27] Later ecclesiastics, including Saint Augustine, would disparage the Pauline apocalypse. Yet this did not prevent it from heavily influencing an Indigenous-authored Nahuatl sermon from sixteenth-century central Mexico. Here, Paul and his surroundings adopt Indigenous characteristics and customs to create a wholly Nahua version of the account but one that still encourages Christian behavior.[28]

The visions of John and Paul certainly had an impact on medieval culture. Yet, as scholars have noted, others including Joachim of Fiore and Peter John Olivi (1248–1298) played a key role as contributors to medieval eschatology and the apocalyptic beliefs of many ecclesiastics who were later sent to the New World. Himself a Cistercian abbot, Joachim held a reformist's view of the Apocalypse that, as we saw above in his interpretation of the millennium, differed greatly from previous interpretations. Saints John and Augustine viewed the Apocalypse in a Jewish-Christian way that held the coming of Christ as a saving and cleansing act to a world that had reached its apex of wickedness and corruption. Joachim, however, placed the world and its events in a historic lens that experienced various "purifying catastrophes" as it advanced through progressively improving stages until reaching the Third Age of the Holy Spirit.[29] Joachim's various commentaries on the Bible and the book of Revelation gained momentum after his death and evolved into the popular argument that the Third Age of the Holy Spirit would be governed by the monastic orders and their spiritual Church instead of the carnal, clerical Church.[30]

Peter John Olivi likewise composed a commentary on the Apocalypse that was heavily influenced by the work of Joachim. For Olivi, Joachim and the birth of the Franciscan order were essential in initiating a new period of Church history. Like Joachim, Olivi stressed historical themes to predict upcoming events. For example, following patterns of persecution predicted by prophets of old, the Spiritual Franciscans would likewise receive persecution from "carnal Christians," and even the pope.[31] Moreover, Olivi, like Saint Bonaventure and others, recognized Saint Francis as the angel who opened the sixth seal, which he associated with the preaching of the Gospel throughout the world.[32] It should come as no surprise, then, that such teachings found eager recipients in Spain and many of the early Franciscans sent to evangelize New Spain and conquer its souls for Christ and who would rework existing, Old World millennial and apocalyptic ideologies to fit a New World setting.[33]

The Apocalypse and the Spanish Military and Spiritual Campaigns

One of the reasons apocalyptic thought survived the millennia surely concerns its ability to renew its relevance through everyday events. By the fifteenth century, the region that would become Spain was well immersed in apocalyptic teachings, which were commonly applied to explain political unrest, famine, discovery, and war. For example, the Apocalypse commentary of the eighth-century Spanish monk Beatus of Liebana was likely inspired by the Muslim conquest of the peninsula and the desire to defend orthodoxy.[34]

Moreover, a thirteenth-century physician from Valencia, Arnold of Villanova, inspired by Joachim of Fiore, prescribed a role for the Aragon monarchy that included the retaking of Jerusalem and a global Christian empire.[35] Such apocalyptic prophecy frequently included the retaking of Jerusalem as requisite for the millennial Christian kingdom and the return of Christ. Not surprisingly, the Reconquista, or the Christian reconquest of Iberia from Islam, was often painted in the renewal light of the Apocalypse or at least divine endorsement, as was the unification of Spain under the Catholic Isabella and Ferdinand.[36] In addition, and similar to the reconquest of Granada in 1492, many viewed the fall of the Moorish city of Oran in 1509 to Cardinal Francisco Jiménez de Cisneros through an apocalyptic lens. One scholar stated that the capture "raised hopes in Spain that Islam would finally be vanquished, Jerusalem would be conquered and all humanity would be converted to Christianity."[37] Certainly such everyday events gave new lifeblood to millenarianism and apocalyptic beliefs in the minds of many.

Another example concerns the expulsion of the Moriscos from Spain, which began in 1609 under Philip III. A few decades after the 1492 reconquest of the final Muslim stronghold in Granada, Spain, gave the Moors a choice: to either convert to Christianity or accept exile. Those that converted became new Christians, or Moriscos. Yet many viewed it as a hopeless case, and religious intolerance and zeal eventually brought about their expulsion. The act did not escape criticism, and Catholic apologists defending the ejection found an invaluable stockpile of ideological ammunition in apocalyptic prophecies. Apocalypticism not only provided justification for the seemingly inevitable expulsion of the Moriscos but also allowed Seville to be referenced as the site of the New Jerusalem and Spaniards to become the new Chosen People. Some even held Ferdinand to be the New David—a messianic figure destined to initiate the millennium.[38] This messiah-king theory derived from the Middle Ages and became applied to various rulers, including Ferdinand and Isabella, whom Mendieta proclaimed would begin to cleanse the world of heretics and nonbelievers.[39] In short, apocalyptic belief thrived in Spain and became useful in justifying its past while promoting its proclaimed superiority as *the* Christian nation that would usher in the Apocalypse.

Because the discovery, colonization, and evangelization of the New World is best viewed as an extension of the Reconquest, it is not surprising that the Apocalypse likewise played an important role. From the beginning it seems that Christopher Columbus saw his role as explorer as hastening the apocalyptic prophecy of the conquest of Jerusalem and the spread of Christianity.[40] In a letter from his first voyage to the Spanish monarchy, he expressed his hopes that the forthcoming riches from his discoveries would allow that "within three years the King and Queen could undertake to prepare to conquer the Holy House . . . that all the profit from this enterprise of mine should be spent in the conquest of Jerusalem."[41] So adamant was he regarding the imminent End of Days that he, on multiple occasions, encouraged the Spanish monarchy to conquer Jerusalem and hasten the Second Coming of Christ. Having had a close relationship with the Spiritual Franciscan tradition and versed in Joachimism—although probably never actually reading his writings—Columbus came to view his discoveries and voyages through an apocalyptic lens.[42] This lens enabled him to claim, "Of the New Heaven and New Earth of which our Lord spoke through Saint John in Revelation (having formerly spoken through the mouth of Isaiah) He made me His messenger and revealed those places to me."[43] Columbus even composed *The Book of Prophecies*, which although unfinished, housed a collection of apocalyptic writings.[44] For the Genoese explorer, the discovery of the New World fulfilled apocalyptic prophecy.

The organized evangelization efforts in New Spain likewise began with an apocalyptic emphasis. In the Gospel of Matthew, Christ declares, "this gospel of the kingdom will be preached throughout the world as a witness to all nations, and then the end will come."[45] This and other biblical passages helped germinate the belief that before Christ returned to earth, Christianity needed to spread throughout the world and all its "heathens" must be converted—a belief emphasized and linked specifically to the Franciscans by Joachim, Olivi, and others.[46] And so, after the Aztec capital of Tenochtitlan fell in 1521 following a military siege, the evangelization effort began in earnest. The religious orders served as vanguards to the Faith with the Franciscans sending Pedro de Gante and two others in 1523 and then twelve more in 1524 in symbolic deference to Christ's twelve apostles. The Dominicans and Augustinians arrived shortly thereafter in 1526 and 1533, respectively, with the Jesuits obtaining their foothold in 1572.[47]

The Franciscans and their pseudo-Joachimist, apocalyptic ideologies greatly impacted the evangelization program established initially.[48] And understanding the historical context from which emerged the early Franciscans sent to New Spain illuminates the apocalyptic undertones of the mission. In the centuries prior to their New World mission, reformist and revivalist movements in the order had reinvigorated the Franciscans, particularly in Iberia where approximately one-third of their European members resided.[49] The beliefs of many of the early Franciscans sent to New Spain descended from Saint Francis, who received inspiration from Joachim-like teachings and those in the Spiritual and Observant movements in the order, who emphasized the importance of poverty and an apocalyptic interpretation of history where events are placed into ages—an interpretation only revived further with the discovery of the Americas and their Indigenous populations.[50]

Indeed, the fifteenth-century Observant movement grew out of the writings of the earlier Spiritual Franciscans.[51] Eventually, the Observants would provide the majority of the Franciscans sent to New Spain.[52] Add to all of this that the thirteenth-century "Seraphic Doctor" of the Church, Saint Bonaventure, identified the founder of the order, Saint Francis, as the angel referenced in Revelation 7:2, which reads, "And I saw another angel ascending from the east, having the seal of the living God." Francis, with his stigmata, or "seal of the living God," was this apocalyptic angel.[53] In the end, the opportunity to evangelize a new population seen as misguided yet innocent and to erect among them a New Church, governed by the friars and restored to its original primitive purity and humility, and devoted to ushering in a new age, was an opportunity too precious to miss; it would fulfill all medieval prophecy and hopes.[54]

Leading up to the New World mission, various reform movements occurred among the Spanish Franciscans during the fifteenth century, which eventually allowed the dominance of the Observant Franciscans and their emphasis on religious asceticism. The Cardinal Cisneros and fray Juan de Guadalupe were important advocates in this return to simplicity and humility in Spain.[55] After all, according to Christ, the End of Times would bring about the rule and exaltation of the world's most humble where the meek would inherit the land (Matt. 5:5), and Spain needed to be prepared.

In the midst of such reforms, Guadalupe established houses in Extremadura where he and his followers could practice a rigorous form of religious asceticism they deemed to most closely follow the Rule of Saint Francis and Christ. Like Francis, Guadalupe was influenced by the teachings stemming from Joachim, and millenarianism played a role in his movement. Eventually, the houses and their respective custodies would form the Franciscan province of San Gabriel of Extremadura. Most of the early Franciscans sent to New Spain derived from this province.[56]

As scholars have outlined, fray Francisco de los Ángeles Quiñones viewed Cortés and his conquest as opening up fertile grounds for evangelization, and Quiñones desired to preach in New Spain. His appointment as minister general of the Friars Minor in 1523, however, required him to stay in Spain. In his place, fray Martín de Valencia organized a group of friars that would represent the first structured contingent of missionaries in Mexico—the Twelve. Not surprisingly, Valencia selected friars from the province of San Gabriel.[57]

Quiñones then gave the group their orders. Known as the *Instrucción* and *Obediencia*, the "instructions" and "admonitions" would establish the mood of early evangelization—and among other things, the mood was apocalyptic. Quiñones relates his friars to the workers in the Parable of the Laborers, who worked during the eleventh hour in the lord's vineyard or the kingdom of heaven. Like the lord of the vineyard, Quiñones called his fellow Franciscans to labor for souls in the kingdom of heaven in the eleventh hour before Christ's return and, as he states, during a time where the "last end of the age is approaching and is growing old."[58] Regardless of how each friar viewed his own mission to the New World, the Apocalypse informed the overall initial venture.

The Twelve were chosen to mirror the historical, apostolic twelve chosen by Christ and also the twelve followers of Saint Francis when he developed the order.[59] Moreover, according to the view of the sixteenth-century Franciscan Diego Valadés, although the devil used Martin Luther to damn countless, fray Martín de Valencia would save even more and help establish "the New Church."[60] Valencia himself experienced the fulfillment of historical prophecy. When at the monastery of Santa María de Hoyo in Extremadura, Valencia meditated upon the conversion of all the world and Psalm 59, which states, "that men may know that God rules in Jacob to the ends of the earth."[61] He asked, "Oh, and when will this be! When will this prophecy be fulfilled? Would I not be worthy to see this conversion as we are already at the evening and end of our days and in the last age of the world?" Eventually, God showed Valencia multitudes of non-Christians being converted, for which he praised heaven. Once in New Spain, Valencia claimed to have seen his vision come to fruition.[62]

It is important, however, to recognize that although frequently referenced by the homogeneous phrase "the Franciscans," the order and those evangelizing New Spain varied in beliefs, actions, and apocalyptic zeal. Such diversity was not new. Indeed, the Spiritual Franciscans who embraced a form of the Joachimite spirit were deemed unorthodox by Pope John XXII and disbanded in 1317, although the Observant Franciscans continued to breathe life into apocalypticism.[63] Regarding the Franciscans in Spain, Steven Turley notes that "within the 'united' Franciscan order at the start of the mission, many different kinds of friars existed: Guadalupan *descalzos* . . . recollects . . . Observants governed by still other statures, and even "crypto-Conventuals."[64] Paradoxically, Saint Francis emphasized two seemingly contradictory practices for the order: missionary work and solitude. Some who came to evangelize New Spain embraced an active ministry, while others preferred solitude and found that active ministry conflicted too much with such goals. And some, finding no middle ground, desired to abandon the mission and return to Spain.[65]

Just as they had before, then, the actions and beliefs of the early Franciscans differed, and although they all believed their work to be furthering the kingdom of God, not all believed in the same method. Indeed, sixteenth-century Franciscans held diverse ideologies, and some even fell under the scrutiny of the Inquisition. With regard to the Apocalypse, Maturino Gilberti expressed millenarian beliefs radical enough to warrant an investigation by the Inquisition, who claimed that Gilberti preached an exclusive salvation for friars and their followers during the Apocalypse.[66] In the end, although many of the early Franciscans sent to evangelize shared apocalyptic and eschatological aspirations, their ideological and devotional frameworks differed.

In addition to the variation within the order is the certain differences among the other orders.[67] Scholars of medieval apocalyptic discourse note that both Franciscans and Dominicans claimed that their orders had origins in the Apocalypse and shared many of the same discourses in their treatises. Indeed, some Dominicans engaged aspects of Joachim's eschatological view in supporting their order. Moreover, throughout the Middle Ages, many viewed the efforts of both orders to renew the Church as hastening the inevitable end.[68] However, over time it was easier for the Dominican order to remove itself from such immediate apocalyptic interpretation, particularly as Thomas Aquinas increasingly inspired the order. Bonaventure's connection of Saint Francis to the Apocalypse, however, made an apocalyptic rhetoric harder to avoid for the Franciscans.[69]

That said, it appears that many of the first Franciscans viewed the Indigenous people as virgin soil in which to plant a pure version of Catholicism, a New Church, untainted from the ailments that plagued the Old World and previous efforts of renewal. These and subsequent friars saw the hand of God preparing such soil through a variety of events, ranging from the commission of his servant Cortés, to the supposed prophecies of Nahua and Maya priests regarding the arrival of the Spaniards and Christianity, to sending devastating diseases according to his "secret judgments."[70] In light of such divine preparations, Indigenous people simply required proper education to rid themselves of traditions wrought by the devil's deception. Thus, prior to their daily chores, common Nahua and Maya children were to assemble at the local church each morning to learn the basic prayers and teachings of Catholicism. Yet the friars viewed the youth of the Nahua and Maya elite as having the greatest potential as future leaders, assistants, and allies, and such were destined for the schoolroom. Here, in the friars' makeshift boarding schools, they received instruction in Catholic doctrine and how to read and write in Nahuatl, Latin, and Spanish.

Many viewed the education of Indigenous people as essential to the formation of the New Church. In the minds of some friars, including Martín de Valencia, the baptism and intellectual conversion of Indigenous people would aid to usher in the Second Coming. Among their converts, the friars could create the idyllic Church of the past, stripped of pride and avarice and mirroring that imagined from the Bible.[71] Or as the bishop of Michoacán, Vasco de Quiroga, put it, "to plant a type of Christians . . . like those of the Primitive Church."[72]

Well known among the early Franciscans was Gerónimo de Mendieta. With his *Historia eclesiástica indiana*, Mendieta would interpret the discovery and subsequent military and spiritual conquest of Mexico in apocalyptic fashion. The efforts of the Franciscans were sanctioned by God himself, and those that questioned, opposed, or even delayed such efforts—even royal officials—were condemned unabashedly. And the Indigenous people, with their friar instructors, were to form a perfected, New Church.[73] The setbacks in establishing this New Church both frustrated and reinvigorated fray Bernardino de Sahagún. In the prologue to his 1585 *Arte adivinatoria*, he declared that God gave the Roman Pontiffs and the Catholic Church the duty to fulfill the prophecy given to the Old Testament prophet Jeremiah to rule "over the nations and over kingdoms, to root up and to pull down, and to waste, and to destroy, and to build, and to plant."[74] In the end, however, with the futility of early education efforts to eradicate idolatry evident, Sahagún lamented that the New Church, so often cited in the correspondence of the early Franciscans, was "founded on lies."[75]

For Mendieta, renewal included the education of a humble, primitive lifestyle, and he references a few cases of Indigenous followers. In one instance, a Nahua, Balthazar, established a settlement he called Chocaman, or "place of weeping," where he and his followers could focus on their commitment to God and eremitic spirituality away from the world. In another, Juan, desired so much to remain chaste that he prayed for God to give him some infirmity that would discourage his parents from finding him a match. God acquiesced and "blessed" Juan with an ailment of the throat, which deformed him in a way that led his parents to give up on him being married. Mendieta proclaimed that if all friars were similarly devoted, "the order of Saint Francis on earth would shine brighter than the sun."[76] Such behavior reflected that of the early friars who often walked barefooted in ragged clothing and engaged in frequent fasting and even corporal mortification.[77]

A tangible fruit of such attitudes of renewal certainly included the establishment of the Franciscans' first institution of higher learning for select noble youth and promising students, the Colegio de Santa Cruz in Tlatelolco, established in 1536. The boarders received lessons in myriad disciplines including music, humanist philosophy, grammar, arithmetic, logic, and theology. The college would not only produce the Indigenous assistants the friars so desperately needed to realize evangelization but also initially produce an educated Indigenous government.[78] Although the epidemics of the sixteenth century and decreasing funds led to the school's decline by the seventeenth century, the institution and others like it armed Indigenous people with knowledge not only of Catholicism but also the workings of Spanish society. Moreover, within its walls, Nahuas and friars produced some of the most beautiful examples of Nahuatl religious texts destined, as friars Alonso de Molina and Juan Bautista Viseo stated, to assist in the foundation of the New Church.[79]

Similar schools for Indigenous people appeared throughout central Mexico and Yucatan. Although the larger convents boasted sizable schools for nobility, many were modest rooms attached to the town church where an Indigenous instructor would walk the youth of the town through the basic prayers and doctrines. A select few became *indios de confianza* trained in reading and writing. These persons, like the Maya *maestros* of Yucatan and the Nahua *fiscales* of central Mexico, would serve as general assistants to the local ecclesiastic in charge of the town, performing tasks in the frequent absence of the priest. As one Franciscan commented, "They are already instructed in Christian doctrine, and the sons teach their parents privately, and publicly from the pulpits in a marvelous manner, and many of them are teachers of the other children."[80] Baptizing, confessing, and assisting to achieve a good death for those in their last extremity all fell under the purview of such Indigenous surrogate priests, as did the Christian instruction of the youth and the training of subsequent assistants and *escribanos* (scribes).[81]

Such knowledge proved vital to negotiating the new and challenging colonial world. As one scholar stated regarding the Nahua, but also easily applied to Mayas, "With European invasion, the Nahua experienced a true apocalypse: war, famine, and disease, followed by the imposition of a new social system."[82] Indeed, as illustrated above, the Apocalypse served not only to encourage Christian behavior but also to justify Spanish expansion and domination over land and people. Yet, as will be seen throughout this book, Christianity and its eschatology could also shelter elements of preexisting worldviews, which explained the new colonial era along familiar lines allowing some continuation of the old within the new. After all, adaptation and resilience have been the hallmark of Mesoamerican peoples for millennia.

Thus, in these early colonial schools many Indigenous students and their successors came to view the present through both Apocalyptic and traditional lenses. In addition to the didactic eschatological texts examined in this book, Nahuas and Mayas—particularly those suffering through the epidemics of the sixteenth-century—produced other works betraying the impact of the Apocalypse. For example, Book Twelve of the *Florentine Codex*, its images, and its omens explained the conquest through Catholic eschatology and preexisting forms of divination and symbolism; paintings and frescoes frequently blended European apocalyptic imagery with Indigenous motifs; and the Maya Books of Chilam Balam—local, Maya manuscripts containing a variety of texts relevant to the town—included Christian eschatology and Maya worldviews in their texts on creation and renewal.[83] As so often happens, tools of oppression could likewise become instruments in adaptation and regeneration.

But why found the College of Tlatelolco? Necessity played an important role, to be sure. The ecclesiastics were impossibly outnumbered by their Indigenous fold, and the need for assistants fluent in the vernacular encouraged the early schools. So too did the desire to educate the next generation in how to live in *policía cristiana*, or "Christian civility," according to Spanish expectations.[84] After all, good Christians were at the same time good Spaniards or good subjects under the Spanish crown. Such were the motivations for various schools throughout Catholicism's global endeavor resulting, for example, in the African kings of the Kongo establishing various Jesuit schools for youth in the mid-sixteenth century and the creation of schools for Japanese youth to teach them the doctrine, reading, and writing by the 1580s.[85] Sixteenth-century Mexico, however, stands apart. To be sure, the sedentary nature of its Indigenous populations and their exposure to forms of writing prior to Spanish contact distinguished Mesoamerica. Yet the educational scope of the College of Tlatelolco and resulting collaborative texts between teacher and Indigenous student was simply unparalleled in any other part of the world.

Certainly, the humanist beliefs of the Franciscans played a part. In Tlatelolco, Nahuas were to receive education in the Bible, the Fathers of the Church, and Latin, among other subjects—all hallmarks of a humanist education.[86] Furthermore, Nahuatl translations and redactions appeared, or were being prepared, of various humanistic and devotional works including fray Luis de Granada's *Libro de la oración y meditación* and Thomas à Kempis's *Imitation of Christ*; and even Denys the Carthusian's commentary on proper government, "On the Government of a Polity."[87] All such works would have been helpful in training the Indigenous leaders of a renewed and more perfect society. Moreover, the cofounder of the college, Bishop fray Juan de Zumárraga, who subscribed to Joachim-like ideas of the millennium, followed the teachings of the humanists Erasmus and Thomas More.[88]

Yet, as others have done, it is important consider the impact of the millenarian and restorative mindset of the various early friars on Indigenous education and, in particular, the College of Tlatelolco.[89] Certainly, the Franciscan Pedro de Gante thought as much when opening the college's predecessor, the school of San José de los Naturales.[90] How can a new age or the New Church, basking in spiritual insight, be achieved in ignorance? It was necessary, then, to help Indigenous people, at least those nobles among them, to achieve this heightened understanding through education in the schools and to help establish and lead the New Church. Moreover, as Baudot noted, the Franciscans opposed the Hispanization of Mexico, for such endangered their ability to separate Indigenous people from the corrupting influences of Spaniards and the Old World in general.[91] Thus, Indigenous people should be taught in their own quotidian tongue from texts in their own language in order to achieve their religious potential.[92]

Other orders, such as the Dominicans and Augustinians, created schools to be sure, and such orders, as will be seen, likewise employed the Apocalypse in their teachings and ideals. But all lacked the initial aspirations of the College of Tlatelolco, which was designed to create a highly educated Indigenous nobility that would administer in the New Church alongside friars.[93] As mentioned, Franciscans such as Molina and Bautista saw their efforts to produce religious texts as serving in and strengthening the New Church—a motive and term, interestingly, not seen in the texts of other orders.[94] It is possible, although admittedly speculative, that without the millenarian and renewalist mindset of many of the early friars, the Franciscans would have served only to educate Indigenous people in the basic doctrine and would have likely robbed history of the many Indigenous-language masterpieces that emerged through Nahua-friar collaboration. Indeed, of the Nahuatl religious texts printed in the colonial period, the Franciscans authored twenty-four while the Dominicans and Augustinians authored eight and nine respectively.[95]

Apocalypticism and the call for renewal did not restrain itself to central Mexico.[96] The early friars in Yucatan likewise received influence from its reinvigorated zeal, even participating in mass baptisms. Perhaps most (in)famous among the friars was the Franciscan Diego de Landa. Landa began his years in Yucatan as a zealous preacher who, from all accounts, enjoyed his time with the Maya. Yet when evidence reached him of idolatry among his baptized fold, Landa unleashed an inquisition that resulted in the deaths of hundreds and the torture of thousands, not to mention the burning of countless Maya codices. Some scholars have blamed his inquisitorial actions on Franciscan paternalism. Yet recent studies have examined his inquisition within the context of millenarianism and Spanish practices employed during the Middle Ages.[97]

Regardless of Landa's exact millenarian beliefs, the Apocalypse adorned one of his hallmarks: the monastery of Izamal. As Restall and Solari note, inside the massive structure that Landa helped construct in the 1560s is a series of Maya-painted murals appearing shortly after the church was finished. The murals include a representation of the Virgin Mary dressed in a red and blue robe in front of a yellow orb. She was the Virgin of the Apocalypse as recorded in Revelation 12:1: "And there appeared a great wonder in heaven; a woman clothed with the sun, and the moon under her feet, and upon her head a crown of twelve stars."[98] Yet the realities of everyday life seemed to have tempered Landa's optimism. Indeed, it appears that when Landa referenced the *primitiva yglesia* (primitive church) in a 1574 letter to the inquisitors of New Spain, he did so in reference to Christianity's neophytic, not apostolic, nature in the colony, hoping that the Inquisition would provide some much needed support and "suppress and remedy the many evils" that existed.[99]

An important point needs to be reemphasized here: not everything concerning sixteenth-century evangelization can or should be connected to millenarianism, nor did all friars associate the opportunity to build the New Church, or even efforts to restore the primitive church of the Bible, with a fast-approaching apocalyptic end.[100] Indeed, although examples exist of various sixteenth-century friars connecting their proselytizing work with the New Church, most left no record indicating that they thought a "Millennial Kingdom" was right around the corner. For example, in a 1562 letter to the king, the first bishop of Yucatan, fray Francisco Toral, expressed his dedication to his evangelical work: "Certainly I will work until I die to serve our lord and your majesty in that New World and Church," and that his and the labor of the friars will be "for the good of that New Church."[101] Toral seemed to view his work as contributing to the establishment of a renewed church and era but, similar to Sahagún, avoided the urgent tone of millenarianism. Eventually, and along with millenarian beliefs, the idea of a New Church increasingly lost momentum as the colonial period progressed. Indeed, the eighteenth-century Franciscan Pedro Beltrán de Santa Rosa never mentions the New Church when composing his religious texts in Yucatan. Instead, he refers to his Indigenous audience as *pobrecitos* (poor things) on numerous occasions.[102] His omission and opinion are reflective of the majority of seventeenth- and eighteenth-century religious texts.

Although the apocalyptic zeal held by many in the early companies of friars waned by the mid-sixteenth century, the harsh realities and struggles of colonial life continued to sustain the doctrine of the Apocalypse.[103] Moreover, the utility of the Apocalypse, and Christianity in general, in forming a population obedient to Catholic and Spanish authority surely provided the event relevancy throughout the colonial period.[104] Thus, regardless of the exact apocalyptic and millenarian beliefs of the early friars—many of which are impossible to ascertain for certain—the impact of the Apocalypse remained constant. Every single ecclesiastic to proselyte in the New World believed that his work contributed to building an orderly, Christian kingdom for God that would eventually triumph in the Apocalypse.

Despite the fading of idealistic, even millenarian hopes, certainly a middle ground existed throughout the sixteenth century and entire colonial period between an immediate and delayed Apocalypse. On this middle ground, ecclesiastics could safely believe that the evangelization of New Spain played an important role in preparing the world for an end that would arrive someday in the undiscerned future.[105] As the jurist Juan de Solórzano Pereira stated in his 1648 *Política indiana*, Spain would be the messenger of the Gospel, and "with the preaching of the Gospel to all the world, the Day of Judgment will come."[106] Or, as fray Martín de León stated, the work of preaching the word of God and salvation would continue "until the end of the world."[107] The Apocalypse and the evangelization of the New World truly went hand in hand.

Mendieta relied heavily on an apocalyptic view of history. But by the end of the sixteenth century, history largely had stopped supporting Mendieta's vision of renewal. As Phelan observed, Mendieta finished his *Historia eclesiástica indiana* in frustration and pessimism. God had granted Spain the New World upon which to establish a purified version of Christianity. For their part, the physical and spiritual conquistadors had played their role. Yet the "beast of avarice" had reared its head to exploit Indigenous people and the New World's material rather than spiritual spoils. Philip II was failing his role as king and spiritual leader as was Spain in its charge to convert all humankind to Christianity.[108] But in truth, the Reformation had redirected the attention of the Catholic monarchs back to Europe, Asia was providing a new option for converts and renewal, and those friars destined for the Americas brought with them a much more basic and practical ideal of conversion.[109] Mendieta's sixteenth-century version of the millennial age spoken of in various forms by Joachim, his later followers, and the Spiritual and Observant Franciscans would have to wait.

But waiting was not on the mind of Marshall Applewhite in 1997. Years ago, Applewhite began examining the teachings of Saint Francis and the book of Revelation.[110] Ultimately, he viewed himself and his companion, Bonnie Nettles, as the two witnesses or prophets described in Revelation 11:3–12 and destined to die only to be resurrected and ascend to heaven in glory. Applewhite and Nettles thought their ascension would be to a spacecraft that would transport them to heaven. Although most rebuffed Applewhite and Nettles, their proselytizing earned them a small number of followers. When Nettles died in 1985, Applewhite believed she had progressed to the Next Level.

The new millennium approached, a sign in the heavens appeared, and the time came. The highly visible comet Hale-Bopp was to pass closest to the earth in March 1997. Applewhite believed a rumor that the comet hid a spaceship in its tail and thought that Nettles, and the extraterrestrial human known as Jesus Christ, could be aboard awaiting him and his followers. In late March 1997, Applewhite facilitated the mass suicide of himself and his thirty-eight followers in a mansion of Rancho Santa Fe, California, to ascend to the spaceship—a sort of "technological rapture"—and avoid the impending Apocalypse.[111] At the time, I was a teenager living nine miles away; I still remember the newspaper headlines describing the "Mansion of Death."[112] The Apocalypse had suddenly become very real and relevant again.

Present-day calamities, wars, and misfortunes frequently summon the Apocalypse and betray its fluid and mercurial ability to appear throughout the ages and regions of the world. The Apocalypse is at the heart of diversity in the Catholic Church. Throughout the Middle Ages it could both justify and foretell the dominant spread of Roman Christianity while paradoxically associating the Roman Church and its institutions with the Antichrist deserving of eradication.[113] Perhaps never at any given time in the history of Christianity did one single interpretation of the event exist. And despite Joachim's general influence, many Church authorities disagreed with his views or, at the very least, selectively chose which views to endorse.[114]

The Apocalypse, versions of millenarianism, and the effort for renewal found in the early stages of New Spain's evangelization certainly did not begin in the Americas.[115] Such ideas had existed in the Old World long before, where they experienced the ebb and flow of interest and attention eventually culminating to provide the theological fodder that drove exploration and early evangelization efforts. Indeed, the efforts of renewal seen in New Spain are echoes of those attempted previously in Europe, albeit with a new population and some new techniques. As the millenarianism and renewal efforts met the same fate they suffered in Europe, ecclesiastics increasingly turned to the Apocalypse for its utility in teaching the doctrine that would form a righteous, Christian fold obedient to Spanish colonialism and prepared to meet their own, personal apocalypse (the topic of the next chapter). Such eschatological instruction would create a righteous congregation that could stand resurrected next to Christ during the actual End of Days, whenever that might be.

In a way, the remainder of this book attempts to follow the advice of Sahagún who encouraged a move beyond the illusion of a quick fulfillment of millenarian prophecy in order to produce a truly converted Indigenous Christian through detailed instruction. In his exposure of this illusion is his plea for more instruction on eschatological topics including death, the immediate afterlife, the rewards of heaven, and the punishments of hell.[116] The following chapters illustrate this important step in the evolution of the Apocalypse as Nahuas, Mayas, and ecclesiastics reworked and preserved an Old World Apocalypse and its teachings to accommodate its New World setting, thus providing the instruction Sahagún so desperately wanted.

≈ 2 ≈

The Personal Apocalypse

The First Judgment, Limbo, and Purgatory

At the moment of death, each man has his Apocalypse.

Homero Aridjis

Death is scary for many of us. We hate everything about it, really. From the aging process to the uncertainty of what happens after death, humankind has often been preoccupied with delaying the inevitability of death and its finality and uncertainty—delaying, in short, our own personal apocalypse. Advances in medicine have increased life expectancy in the United States to nearly seventy-nine; an increase of about ten years since 1959.[1] Not only are people living longer, but we look younger longer, too. The signs of death within our own body—wrinkles, graying hair, sagging skin, and so on—can be delayed and, in some cases, reversed due to anti-aging creams, injections, and plastic surgery. Ironically, this process of delaying and avoiding death often makes death that much scarier. Whereas death was a common part of life throughout the course of human history, such has greatly receded in present day to the point that many people think nothing of going to the store and buying a chicken breast for dinner but would be made ill—even offended—to see a chicken killed. Modern society's unfamiliarity with death only worsens our fear. In short, many today remain scared to death of death.

Humankind's general trepidation about death—the personal apocalypse—and the uncertainty it breeds was not lost on Christianity. Used properly, the fear could win over an audience's attention (always a struggle during a sermon) and encourage proper moral behavior. In Catholicism, everyone experiences two moments of judgment. The first occurs at one's death and is a particular, or individual, judgment. This judgment determines the eternal residence of the soul: either to heaven—perhaps with a stop first in purgatory—or to hell. The second moment is more of a reveal than a judgment, which occurs during the final, or universal, judgment. Here, everyone is brought before Christ where, in front of all humankind, the "the truth of each man's relationship with God will be laid bare," confirming the sentence previously awarded during the particular judgment.[2] Descriptions of the torture and suffering awaiting those who disobey God's law would not only grab the attention of parishioners but also scare them into living a Christian life to avoid both an unfortunate experience during their first, or particular, judgment and having such confirmed and extended at the Final Judgment of the Apocalypse.

After an introduction to the Old World concepts of the particular judgment, purgatory, and limbo, this chapter examines various examples from Nahuatl and Maya texts to demonstrate the instruction received on these topics. The following explores how European, Nahua, and Maya worldviews combined to create the narrative and rhetoric of each sermon that, in itself, represented a new step in the evolution of the Apocalypse and its eschatological teachings. To be sure, death and its immediate consequences were powerful motivators and, thus, throughout the colonial period, occupied the pages of ecclesiastical texts that were intended for Nahuas and Mayas alike and that instructed them why most everyone should fear death.

The First Judgment, Purgatory, and Limbo

Two biblical passages in particular encouraged the Church to believe in a particular judgment and subsequent fates for the soul upon death. The first comes from Christ's parable of the rich man and Lazarus. In the parable, the rich man spent his days in luxury while Lazarus begs in vain at his gate. Upon death, the rich man found himself in hell (Hades), amid the flames, and sees Lazarus in Abraham's Bosom—often called the limbo of the

Fathers—a place within the next life that the Church believed to be where the righteous awaited Christ and his harrowing of hell.[3] The rich man petitioned Abraham to send Lazarus, "that he may dip the tip of his finger in water and cool my tongue; for I am tormented in this flame." But Abraham explained the futility of such a request as the rich man had received his reward during life, and an unbridgeable gulf divided the two men.[4] The second example derives from the crucifixion of Christ. His crucifixion took place between two "criminals," and during the ordeal, one mocked Christ while the other petitioned his good graces. To the latter Christ said, "Amen, I say to you, today you will be with me in paradise."[5]

Both passages allowed the Church to promote an initial, particular judgment upon death, which occurs prior to the resurrection and Final Judgment and determines the placement of one's soul and its reward or punishment.[6] Yet the specifics of such an intermediate afterlife increasingly became a topic of debate between the second and fourth centuries. Various Church Fathers, including Saints Ambrose and Augustine, offered their opinions on the organization of the afterlife following the particular judgment and the punishment or reward of the soul upon death. For example, in his works *The Confessions* and *The Enchiridion*, Augustine suggests four divisions in the afterlife: paradise for the exceptionally righteous; hell for the truly wicked; and two for the partly wicked and the partly righteous that can be reached to various degrees by the prayers of the living.[7]

Such debates combined with ancient beliefs from the Egyptians, Greeks, Romans, and others regarding the reward and punishment, and sometimes purification, of the soul after death to nurture the idea of purgatory and limbo. Jacques Le Goff claims that "until the end of the twelfth century the noun *purgatorium* did not exist: *the* Purgatory had not yet been born."[8] Although some medievalist disagree with the time frame and nature of the emergence of purgatory, its popularity and doctrinal maturity beginning in the twelfth century is evident.[9] Stories of visions of purgatory spread with increasing popularity, from the vision of Dryhthelm appearing in Bede's eighth-century *Ecclesiastical History of the English People* to the twelfth-century tale of *St. Patrick's Purgatory* and Dante Alighieri's fourteenth-century *Divine Comedy*. And as purgatory began to take shape, it also became intimately connected with the living whose prayers and works could assist the suffering souls to pay their spiritual debt and become clean.[10] Indeed, the word "purgatory" derives from the Latin *purgo*, "to wash, to clean," and the Nahuatl translation most often appears as *nechipahualoyan*, "place of purification or cleaning"; the Maya simply used the loanword *purgatorio*.

Importantly, the Council of Trent (1545–63) endorsed the already accepted existence of purgatory and the potential to assist its tortured souls.[11] An important avenue for this assistance derived from requiem masses requested in wills and prayers offered by the living. By the twelfth century, confraternities had become popular for the assistance they provided to the postmortem soul, and masses for the deceased were a familiar feature in most areas.[12] In the fifteenth century, Thomas à Kempis's popular text, *Imitatio Christi* (Imitation of Christ), later translated into Castilian in the late fifteenth century, helped spread a movement encouraging a meditative and personal experience with God known as the *devotio moderna*.[13] The *Imitatio* contained the counsel, "It is better to atone for sin now and to cut away vices than to keep them for purgation in the hereafter. . . . One hour of suffering there [in purgatory] will be more bitter than a hundred years of the most severe penance here [on earth]."[14] By the sixteenth century in Spain, cofradias, masses, and prayers for those in purgatory were a common staple in wills. Even spiritual apparitions from those in purgatory to the living became more commonplace as tortured souls plead for assistance from those with the means to give it.[15] In short, purgatory, as a result of the particular judgment, had become a well-known fixture in the doctrine of Christianity.

But what of limbo? Although the Gospel of Luke placed the righteous who died before Christ in Abraham's Bosom, speculation continued—and continues today!—regarding the fate of unbaptized infants. As Henry Ansgar Kelly explains, Saint Augustine claimed that unbaptized infants were damned and punished but only in the slightest form. Later, Peter Lombard and Thomas Aquinas posited that although denied an eternal abode with God, they existed "without any other pain of fire or conscience." Church councils over the ages largely confirmed this lessened state of punishment for unbaptized infants but, unlike purgatory, failed to confirm the doctrine of a limbo for infants.[16]

In sum, at the time of their arrival in New Spain, Spanish ecclesiastics brought with them a general view of the immediate afterlife that included the limbo of the Fathers; the limbo of infants; purgatory; and hell itself.[17] Unsurprisingly, then, such topics crossed the Atlantic to become a familiar aspect of Christianity to Nahuas and Mayas. Indeed, bequests for the care of the purgatory soul appear in nearly every Nahua and Maya will authored throughout the colonial period. As demonstrated below, numerous religious plays, sermons, and exempla (illustrative stories) on the particular judgment, purgatory, and limbo instructed Nahuas and Mayas who were no strangers to death.

Familiar with dramatics, both Nahuas and Spaniards employed some form of religious theater prior to their contact. Nahua deity impersonators, *ixiptla*, would dress the part of a particular god to become that divine being in ceremonies that retold historical and mythical events. Spanish actors of religious dramas likewise played roles in recreating biblical and historical events. In the initial years of Mexican evangelization, "Aztec and European traditions merged in the invention of Nahuatl theater, the first true American theater."[18] Not surprisingly, Nahuatl theater's religious dramas included those illustrating to a Nahua audience the importance of living a Christian life so as not to receive a poor particular judgment and subsequent punishments.

Such was demonstrated in the drama *How to Live on Earth*. In the play, Lorenzo and his wife, decide to place the things of God above earthly riches, pray for those souls in purgatory, and confess their sins before the priest. In contrast, a disrespectful youth slaps the faces of his father and mother and fails to cross himself before sleeping. All three go to purgatory upon their death and await their judgment. When Christ calls for their souls, "those who have loved one another well on earth" (presumably Lorenzo and his wife) go to heaven. However, regarding the wicked youth, Christ orders the demons, "Come. Take him there to the fiery crag. Hang him, beat him, rip him apart there, because it is I whom he slapped in the face, I whom he offended."[19]

A similar theme is repeated in the play *Souls and Testamentary Executors*, relating the fate of the soul upon death and the moral necessity of executors of wills to fulfill the wishes of the dead. Here, don Pedro and his wife express their concern for those in purgatory and their suffering. A demon attempts to deter the wife from entering the church, but the priest assures her of the benefits of praying for the dead in purgatory: "When your earthy life comes to an end they will speak on your behalf so that God will favor you." Meanwhile, a widow and two executors of a will fail to uphold the wishes of the dead and pray for him even though the widow had a vision of her husband "greatly suffering" in purgatory. Instead, the trio spend the money set aside for the deceased's Mass on themselves. Eventually, Christ orders demons to bring him the widow and negligent executors. Saint Michael and Lucifer then discuss their obedience to the Ten Commandments and Five Commandments of the Church while reading a document recording their sins, a book of life of sorts. Their wickedness proven, Christ orders them to hell where they are placed on a wheel of fire, "into the place of fire-blackened water, into the house with tubs of fire" to be greatly tormented.[20]

Outside religious drama, the particular judgment and purgatory make regular appearances in nearly every Nahuatl book of sermons, catechism, and confessional manual. And although scholars must fish in a more limited documentary pool, Maya religious texts likewise give the topics proportionate attention. Yet, as demonstrated in the examples that follow, each religious text differed in the focus and detail such subjects received.

Nahuatl and Maya texts devote few words to Abraham's Bosom and the limbo for infants. Most texts' limited coverage of these limbos focuses on Abraham's Bosom due to its reference in the fifth Articles of Faith pertaining to the humanity of God and discussing Christ's harrowing of hell and resurrection. For example, in addressing the fifth Articles of Faith in his 1577 Nahuatl *Sermonario* (book of sermons), fray Juan de la Anunciación discusses the four areas of the afterlife. After describing hell and purgatory he moves on to limbo:

And next to purgatory there is also a place called limbo where the tender, unbaptized children go. They are not burned nor are they afflicted by anything, but all that they suffer is that they never ever will see our lord God. And also there was a place also called limbo, or *Abraham's Bosom*, it means in the arms of Abraham. There, the entirely clean soul of our lord Jesus Christ descended, it was going along fully united with his divinity. And there, there was no eternal suffering at all as there is in hell. Nor is there any suffering as there is in purgatory. Nor also was it [the soul] placed there forever, as the tender, unbaptized children who are eternally placed in another limbo.[21]

The Dominican Domingo de la Anunciación described Abraham's Bosom with a bit more dire prose in his 1565 doctrina describing it as *tlayohuayan, mixtecomac* (a place of darkness, a place of fogginess).[22] And fray Martín de León describes it as a *mictlan teilpilcalli* (hell prison), where the saints and righteous fathers awaited Christ.[23] Most texts referenced limbo in association with Abraham's Bosom, not the limbo of infants, and most texts simply refer to it as a place in *mictlan* (hell). No doubt the Nahua and Maya, like many today, had vague understandings of limbo. Interestingly, in 2004, Pope John Paul II asked the International Theological Commission to reexamine the limbo of infants. In 2007, the commission produced a statement confirming "serious theological and liturgical grounds for hope" for the fate of unbaptized infants, while categorizing their limbo as a "theological opinion."[24] Although never truly existing as a confirmed doctrine, it would seem that limbo is on the "edge" of people's beliefs.

Overall, then, the concept of a first and particular judgment followed by the placement of the soul was taught to the Nahua and Maya. Yet, as will be seen, the level of exposure, detail, and explanation varied from text to text and culture to culture as authors negotiated between European and Mesoamerican worldviews and colonial realities to convey their messages.[25] The following provides a few of many examples.

Purgatory and the Exemplum of Saint Vincent Ferrer in Bautista's 1599 *Confessionario*

As mentioned in chapter 1, some theologians identified Saint Francis as an apocalyptic angel. Yet he was not the only one. Many also believed the Dominican friar Vincent Ferrer (1350–1419) to have been an "Angel of the Apocalypse," destined to warn everyone regarding the Day of Judgment. Vincent was renowned for his miracles and missionary work. One of the wonders most oft recounted in text and imagery concerns an insane mother who dismembers and cooks her own baby for the dinner of the saint. After Vincent prayed over the body parts, they reunited, and the infant lived without any blemish. He attempted such a miracle of reunification in his efforts to end the Western Schism (1378–1414)—a period when up to three popes claimed the papacy. In his missionary work, he employed a message forewarning the rapid approach of the Apocalypse to convert Muslims, Jews, and others. His reputation as miracle worker and apocalyptic preacher carried his legend across the Atlantic to the New World.[26]

Various Dominican churches and provinces in the Americas held the name of Vincent Ferrer, and numerous publications containing his sermons appeared in colonial repositories. As Laura Smoller notes, one of the more popular colonial publications concerns a novena to the saint published in Mexico City, Guatemala, Lima, Buenos Aires, and Puebla from 1710 to 1850, which was, apparently, responsible for numerous miracles. And his visual representation appears on media from small retablos to large canvases adorning churches.[27] One example derives from the seventeenth-century artist Cristóbal de Villalpando, who practiced his craft in Mexico City and Puebla. As an apocalyptic angel, Vincent is given wings and is gazing over his shoulder at Christ presiding over the Last Judgment with Mary as intercessor. In front of Vincent is the miraculously restored baby holding the spit once used to cook its body (see figure 2.1).[28] Yet Vincent, his sermons, and his life also appeared in Indigenous-language texts. His eschatological sermons influenced the sixteenth-century Nahuatl author, Fabián de Aquino, who wrote two Antichrist plays.[29] Moreover, stories of his life appear in confessional manuals including fray Juan Bautista's 1599 *Confessionario*, the text examined here.[30]

Juan Bautista Viseo was born in Mexico in 1555 and became the most productive Franciscan author of Nahuatl texts during the colonial period. At age fifteen he joined the Franciscan order and began his studies in the convent of San Francisco de México under the tutelage of the Nahuatl scholar Miguel de Zárate, among others. Bautista served in a variety of positions including guardian (religious superior) at the College of Tlatelolco from 1598 to 1603 and lecturer in theology at the same. His relationship with the college remained close, and there he collaborated with both friar and Nahua to publish a variety of Nahuatl texts, including his *Confessionario*.[31]

Attempting to encourage a complete confession and performance of penance, Bautista employs the saint not for his miracles but for the vision

Figure 2.1 Cristóbal de Villalpando, *San Vicente Ferrer*. Reproduction in *Arte y mística*.

granted to him of his sister in purgatory. Medieval accounts and stories of visions of souls in purgatory and apparitions were not uncommon, although their frequency diminished in sixteenth-century Spain in light of the distrust of lay visions.[32] As the traditional, European story goes, Francisca fell victim to rape from her merchant husband's slave and became pregnant. After poisoning the slave and aborting the pregnancy, she concealed her sins from everyone and only later confessed to a strange priest who "was

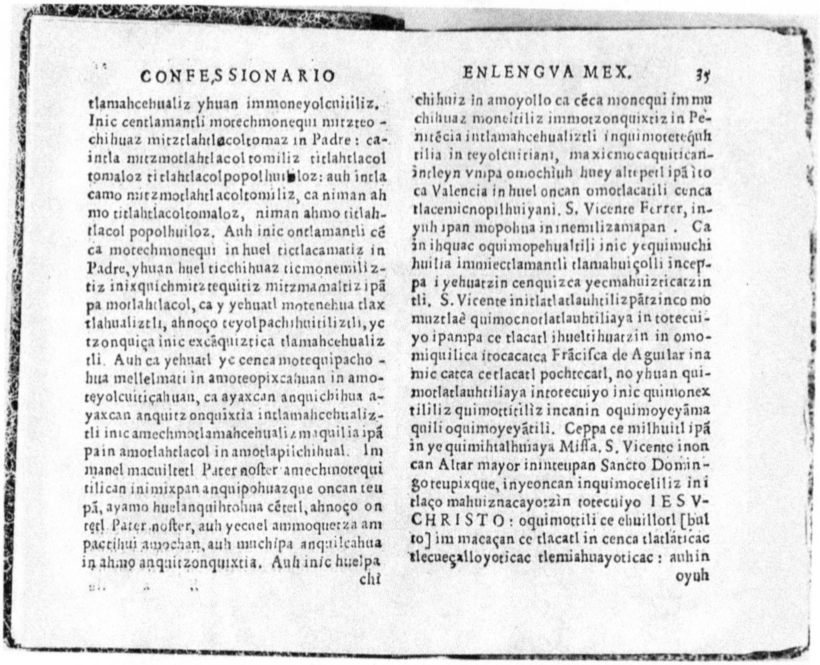

CONFESSIONARIO

tlamahcehualiz yhuan immoneyolcuitiliz.
Inic centlamantli motechmonequi mitzteo-
chihuaz mitztlahtlacoltomaz in Padre: ca-
intla mitzmotlahtlacoltomiliz titlahtlacol
tomaloz titlahtlacolpopolhuiloz: auh intla
camo mitzmotlahtlacoltomiliz, ca niman ah
mo titlahtlacoltomaloz, niman ahmo titlahtlacol popolhuiloz. Auh inic ontlamantli cē
ca motechmonequi in huel tictlacamatiz in
Padre, yhuan huel ticchihuaz ticmonemiliz-
tiz inixquichmitztequitiz mitzmamaltiz ipā
pa motlahtlacol, ca y yehuatl motenehua tlax
tlahualiztli, ahnoço teyolpachihuitiliztli, yc
tzonquiça inic excāquiztica tlamahcehualiz
tli. Auh ca yehuatl yc cenca motequipacho-
hua mellelmati in amoteopixcahuan in amo-
teyolcuitiçahuan, ca ayaxcan anquichihua a-
yaxcan anquitzonquixtia intlamahcehualiztli inic amechmotlamahcehualizmaquilia ipā
pain amotlahtlacol in amotlapiichihual. Im
manel macuiltetl Pater noſter amechmotequi
tilican inimixpan anquipohuazque oncan teu
pā, ayamo huelanquihtohua cētetl, ahnoço on
tetl Pater noſter, auh yecuel ammoquetza am
pactihui amochan, auh muchipa anquilcahua
in ahmo anquitzonquixtia. Auh inic huelpa
chi

ENLENGVA MEX. 35

chihuiz in amoyollo ca cēca monequi im mu
chihuaz moneltiliz immotzonquixtiz in Pe-
nitēcia intlamahcehualiztli in quimoteteq̄uh
tilia in teyolcuitiani, maxicmocaquitican-
intleyn vmpa omochiuh huey altepetl ipā ito
ca Valencia in huel oncan omotlacatili cenca
tlacenmicnopilhuiyani. S. Vicente Ferrer, in-
yuh ipan mopohua in inemilizamapan. Ca
in ihquac oquimopehualtili inic yequimuchi
huilia immiectlamantli tlamahuiçolli incep-
pa i yehuatzin cenquizca yecmahuiztica tzin
tli. S. Vicente initlatlatlauhtilizpātzinco mo
muztlaè quimocnotlatlauhtiliaya in totecuiyo ipampa ce tlacatl ihueltihuatzin in omo-
miquilica itocacatca Frāciſca de Aguilar ina
mic catca cetlacatl pochtecatl, no yhuan qui-
motlatlauhtiliaya intotecuiyo inic quimonex
tililiz quimottitiliz incanin oquimoyeyāma
quili oquimoyeyātili. Ceppa ce milhuitl ipā
in ye quimihtalhuiaya Miſſa. S. Vicente inon
can Altar mayor ininteupan Sancto Domingo teupixque, inyeoncan inquimoceliliz in i
tlaço mahuiznacayotzin totecuiyo IESV-
CHRISTO: oquimottili ce chuillotl [bul
to] im macaçan ce tlacatl in cenca tlatlaticac
tlecueçalloyoticac tlemiahuayoticac: auh in
oyuh

Figure 2.2 *Confessionario en lengua Mexicana y Castellana,* 34v-35r. Courtesy of the John Carter Brown Library.

in reality a devil." Three days after her confession, she died and landed in purgatory. The tormented Francisca appeared to her brother surrounded by flames and eating a tanned baby boy (*atezado niño*) whom she held in her hands only to vomit him out whole again. She pleaded for his help in ending her torments. Vincent offered forty-eight masses for her soul. Upon their completion, Vincent saw his sister adorned with a crown of flowers ascend with angels to heaven.[33]

The version appearing in Bautista's *Confessionario* is a simplified, less graphic version neglecting the salacious details of Francsica's rape, abortion, and the cannibalistic image of her eating her aborted child in purgatory. The text also leaves out the detail of a devil disguised as a priest, perhaps not wanting to foment suspicion or distrust regarding confessors. In the Nahuatl text, Vincent inquires of God regarding the state of his deceased sister. In response, the burning image of his sister appears to him, lamenting her failure to complete the penance her confessors gave her while alive, resulting in her torment in purgatory. Vincent performs forty-seven masses on her behalf, leading in her liberation from purgatory and ascension to heaven.

Interestingly, the tale also appears later in a Jesuit manuscript collection of eighteenth-century Nahuatl sermons whose unknown author admits having referenced sixteenth-century authors including Bautista. The Jesuit rendition of the exemplum certainly drew upon Bautista's work—oftentimes verbatim, at other times modified, but in all cases the moral remains the same.[34] Similar to Ignacio Paredes's eighteenth-century attempt to model his Nahuatl after the masters of an earlier age (seen below), the Jesuit text includes plenty of couplets and triplets reflecting the traditional rhetorical style of Nahuatl, employing parallelisms.

For example, when Francisca appeared before Vincent, the Bautista and Jesuit texts both describe her burning image with the triplet *tlatlaticac, tecueçalloyoticac, tlemiahuayoticac* (she stood burning, emitting flames, casting flames). Other times, the Jesuit text seems to overcompensate in its attempts to reflect a sixteenth-century discourse. In the Bautista text, when Vincent sees his sister's burning image, he wonders at how this could be, replying to his sister in a series of couplets *cenca qualli yectli motenyo motoca, yhuan motley momahuizço* (your reputation, your name, and your honor, renown, was very good, righteous). It appears that the Jesuit text intended to amplify the phrase by removing the *yhuan* (and) to allow for the uninterrupted quadruplet *motenyo, motoca, motley, momahuiço* (your reputation, your name, your honor, your renown).[35] In the end, both renditions of this exemplum reflect the parallelism so often seen in early colonial Nahuatl rhetoric, albeit with the Jesuit text doing so retroactively.

Moreover, both texts allow for the influence of the Nahua worldview on that of the Catholic. For example, Francisca appeared to Vincent as an *ehuillotl*, which the Bautista text describes with the subsequent Spanish word of *bulto*, "image" or "shape." Nahuas employed ehuillotl as wooden effigies of war victims that were burned in honor of their remembrance. Colonial documentation suggests that ehuillotl could also be honored as deities and received offerings in their own right.[36] Sahagún stated that "the idolaters called to and served wood, stones, figures made of sticks [*ehuillome*], devils, and idols."[37] Knowing that Bautista often employed Nahuas to help compose his texts, it is not difficult to imagine a collaborator explaining the burning, purgatory image of Francisca with the closest Nahua equivalent: the ehuillotl. This is not to say that the Nahua amanuenses mistook Francisca for a sacrificial victim. Only that they employed an item from the preexisting worldview to make sense of the new, consequently ensuring the survival of the term with a meaning left to the reader or listener to decide.

In another instance, the text relates how people negligent of their penance will make images of themselves in purgatory. Although this may sound strange to most, it would have made sense to a Nahua as the word employed is *ixiptlayotia*, or "to make an image or representation of oneself." As mentioned, in the ritual world of the Nahua, an *ixiptla* is an "impersonator" or "image," typically of a deity. Human ixiptla wore the regalia of the deity they were impersonating to actually become that deity's embodiment.[38] Thus, when a person negligent of their penance creates a noncorporal ixiptla of themselves in purgatory, they become that image to experience the torments of hell personally. In truth, the Nahua concept of ixiptla provided an excellent vehicle through which to describe one's presence in purgatory.

In the end, the power of Vincent's masses aiding his sister's purgatory soul allowed the saint to become part of the trental mass tradition. Trentals represent a collection of masses offered on behalf of a soul in purgatory typically over the course of thirty days and were common in medieval and early modern practice.[39] The mass cycles of Vincent formed part of such a European tradition that likewise experienced popularity in central Mexico. So much so that the Third Mexican Provincial Council of 1585 issued a decree that priests stop saying these trentals, "called San Amador, nor those of El Conde, or San Vicente," in attempts to follow the mandate of the Council of Trent and eliminate "the many abuses and superstitions that some of the faithful have introduced because of their ignorance and excessive affability."[40] Despite the decree, the popularity of such mass cycles apparently continued as the Fourth Mexican Provincial Council of 1771 repeated the prohibition.[41]

The popularity and reputation of Vincent, then, makes his inclusion in Bautista's confessional manual a logical one. The exemplum provides a clear and descriptive lesson on the role of purgatory in cleansing the soul and the importance of completing one's penance prior to the particular judgment in a shortened story familiarized for Nahua parishioners who were unlikely to forget it.

Fray Juan Bautista, 1599 *Confessionario* 34v–36v

And so that your life will be satisfied, it is very necessary that the penance, *penance*,[42] that the confessor assigns will happen, occur, be completed. May you all listen to that which happened there at the great altepetl called Valencia where the very blessed Saint Vincent Ferrer was born, and as is related in the book on his life. At that time when he began to perform many miracles, once the entirely good, respectable Saint Vincent in his daily prayer was asking our lord concerning someone, his dead older sister, Francisca de Aguilar was her name, her spouse was a merchant, and he was pleading unto our lord for her that he would show him, reveal to him where he [God] placed, put her. Once, on one day when Saint Vincent was saying Mass at the main altar of the church of the priests of Santo Domingo, when he was about receive the precious, honored body of our lord Jesus Christ he saw a shape, *a form*,[43] as if a person stood greatly burning, emitting flames, casting flames. And after Saint Vincent received communion, he invoked the shape in the name of God that by the order of God it would say and satisfy his [Saint Vincent's] heart regarding who it was and that which it sought, desired. The shape answered and thus said, "I am your older sister; I am Francisca de Aguilar."

Thereupon Saint Vincent replied, responded, "How are you suffering, becoming fatigued with very great affliction, torment? We ourselves know that while you went about on the earth you were very good, righteous, and your reputation, your name, and your honor, renown, was very good, righteous."

"May you not be very scared, frightened because of how you see me," the shape said, "because I was not eternally condemned, cursed so that always, forever I will be afflicted with torments, with pain because I merely neglected it, left incomplete the penance my confessors gave me, assigned to me; I did not fully complete it, finish it while on earth; I will be tormented, cleaned in the place of cleansing [purgatory] until the end of the world, the Day of Judgment."

Then Saint Vincent answered, he said, "Perhaps it is possible that I can help you so that you can be liberated from the torment, pain, suffering?"

His older sister answered him, she said, "Yes, it is possible for you to help me if you perform a mass on my behalf."

Then, Saint Vincent performed forty-seven masses. Immediately his older sister revealed herself, appeared to him, she was accompanied by the many angels and saints that were with her. She thanked and was grateful to the saint, her brother for what he did for her. Thereupon, she left and ascended to heaven to go and enjoy the deity lord, many angels and saints go to accompany her, gather around her, scatter themselves around her.

Oh my precious children, right there you see two things. The first, it is very necessary that you do, complete the *penance* that the priests, confessor give you so that you become deserving, thus you were forgiven of your sins. But if you merely neglect it, leave it undone, you will absolutely be locked up for a very long time and make an image of yourself there in the place where people are cleansed, *purgatory* with great torment, great pain. Second, because your spirit was delayed, the Mass is a very great, very precious medicine (since, then, a sacrifice was made, even our lord Jesus Christ) so that it helps and frees the souls that went to torment, become clean in purgatory. May you not forget them, neglect them at times, but always plead to God for them so that afterwards they will be, appear as your helpers, intercessors before God when he generously allows that you are detained there [in purgatory] and while you are being entirely cleaned, made completely good so that truly you will see, be happy with, and enjoy your deity, your ruler God there at his place of enjoyment, *glory*.

The First Judgment, Limbo, and Purgatory in Paredes's 1759 *Promptuario*

The Jesuit Ignacio de Paredes published a variety of Nahuatl works in his lifetime but none more extensive, more thorough, than his 1759 *Promptuario manual mexicano*. Designed with the intent to help ecclesiastics and Indigenous people alike, the *Promptuario* contained nearly 480 pages of sample sermons for every Sunday of the year and an additional one regarding the Virgin of Guadalupe. Yet Paredes was not only thorough. He was a purist. In his introduction to his sermonary, he declares his intent to use only a pure and genuine form of Nahuatl that he deemed more effective in transmitting the Christian message and as reflected by great authors, such as friars Alonso de Molina and Juan Bautista and fellow Jesuit Horacio Carochi, while omitting contemporary language he considered "barbarous."[44] In short, Paredes desired his sermons to reflect Nahuatl's rhetorical and metaphoric prose of the early colonial period—demonstrated in the previous Bautista text—not that of eighteenth-century Nahuatl. He succeeds only in part, but his efforts are reflected in the parallelism and synonym or quasi-synonym strings that follow describing the first judgment, purgatory, and limbo.

Within his eighth and ninth sermons, Paredes addresses Christ's descent into hell after his crucifixion and the first judgment, providing an expanded version, of sorts, of Anunciación's discussion. In his eighth sermon, Paredes describes the four residences of the souls of the dead as being located in the center of the earth—a common assumption in Europe at the time, masterfully articulated in Dante's *Divine Comedy*.[45] Paredes employs Nahuatl rhetoric using a string of descriptors to describe such a residence as *tlayohuallotitlan, cehuallotitlan, mixtecomactitlan* (a place of darkness, a place of shadows, a place of fogginess). He then explains the four residences in hell. The first part, limbo, is inhabited by the unbaptized. Reflecting a middle ground, perhaps, between Augustine and Aquinas, Paredes states that such souls are not tormented with physical pain, but because they will never again see the face of God, *cenca huel tonehua, patzmiqui, chichinaca, ihuan mocococapoloa* (very greatly are they tormented, are in anguish, hurt, and afflicted). Unlike Anunciación, Paredes emphasizes the suffering of the unbaptized. This, then, provides a segue of sorts as Paredes refers Nahuas to consult his catechism, published the previous year, for instructions on how to baptize infants in their last extremity and emphasizes that no prayer from the living can save the deceased unbaptized child.

The second part of hell Paredes discusses is purgatory, which he variably calls Nechipahualoyan (the place of cleansing), Netlechipahualoyan (the place of cleansing with fire), and Neyectiloyan (the place of restoration)—all apt descriptions. Colonial texts nearly exclusively employ fire when describing the torments of purgatory. For Paredes, he plainly states that the souls *tletica ihuan nepapan tonehuiztica tlaxtlahua, ihuan mocenchipahua* (pay and completely cleanse themselves with fire and various torments). Not all authors chose such restraint when describing purgatory. In his sixteenth-century collection of sermons and plays, Nahua author Fabián de Aquino added a bit more detail describing purgatory as a *uey oztotl yn yeuatl yn oztotl: yuhqui Cenca uey amanalli mochiuhtica tentica yn tepoztleyatl Cenca tetlayhiyouilti yn euatl yn uey amanalli* (large cave, a cave like unto a large pool made of, full of metal-fire-water; the large pool is something that greatly torments).[46]

Paredes's discussion on the torments of purgatory is brief with a primary emphasis on the role the living play in helping souls in purgatory. Later in his ninth sermon, Paredes relates an exemplum to paint purgatory as both an inevitable and awful place. In the story, a righteous priest died and was sent to purgatory to pay off his debt of sin. Later, he appeared to a fellow priest and pleaded for his help so that his soul could quickly leave purgatory. Paredes's point: if purgatory was bad for a good priest, how much worse for the average Nahua, and therefore everyone should confess their sins to lessen the severity of God's judgment.

Paredes finishes his tour of the immediate afterlife with hell itself, for those who died in mortal sin, and the Bosom of Abraham, where the righteous awaited Christ's visit to and harrowing of hell following his death. Regarding the latter, the text explains how this place is uninhabited today. Moreover, it details how, following his visit to hell, Christ resurrected and appeared first to his mother, Mary, and then to his disciples. Christ's immediate visit to his mother was—and is today—considered factual by many, including Luis de Granada, who includes the event in his 1594 *Libro de la oración*, although the event is not mentioned in the Bible.[47] Such a belief not only shores up the relationship between son and mother—a relationship vital in the intercessory powers of Mary—but also could explain why Mary never visited the tomb to finish anointing and preparing her son's body with the rest of the women on Sunday.[48]

The ninth sermon recaps much of the eighth while emphasizing the particular judgment. Paredes states that God's judgment made immediately upon dying is eternal and cannot be undone: *ca aic cahuiz, aic polihuiz; ca zan cemmanca yez, cemmanca neltiz* (never will it be abandoned, destroyed; forever it will exist, forever it is true), and that such judgment will remain during the second, or final judgment.

Overall, these two sermons provide a to-the-point description of the first judgment, purgatory, and limbo, which lacks much of the creativity and overall engagement with the Nahua worldview found in Bautista's and earlier texts. Although the content is firmly rooted in the Old World, its delivery to a New World audience does has an effect on the sermon beyond rhetoric. For example, the text employs terms familiar to Nahua culture such as *tlatoani* (lord or ruler) to describe God as Tlatoani Dios (God the ruler) and mictlan (place of the dead). In all Nahuatl texts, mictlan is used to represent hell. In the Nahua worldview, nearly everyone went to mict-lan after death regardless of morality—it was a neither good nor bad place and often described as cold and dark. It was certainly not the fiery furnace of tortures so often depicted as the European hell, although it did share its dismal and dark features, perhaps encouraging the numerous descriptive references and strings of couplets found in colonial texts, including Paredes's.[49] Regardless, these sermons are an excellent eighteenth-century example of Old World theology presented in a New World rhetoric in efforts to familiarize the Apocalypse to a Nahua audience while instructing on its Christian characteristics.

Ignacio de Paredes, 1759 *Promptuario*, 58–71

Concerning this [Christ's descent into hell] you must understand, my child, that the place where the spirits, the souls reside of those people who have already died is divided into four places.[50] The four parts where the souls reside is inside the earth, it is located in the center of the earth. Because of this, there is absolutely no brightness, no light exists, but they are immersed in really a place of darkness, a place of shadows, a place of fogginess. The first part where the souls of the dead people reside is called *limbo*. And there God casts the spirits, the souls, of those people who were not baptized and during their life never ever committed their very own sin, personal fault, but only attached to them was original sin that was inside them when they were conceived and when they were born. And truly this original sin is erased immediately with baptism. The one who dies in this sin truly can never ever be saved, it is impossible for them to enter into heaven and be happy in the presence of God. Even though the souls there are not tormented with fire, with various torments, truly, my children, very greatly are they tormented, in anguish, hurt, and afflicted because they do not see the beautiful face of God their creator. So because of this, may you really see to it, my child, that you let no child die before it is baptized! And if some child is very sick and is about to die, then may whichever learned person, be it a man or a woman, baptize it. And if no one else appears to baptize it, even though it is the child's father or mother, let them baptize it as is said in the Mexica learning guide, *catechism*.[51] Also there [in the catechism] may you learn, my children, how to baptize someone so that you can help the little children and by means of you they will be saved.

The second part where souls reside is the place of cleansing with fire, *purgatory*. There the souls of the righteous are cast who have died but here on earth they did not completely accomplish their penance for their sins. And there in the place of cleansing they pay and cleanse themselves with fire and various torments, then they immediately go straight to heaven. And concerning this, you must know, my children, that we people on earth alone are able to help the souls that are suffering in the place of restoration, *purgatory*, through prayers, masses, candles, and various other good works, but not in any way the other souls of children or non-children dwelling in another part. Thus, concerning the dead children, absolutely no good is done for them from whoever prays to God or has masses performed or lights *candles*. If, however, they [the children] were baptized, they are already there in heaven where truly they do not need anything for their aid, but if they were not baptized, it is thus absolutely impossible for them to be helped. And thus they are helped in vain; that which is prayed is merely not considered.

The third part where they [the souls] reside is called *hell*, where the eternally cursed souls of those who died in mortal sin are thrown, hurled. And there they will always, really, completely be tormented, afflicted, and made to suffer with fire and various eternal pains. And truly, my children, their torment, eternal death, never will end, leave, finish, but will be perpetually, eternally made to last a long time. Oh my children, it is something really frightening, really saddening, really anguishing. Because of this, let us not sin, may we always feel remorse for our sins and live well before God.

The fourth part where the souls resided is called the *Bosom of Abraham*. There went the souls of the righteous fathers and the other just people who died in very complete cleanliness. Even though they never ever had sins,[52] they absolutely never went to heaven [as now] because heaven was still closed until our savior Jesus Christ would open it with his precious death, because of which God would pay the debt of our sins. And thus, when whichever just person was dead, they did not go to heaven but were lowered to reside with the righteous fathers there in Abraham's Bosom; and there they were kept the whole time until our savior would die for us. And after he died for us in this way, then immediately he descended in order to console them and take them with him to heaven; thus he did when he ascended to heaven. But now, after our savior died, none of the souls descend to, are placed in the place of the righteous fathers.

And now it is not inhabited, it is abandoned. After the third day, on Sunday, really early in the morning our savior rose here on earth and with him the souls of the righteous fathers rose also from their place where they were imprisoned in the Bosom of Abraham. And the precious soul of our savior arrived there at the sepulcher where his precious body was laying and by his very own power again entered inside his dead body, again united it, he gave it life, and with great joy he spontaneously resurrected.[53] And, in addition, with him were resurrected many of the beloved people of our savior. *Many bodies of the saints that had slept arose.*[54] Thereupon, he went to appear to his precious, honored, sad mother, and afterwards the other people, his disciples or his beloved. . . .

Concerning this Article of Faith, we are to know, my child, that when each person on earth dies, when their spirit, their soul abandons their body, then their soul is ordered to appear before God and God will judge them. And if they died well, then their life ended on earth in divine goodness, *Grace*, and never ever will it be in debt on account of their sins; truly God will then forever give them eternal happiness, *glory*. And if they died well but not fully pure on account of the penance they did for sins here on earth, truly God throws their soul down to the place of purification, *purgatory*, where it is purified with fire, and then goes straight to heaven. Likewise, if a person on earth never ever had their very own sin, such as little children, they already have original sin because it was made inside people, and [if] they are not baptized and die in this way, then our lord God casts their spirit, their soul down to where the unbaptized little children are, called *limbo*.

And lastly, if a person on earth dies in mortal sin, then God casts the soul of this sinner down to the abyss of *hell*. And there truly forever it will burn, be tormented, be punished. Likewise, we are to know, my child, that it is really very truly just, that never ever will God end or reverse that which he already sentenced, established, because the word of God is eternally just—never will it be abandoned, destroyed; forever it will exist, forever it is true. This is how it will be on Judgment Day; in no way will the judge, God, destroy what he already sentenced, established, all remains unchanged, forever it will be unchanged.

However, truly there is still another universal judgment God the tlatoani [ruler] established so that everyone on earth and in heaven will appear in his divine presence. There, he will come to show them his just government, mercy, and various gifts. And again our lord Jesus Christ will judge them in front of everyone so that the righteous will be glorified, praised in front of everyone and also the wicked will be shamed, entirely cursed in front of everyone because of their sins; God will find out about, become acquainted with all people. And the eternal judgment will happen when he goes to end, completely destroy all of this earth. . . .

My child, may we place inside our hearts and take as an example that which I am about to relate to you. Here on earth a priest was living, he was serving God.

And when he died, his soul appeared to another of his fellow priests and this is what he said to him:

"Oh, Oh," he cried out to him, "how really very frightful is the judgment of God because it examines the many things—good or bad—that people did during their lives. I myself, by means of the precious blood of our savior Jesus Christ, was saved. However truly our lord God cast me down to the place of cleaning, *purgatory*, so that there I would achieve my payment for my sins. Therefore, help me before God so that I can leave there soon!"

He said this and immediately thereafter departed from his presence and disappeared. May we open our eyes, my child, may we fear the entirely just judgment of God! May we judge ourselves today so that God does not judge us harshly! *But if we would judge ourselves, we should not be judged.*[55] I mean to say, may we confess with truthfulness our sins today and in no way hide them so that we will merely be judged with discretion and so that here on earth we will merit God's purification, *Grace*, and afterwards his eternal happiness, *Glory*. Amen.

The Two Judgments of God in Coronel's *Discursos*

Born in Torija, Spain, Juan Coronel became a Franciscan at an early age and traveled to Yucatan around 1590. To assist evangelization efforts, he studied and learned Maya and taught it to others. According to fray Diego López de Cogolludo's *Historia de Yucatan*, Coronel was zealous in both his dedication to teaching the Maya the Christian doctrine and his efforts to teach other friars Maya. He was an Observant Franciscan, and his dedication allowed him to enjoy his poverty, endure injuries with patience, and live solitarily, emerging only to administer the sacraments to the Maya or fulfill his religious duties until his death in Merida in 1651.[56]

Whereas Cogolludo surely engaged in hyperbole when describing his former teacher, Coronel remains a paramount figure in colonial Maya literacy for his publications. In 1620, his publications included a Maya grammar, a book on Christian doctrine (*Doctrina christiana*), and a collection of sermons (his *Discursos predicables*). His doctrinal works were designed "for the consoling of the natives, so that they have something interesting and advantageous printed in their language."[57] Coronel's *Discursos* represents the earliest surviving and longest work printed in Yucatec Maya during the colonial period and is a fascinating insight into text production and intertextuality in Yucatan.

It was not uncommon for ecclesiastics and Maya alike to borrow material from their predecessors and contemporaries, update and amend the contents somewhat, and then publish or recopy them anew. This provided material for printed texts and allowed for the preservation of existing manuscript works. And this intertextuality is seen in the existence of various sermons and texts on the Creation, *The Fifteen Signs before Doomsday*, the Mass, and others found throughout printed and manuscript works in Maya—in other words, official and unofficial works—which testifies to the degree of text sharing evident in Yucatan. Likely created in the early friars' schools among ecclesiastics and Maya, these texts circulated in written and oral mediums to be copied, edited, amended, and recopied throughout the colonial period. For example, a text on the end of the world titled *The Fifteen Signs* (see chapter 3) appears in four separate Maya manuscripts. Another example includes a Maya narrative on the creation of the world often called the "Genesis Commentary." This text appears—albeit with various orthographic and textual modifications—in four Maya manuscripts as well: the Teabo and Morley Manuscripts, and the Chilam Balam manuscripts of Kaua and Chan Kan.[58]

Coronel's *Discursos* seems to have included some texts that likewise enjoyed circulation among ecclesiastics and Mayas. Parts of the *Discursos* appear in various Maya-authored, forbidden texts such as the Books of Chilam Balam and Maya Christian copybooks—Maya-authored manuscript collections of Christian texts—thus testifying to the diverse makeup of Coronel's text and the wide circulation of certain religious texts among Maya and ecclesiastic authors throughout the colonial period.[59] Moreover, decades prior, fray Diego de Landa collected some handwritten sermons in Maya containing questionable material. René Acuña rightfully suggests that Coronel's subsequent *Discursos* drew from this corpus of handwritten sermons.[60] Indeed, Coronel stated that his desire was to "bring to light various papers that [he] had collected and copied that the old priests had written, amending some things that in this era are not used, and correcting that which was not true."[61]

Furthermore, passages from the *Discursos* are found verbatim in the Motul dictionary likely compiled circa 1600 from both previous texts and field notes, thus further illustrating the eclectic nature of the *Discursos* (and the Motul).[62] Although Coronel awards the authorship of such papers to previous ecclesiastics, almost certainly Maya collaborators and ghostwriters played a role. Thus, the *Discursos* is an eclectic text representing the work of others and Coronel alike.

In the end, Coronel's *Discursos* serves as another step in the preservation, iteration, and modification of Maya religious texts, some of which contain sixteenth-century roots. Alteration is a necessary step in this process and is one that likewise affected Coronel. Over one hundred years after the publication of *Discursos*, fray Pedro Beltrán de Santa Rosa María would publish his *Doctrina*, based largely on Coronel's work, and correct various Maya terms Coronel employed: some words were originally correct and time had altered their meanings; some conveyed inaccurate meanings from the beginning. In one example, Beltrán criticizes Coronel's use of "Dios Citbil" for "God the Father" claiming that *citbil* referred to a Maya deity that was worshiped in secret in the eighteenth century. Despite Beltrán's objections, the phrase appeared throughout the colonial period in various Maya-authored works including last wills and testaments.[63] Regardless, in the endless process that is text production, emendation, and circulation in Yucatan, Coronel corrected and compiled previous texts in his *Discursos*, allowing Beltrán to do the same in his *Doctrina* nearly five generations later.

Eschatological sermons are certainly present in Coronel's *Discursos*. Included among such sermons is the following text on the particular and universal judgments. After outlining the basics of both, the text justifies the need for a universal judgment, which admittedly, only confirms that of the particular judgment. The text gives two reasons. The first is so that the righteous can be redeemed publicly; the second is so the wicked are punished publicly. Both serve to show the world that God is just, and that no secret deed—good or evil—will remain hidden during the Final Judgment.

To be sure, the sermon follows standard Christian doctrine. Yet Maya elements influence the text as well. Indeed, the text resembles those in Nahuatl from the sixteenth century that employed Indigenous authors and a generous amount of description to make sense of unfamiliar Christian concepts. Death is described as *chochpahal tu cucutil*, or "the loosing from the body," and the biblical idea of an ironic reward and punishment for the righteous and wicked, where the avaricious rich are cast down and the righteous poor are exalted—or, as Christ put it, "the last will be first, and the first will be last"[64]—is described as simply being "backwards." The Maya use of oral narrative is likewise reflected in the discourse of the wicked as they comment on this unfortunate turn of events. And even a bit of the humor and sarcasm characteristic of the precolonial and colonial Maya appear as the wicked admit that God despises and rolls his eyes at them.[65]

Fray Juan Coronel, 1620 *Discursos predicables*, 82v–84r

Two judgments of God, particular and general.

Perhaps someone will say maybe a person is not judged upon death and their loosing from the body? What is the reason for the coming judgment there at the end of the world? At that time, each person is judged upon death and their soul is sent by God to whatever place is fitting for them to go because of their works or if they died in sin, thus they go to the happiness of heaven or the suffering of purgatory to do penance if they have not completed paying their debt for their sin while living on earth. Although the souls are judged while separated from their bodies, this is not the final judgment. Our lord God will perform the universal judgment when the world is destroyed; this, then, is the last standing up[66] of all people to be judged. And there are two kinds of purposes our lord God desired at the coming judgment.

The first is so that it is seen how really just is the judgment of God, for the judgment and examination that the people on earth really receive is backwards also, for as he commands the dead to live it is necessary for him to command that the honorable and those that sit in great seats be torn down; it is fitting also that the others be judged in reverse and also all they receive. However, as God judges, each one sits in their seat and receives their gift, each person, as it suits him whether their works be good or bad. For this reason, when they see the righteous being taken by God they will say,

"These people we shamed, while living on earth back then they desired nothing of worth. See how they are taken and chosen by God. But as for us, honor and glory was our lot on earth back then. Really we are despised by God and he rolls his eyes at us."

By chance they will say this in real fury and being sorrowful and they scream because of what they see. You see how it [the righteous and wicked] is divided and the wicked are reduced to nothing in their judgment and examination.

Here is the second thing that our lord God desires at his coming universal judgment. This is that the sin of the sinners becomes apparent before the eyes of the all the world, that they are punished before all people; soon you will know. The punishment of the robber or the murderer of some person is not hidden nor is how they are punished kept secret. But there in the public square they will be punished. Their error will be proclaimed and all people summoned will see them be punished. Likewise for them that, although dead, still have hidden that for which they are judged and punished. This is the reason, the will of God for his coming, universal judgment: so that they are punished publicly.

When the judgment is finished, that travel of the sun and the rotation of the heavens and also the fruiting of trees will cease because since the people have ascended from the face of the earth, the living things on the face of the earth are not worth anything.

The First Judgment and Purgatory in an Anonymous Maya Text

As mentioned, the utility and universality of death allowed the topics of judgment and life after death to frequently occupy the pages of those few colonial Maya religious texts extant today. The friars in central Mexico and Yucatan, the latter predominantly Franciscan, drank from similar theological wells of inspiration fed by European texts and traditions. The practice, exemplified by Bautista above, to use exempla to relate the horrors of a poor first judgment and purgatory, extended beyond central Mexico. Maya exempla found in both Coronel's 1620 *Discursos* and the Morley Manuscript—a late-eighteenth-century, Maya-authored copy of a likely sixteenth-century original—relate the stories of individuals who failed to make a complete confession and now suffer in purgatory or of the pains of purgatory in general.[67] In one story a man elects to spend one day in purgatory rather than endure one year of sickness on earth. Yet while in purgatory he lamented that one brief moment felt like many *katuns*—in the Maya calendar, one katun equaled 7,200 days. All such stories drew from European works but appear with a Maya influence.[68]

An anonymous collection of Maya sermons housed in the Kislak Center for Special Collections at the University of Pennsylvania provides additional detail on the subjects of judgment and purgatory. Largely overlooked by scholars, the collection survives as a copy made by the nineteenth-century

Mayanist Karl Hermann Berendt from "an old manuscript in quarto" in the library of the bishop, Crescencio Carrillo y Ancona, and it includes his notes detailing his opinion that the manuscript from which he copied derived from the second half of the eighteenth century.[69] Without the original, the authorship of the text remains specious, although Berendt notes the orthography of various hands throughout. That said, an entry appearing early in the manuscript states, "Book of sermons translated into Maya for the Indians of the towns and the priests."[70] Indeed, the sermon's accurate and frequent use of Latin suggest some degree of involvement by a Spanish ecclesiastic.[71]

Although the sermon covers all the basics of the afterlife that we have seen in other texts, it also decides to emphasize certain points throughout its tour. For example, when describing the "second room" of limbo as the abode for unbaptized children, the sermon, like Paredes, instructs that although the children are not tormented by fire, they face the greater suffering of never being able to see God again. However, the Maya sermon then takes this tragedy to condemn those who would cause abortions, "because it kills the soul." Although uncommon in this context, the colonial concern toward abortion appears in confessional manuals. Fray Alonso de Molina's 1569 Nahuatl confessional manual included a series of questions to uncover if women drank something or squeezed their belly or performed hard work when pregnant to abort the fetus.[72]

Throughout, the sermon highlights the duality of the suffering in purgatory and hell as a physical torment and emotional distress for not seeing God, underscoring the severity of the latter. This line of discourse is familiar in European texts. For example, Augustine described the absence of the soul from God as a second death resulting in "eternal punishment"— a punishment both he and Aquinas call the pain of loss. Indeed, Granada dedicated a section to the *dos penas que ay en el infierno* (two pains that are in hell) in his sixteenth-century *Libro de la oración*.[73] The Maya sermon notes that the worst offenders in hell are Christians who "did not fulfill the thing they promised at holy baptism." The topic of the "negligent Christian" seemed a popular one in Maya texts as it took form as an exemplum in both Coronel's *Discursos* and the Morley Manuscript.[74]

The sermon also addresses the benefits of indulgences in reducing suffering in purgatory and earned through a variety of means including "when

Figure 2.3 Arma Christi mural in the cloister corner of Dzidzantun.
Photograph by Amara Solari.

five altars are visited, or the stations of the holy cross, called the *via sacra*, is walked." Colonial processions celebrating the Passion could follow a path to five stations dedicated to the five wounds of Christ, often leading the participants to four outdoor *posa* chapels in the atrium and an interior altar of the church, as was done in Dzidzantun (see figure 2.3).[75] Processions could also follow the stations of the cross oftentimes erected outside the church, which depicted various scenes of the crucifixion—a practice popular among many today in Latin America.[76] Details on the devotional processions of the Yucatec Maya are sparse. Yet the sermon suggests that its particular Maya audience was familiar with such processions.

Finally, the sermon concludes emphasizing the reward awaiting those who pray for souls in purgatory. Here, the sermon employs an exemplum describing a king who spent all his money on the benefit of purgatory souls. Disgruntled by their king's generosity, his soldiers left and convinced a rival king to conquer the generous ruler. When the two kings met on the battle-field, the righteous king was joined miraculously by an innumerable host of soldiers of freed souls from purgatory which frightened the rival king who subsequently pledged his eternal friendship.

A similar exemplum exists in a fifteenth-century manuscript where a man is rescued from his attackers by the purgatory souls he had previously helped.[77] Once again, the story-like genre demonstrates its appeal to the Nahua and Maya.

Maya elements likewise influence the eighteenth-century sermon. Some impacts are expected, such as the sermon's use of Maya terms to convey Spanish and Christian concepts. The traditional Maya ruler, or *ahau*, becomes a king, and *metnal*, which—similar to mictlan, represents the abode of the dead although not necessarily a place of torments—becomes hell.[78] Moreover, like most cultures, the Nahua and Maya had limited literacy and largely conveyed information orally. This influenced colonial texts and is seen here in the abundant dialogue found in the sermon as, in one case, purgatory souls cry out to the reader for help.[79]

Yet other, unexpected appearances of the Maya worldview also occur. For example, the sermon explains that indulgences are offered to Christians by the pope. Although often translated with its Spanish loanword, *papa*, Maya translations of "pope" occasionally appear, as both the Teabo Manuscript and the Motul dictionary convey the figure as *yum cab*, "father or lord of the world."[80] Yet in the sermon examined here, "pope" is translated as *noh yum cab*, which can have the literal translation of "great father of the world." However, *cab* is also the word for "bee" and noh yum cab, was also the deity "great lord of the bees." While performing fieldwork in the village of Chan Kom, Robert Redfield cited an *h-men* (local priest-shaman) saying that "the noh-yum-cab is the principal ruler; under him are all the other bees of the world." When moving a hive or founding a new one, ceremonial offerings are made to noh yum cab.[81] Whether the author(s) of the sermon made or knew of this connection is uncertain, yet perhaps the Maya audience would.

Likewise suggestive of Maya influence on the sermon are the creative and descriptive couplets familiar to the Maya. Such couplets, for example, associate the voices of souls in purgatory with "a cold thing, breath [that] penetrates your ears"—an indicator of a bad omen in the Maya worldview—and emphasize the pensive nature of the generous king by stating, "his face drooped as he thought."[82] Regarding this last phrase, a similar one appeared in the Maya-authored Teabo Manuscript in reference to Eve. As she deliberated whether or not to eat the Forbidden Fruit, "she was unsure, she yawned, she is thinking also."[83] In the end, colonial realities and a Maya audience contributed to the formation of this sermon and its medieval teachings on the immediate afterlife.

Anonymous, Eighteenth-Century *Sermones en lengua maya*, 198–209

Sermons regarding souls

Here are the names of these rooms in hell: the two rooms of limbo, purgatory, and hell. For the dead person—whether just conceived by their mother or one hundred years old—when they die, it is never the death of the soul nor is it destroyed; a person only is full of earth, but the soul will never end. The first room in hell, limbo, no one will go to rest there. It is empty, because this room was designated for the souls of our holy fathers before the door to heaven was opened because of the sin of our first father, Adam, back then. And then the holy soul of our redeemer Jesus Christ descended, he died for us, and he brought them out and ascended to heaven with them. Here in the second room of limbo will go the souls of children that died before they received the sacrament of baptism, because this holy sacrament is on the head of all the just, and is the key to heaven. Although there they are tormented without fire, but there is a somewhat greater evil for them which is that they forever cease to see God; this is the reason it is a great sin for a woman to create, to give an abortion because it kills the soul. This is the situation declared by the Holy Mother Church for those that cause abortions.

But to hell will go the souls of all those of evil works, the friends of the devils, because they forgot our lord God and his holy commandments, and also they gave themselves to the word of the devil, and they obeyed what the world and their flesh says. There, they are tormented endlessly, they will not wait to rest, and never will they see the beauty of our lord God. Because of which, although they will observe the day of great judgment, they receive a somewhat great evil concerning it, it is necessary that they receive it; again they come forth on this day but they will see no part of the face of our angry lord God, and in no part do they hear the curse that will be issued to them by our lord Jesus Christ. The worst of these people had faith in God, they were worthy back then, the Christians, they knew they were cleaned by the holy blood of our lord Jesus Christ, but they did not fulfill the thing they promised at holy baptism; they did not mirror his [Christ's] life and his believers.

This great evil will be given to them so that they who were on the road to heaven know that they quickly will go to hell. Oh Christian! See if you live as a nonbeliever; see if you fulfill what you promised to God at holy baptism; observe how you never passed through your life faultless; but if you have taken up bad habits, there is a way for you to be cured, for your soul, for your body, so that God sees you reconciled to him, if not, you quickly will go to hell.

To purgatory will go the souls of the faithful Christians, since they died without completely paying their penance here on earth, because here sin kills the soul, whoever commits it earns eternal suffering. However, the person who confesses to the priest is justified, and if they beg, have pain also in the center of their heart only because they insult God, for them they earn a pardon from God, it also alters this eternal suffering they earned from before and endless torment; if they will endure here on earth and overcome the flesh and fast and punish themselves and give charity to the poor in the name of God, they also earn forgiveness of sins; it is called *Indulgence*, it is offered to Christians by the great pope for whatever good work he commands to be done; as when five altars are visited, or the stations of the holy cross, called the *via sacra*, is walked, here the sufferings of our lord Jesus Christ during his Passion are pondered and given devotion.

Also, there are other regions inside purgatory of immeasurable suffering. There are two kinds of evil in purgatory: the evil of loss and the evil of suffering. Regarding the evil of loss, this is to cease to see the beauty of our lord God. Regarding the evil of suffering, the souls are burned and suffer immeasurably. But it is somewhat as painful as that perceived by the souls that cease to see God because of their love, they hope that they will go and see him, but they never understand that because of this hope, it lengthens the time, it afflicts the soul: *hope that is deferred afflicts the soul*.[84]

63

Because I love you, listen to what is said to you by the afflicted souls that are under the hand of God among infinite torments: *Oh all ye that pass by the way, attend, and see if there be any sorrow like to my sorrow.*[85]

"Oh you wanderer that walks on the path on earth, a cold thing, breath penetrates your ears, you see the light and glory before you, consider, contemplate what you hear about what we endure, see if there is anything similar to our suffering. Have compassion on us. *Have pity on me.*[86] Observe then how you spend today and how we spent yesterday, also if you are wasting a bit of time right now. Know that what things you do [on earth], thus it is done to you when you come here. Know that really we are afflicted, we are miserable, our hands and our feet are tied, we cannot deliver ourselves from this suffering we have, because we are out of time for worthy works; we trust in your good deeds to hurry along our assigned suffering. Perhaps you will give charity and one mass if you can afford it.

"Oh, have compassion on us! We who loved our lord God but in order to complete his justice, *Justice*, we are plunged below the earth waiting for you to alleviate our suffering from us; do not make yourselves deaf, you living, to our poor words, and whatever good work you will do and deliver to God on our behalf to alleviate the suffering, know that you will have a reward."

Oh my beloved! What, then, do we have to say to you for you to finally hear the pleas spoken to you from the fire of *purgatory* by the afflicted holy souls? In order for you to finally believe how it is true what is promised to you if . . . [87] good to them, hear what they did and that they really loved a ruler [ahau], back then.

Whatever money came from his kingdom, back then, he would spend on the work for all the holy souls in *purgatory*, such as masses, and also he distributed it among the poor for their souls, so that he was hated by his soldiers. Then they went to the ruler to another of town, they said,

"As for us, it is not good how we find ourselves. Start wars with our ruler; come, take by force his kingdom there for yourself. Try this now for he is poor, and easily you will win because he is without goods to pay his soldiers."

When the ruler heard these words, he was desiring with vainglory to increase his kingdom, so he sent word to him [the other ruler] that he come forth that day to fight with him. When the ruler received this word, he answered yes; he awaited with his soldiers; in no way did he embarrass himself for the shame brought forth by the competing ruler by not coming forth with whatever soldiers loved him back then, although there were few. He was really remorseful because he thought he would be conquered by his enemy, his face drooped as he thought. Then he saw come, gather, innumerable strong soldiers that positioned themselves among these few soldiers. When he arrived, the ruler who came to take by force his kingdom, he saw that his strength was insufficient in relation to this multitude of soldiers of his enemy. Then he descended from his horse, he alone approached, then he repeatedly hugged the ruler and said to him,

"Friend, forgive my error, I sent for you to come forth and fight with me earlier, but I lack strength compared to you, I was not enough, nor my soldiers compared to your soldiers. Forgive me, we will not fight, not today nor ever. If you need something from me, command that it should be taken from my home, for I am your friend for life."

When he finished, the [righteous] ruler went there, he came to the group of soldiers. Then he said to the governors, captains of this ruler,

"Know that our lord God sent to me [the angelic soldiers], I brought these that you see here to liberate you. These souls you removed from *purgatory* with good works performed on earth. Do not leave to the end to do good for them," he said.

Then he forgave all of them.

See, my beloved, how God rewards good works done for all the holy spirits in *purgatory*. If until now you did not know this great mercy, change today your thinking so that you do all the good you are able to do, so that you are able to earn the removal from you of all the evil here on earth. Oh my beloved, blessed are those who do good; it is not I that said it, from the mouth of our lord Jesus Christ came these holy words: *Blessed are the merciful, for they shall obtain mercy.*[88] Blessed are the merciful for they will merit the mercy of our lord God. As said David, *Blessed is he who considers the poor.*[89] Blessed is the one that gives alms to the poor; there is no other thing that expedites the entering of a person's pleas before God. Because of this, I really charge you to not forget to do good for the all the souls in *purgatory*. This is the end of you hearing about the great good the helper of *souls* merits so that you might earn eternal life and also the blessing of our lord God. *Amen.*

Understanding the personal apocalypse—its first judgment, limbo, and purgatory—is essential to understanding the general Apocalypse, as both are connected. Speaking of Nahua converts in the sixteenth century, fray Bernardino de Sahagún states, "It is also necessary to advise them concerning the dead because they believe in some errors against the Catholic faith."[90]

He proceeds to detail the continuation of beliefs held over from the Nahua worldview in their understanding of hell. One such belief was that all who die go before the lord of hell, Mictlantecuhtli, and his wife, Mictecacihuatl, present themselves as their servants, and make offerings. He also mentions a belief that some in hell are annihilated completely and turn into nothing. Sahagún refutes all such continuations and emphasizes that everyone sent to hell will exist forever to suffer horrible torments and that hell is the jail God uses to punish the wicked and that only he is lord there.[91]

To be sure, this difficulty of separating the European and Indigenous worldviews contributed to the continued appearance of religious texts, such as those examined here, that attempted to mold a Nahua mictlan and Maya metnal into the realms and qualities of the Christian afterlife.[92] Indeed, whereas Maya ecclesiastical texts typically provide more general and limited instruction on Catholicism, within the relatively limited corpus of Maya ecclesiastical texts available today, eschatological topics concerning death, judgment, and the immediate afterlife are well represented and in some detail.

Yet epidemics, particularly during the first century of colonialism, certainly made relevant such eschatological and apocalyptic doctrine. Introduced by conquistadors and their parties and reappearing frequently, disease—coupled with war, slavery, and other factors—reduced the Indigenous population by approximately 90 percent in the first century after contact.[93] Spaniards generally viewed the epidemics that decimated Indigenous populations while seemingly sparing the Spaniards as the will of God. The sixteenth-century historian, Gonzalo Fernández de Oviedo y Valdés, claimed that the demographic collapse "seemed a great judgment from heaven."[94] And conquistador Bernardo de Vargas Machuca claimed that such epidemics provided "evidence of divine will . . . serving to empty the Indies of idolatrous peoples in order to populate them with Christians."[95] With God sanctioning the death of so many, ecclesiastics had many opportunities to make Catholic eschatology pertinent.

Although disease in the sixteenth century certainly made the personal apocalypse a frequent reality—and, on occasion, was related to the Apocalypse itself—it also provided avenues of adaptation and even resistance. A Totonac native near Xicotepec claimed various personas including God himself. Those who believed in him would be healed and saved; those who opposed would be chastised with plagues and other trials.[96] Moreover, colonial works from Yucatan, like the Ritual of the Bacabs and the Chilam Balam of Na, containing incantations and medicinal cures, illustrate the continued importance of local healers and Indigenous worldviews and medical practices.[97] Such examples provide context to Sahagún's concerns about appropriate eschatological instruction to combat errors in belief. Ideally, properly instructed Nahuas and Mayas would turn to God when confronted with death, as when the seventeenth-century governor of Yucatan, Diego Zapata de Cárdenas, reportedly mentioned how Maya towns made vows to various saints during the deadly smallpox epidemics, "choosing them [the saints] as their advocates before the divine presence to achieve health."[98]

The effectiveness of Christian texts on such topics, however, varied among the Nahua and Maya, as it does today among all Christians. While in Chan Kom in the 1930s, Redfield observed a general belief among the Maya regarding the immediate afterlife that included *gloria* for the good, purgatory for those needing to be "burned white" before going to *gloria*, and metnal for the evil. Yet local innovations existed as well. Prayers from the maestro prevent the demons of metnal, who gather at the doorway of house of the dying, from stealing the soul; some sinners become frogs waiting for their admittance into *gloria*; some immoral become whirlwinds upon death; debtors can become deer or turkeys; and reincarnation is a necessity as "God has not enough souls to keep forever repopulating the earth."[99]

Thus, perhaps the continued necessity of such texts and instruction should not be surprising. Such was the case during the colonial period, and such is the case today in many Christian churches. After all, everyone dies, and many find themselves, at some point, pondering about the afterlife and seeking instruction. Recently, CNN published the article "Why is Pope Francis so obsessed with the devil?"[100] It details the pope's efforts to correct the idea among many that the devil is a myth and how to resist him. Along with the devil, it seems many Catholics today view purgatory as simply a figure of speech, and among American Catholics, only 63 percent actually believe in hell.[101] Indeed, it would seem that now more than ever, Christians are in need of instruction regarding the particular judgment, purgatory, and limbo. Perhaps, in an effort to make the afterlife relevant today, the Vatican offered indulgences to ease purgatory suffering for those who actively participated in the Church's 2013 World Youth Day via social media, including Twitter.[102]

Yet in addition to the frequent, nagging concern over one's personal apocalypse is the occasional preoccupation with a global event—the Apocalypse itself. The signs that betray the End concerned the minds of many in the Old World and New, and are the topic of the next chapter.

≡ 3 ≡

Signs of the Times

As the first coming of Christ our redeemer to save us was preceded by
many signs and events, so too at his second coming there will precede
many and marvelous signs.

Bautista

Whoever does not recognize the first coming of the Lord cannot prepare
himself for the second.

Saint Augustine

Of Antichrist is come that shall be keen
And of the dreadful days, fifteen
That shall come before the doomsday
Since of the doom will I say

Cursor Mundi, c. 1300

Influenced by the political and military turmoil in Italy and the doomsday preaching of the Dominican friar Girolamo Savonarola, Sandro Botticelli painted his *Mystic Nativity* at the turn of the sixteenth century (see
figure 3.1). The painting portrays a strange nativity scene with angelic and
demonic characters not seen in usual renditions of the event. On the top
of the painting appears an ominous Greek inscription that reads: "This

Figure 3.1 Sandro Botticelli's *Mystic Nativity*, c. 1500–1501. National Gallery, London (NG1034). Image courtesy Wikimedia Commons.

picture, at the end of the year 1500, in the troubles of Italy, I, Alessandro, painted in the half time after the time; at the time of the fulfillment of the eleventh of Saint John, in the Second Woe of the Apocalypse; in the loosing of the devil for three and a half years; then he shall be chained according to the twelfth, and we shall see him [here a word or two is missing] as in this picture."[1]

Revelation 9 speaks of three woes, which are to precede the coming of Christ. The second involves an army of angels and the death of one-third of humankind. Perhaps Charles VIII's invasion of Italy in 1494 and the sermons of Savonarola helped Botticelli see the Apocalypse in his time. This may also be why the demons at the bottom of the canvas appear bound to poles. Either way, his apocalyptic interpretations and influences are evident and, in a way, the painting is a perfect representation of Advent sermons and their common purpose to remind the audience of both the first and second comings of Christ.[2]

After a brief excursion into the topic of Advent sermons, this chapter provides two examples that contain redactions of the once-popular medieval text, *The Fifteen Signs before Doomsday*. Although occasionally unrecognized by modern scholars examining the New World, the signs were well known among the colonial Maya and Nahua. The first example comes from a Maya-authored manuscript from an unknown province; the second derives from the Franciscan Juan Bautista Viseo's 1606 Nahuatl *Sermonario*. Both provide excellent examples of how *The Fifteen Signs* formed some part of the Advent sermons delivered to the Indigenous populations of central Mexico and Yucatan and influenced their respective Apocalypses.

Advent Sermons

The word "advent" derives from the Latin *adventus* meaning "arrival" or "approach," and since the early years of the Church, ecclesiastical authorities began distinguishing between the first and second advents of Christ. Perhaps the fourth-century Doctor of the Church, Cyril of Jerusalem, said it best:

> We preach not one coming of Christ, but a second as well, far more glorious than the first. The first gave us a spectacle of his patience; the second will bring with it the crown of the Kingdom of God. . . . In his first coming he was wrapped in swaddling clothes in the manger; in his second he will be "robed in light as with a cloak" (Ps. 103:2). In his first coming he "endured a cross, despising shame" (Heb. 12:2); in his second he will come in glory, attended by a host of angels. We do not rest, therefore, in his first coming, but we look also for his second.[3]

Over the years, in the Latin Church Advent came to represent the four Sundays before Christmas and marked the beginning of the liturgical year.

During the early modern period, readings emerged specific for each of the four Sundays of Advent. For the first Sunday, readings often included those of an apocalyptic nature from Luke 21.[4] In colonial Mexico, ecclesiastics, Nahuas, and Mayas produced Indigenous-language texts that included sermons for the season of Advent that largely followed established patterns. Interestingly, Indigenous-language books of sermons intended for the liturgical year are not as common as one would think, with the primary Nahuatl examples appearing in the first half of the colonial period: fray Alonso de Escalona (n.d.); fray Bernardino de Sahagún (1563); fray Juan de la Anunciación (1577); fray Juan Bautista (1606); fray Martín de León (1614); and fray Juan Mijangos (1624). Moreover, only that of Anunciación contained sermons for the Sundays and feast days of the entire liturgical year.[5]

No comparable example of a book of sermons exists for the colonial Maya, nor would any such work exist until 1846, when fray Joaquin Ruz published his *Colección de sermones* for the liturgical year in Yucatec Maya. However, as seen below, Maya authors did preserve in their own manuscript collections a few sermons intended for the first Sunday of Advent. A Maya-preserved manuscript containing a collection of the author-compilers' preferred Christian texts, or Maya Christian copybook, is located in Princeton University's special collections. This collection, titled "Maya Sermons," contains over seventy folios of religious texts and includes a sermon intended for the first Sunday of Advent. This address is likewise cognate with one found in another Maya Christian copybook, the Teabo Manuscript. These two examples are the only colonial examples of Advent sermons in Yucatec Maya of which I am aware.[6]

A portion of the Nahuatl and all of the Maya sermons intended for the first Sunday of Advent engage, either directly or indirectly, a popular medieval text, which is relatively unknown today and called *The Fifteen Signs before Doomsday*.[7] With origins in the early Church, *The Fifteen Signs* became both a popular and diversified text with wide circulation throughout the medieval and early modern periods. Simply put, the signs describe fifteen catastrophic events that herald the Second Coming of Christ. Since Christ himself declared that, regarding the specific day of his return, "no one knows, neither the angels of heaven, nor the Son, but the Father alone," and since he stated that signs would precede his coming, speculation has ruled the day since the dawn of Christianity.[8] This speculative fodder nourished the growth and spread of *The Fifteen Signs*. The signs appeared in the major texts of the era including Peter Comestor's twelfth-century *Historia scholastica*; the thirteenth-century English poem, the *Cursor Mundi*; the supplement to the third part of the thirteenth-century *Summa theologiae* of Thomas Aquinas; and Jacobus de Voragine's thirteenth-century *The Golden Legend* and its Spanish version, the *Flos sanctorum*, among others.[9]

Thus, the eschatological resources available to medieval scholars certainly included the signs, which likewise enjoyed circulation in the Spanish cleric Gonzalo de Berceo's thirteenth-century poem *De los signos que aparecerán antes del juicio*.[10] Berceo introduces the signs with beautiful poetry:

> Señores, si quisiéredes attender un poquiello,
> *Señores, if you would lend some attention,*
> Querríavos contar un poco de ratiello
> *I would recount to you a short while*
> Un sermón que fué priso de un sancto libriello
> *A sermon that was prisoner of a sacred book*
> Que fizo Sant Iherónimo un preçioso cabdiello.
> *That Saint Jerome, a precious leader, made.*
>
> Nuestro padre Iherónimo pastor de nos entienda
> *Our father Jerome, shepherd of our understanding*
> Leyendo en ebreo en esa su leyenda
> *While reading in Hebrew, in that, his legend*
> Trovó cosas estrañas de estraña façienda
> *Put into verse strange things of strange make*
> Qui las oyr quisiere, tenga que bien merienda.
> *That whoever will hear them, will have something good to snack on.*
>
> Trovó[11] el omne Bueno contra todo lo ál,
> *The good man put into verse before all else,*
> Que ante del juiçio, del juiçio cabdal,
> *That before the judgment, the prime judgment,*
> Vernán muy grandes signos, un fiero temporal,
> *Very great signs will be seen, a terrible savage,*
> Que se verá el mundo en presura mortal.
> *For the world will see itself in deadly anxiety.*

Por eso lo escribió el varón acordado,
For that reason the prudent man wrote,
Que se tema el pueblo que anda desviado,
That the people who wander should fear,
Mejore en constubres, faga a Dios pagado,
Improve in behavior, make payment to God,
Que non sea de Xpo estonçe desemparado.
So they will not be soon forsaken by Christ.[12]

Berceo, like so many others of the medieval and early modern era, subscribed to the belief (albeit erroneous) that the signs originated from Saint Jerome (c. 347–420) and the *Annales Hebraeorum* he studied. Granada's sixteenth-century *Libro de la oración* even mentions a few of the signs citing the *Sibylline Oracles* as the source—another common belief in medieval times.[13] Modern studies demonstrate a complex, medieval origin for the signs while demonstrating their continued popularity throughout the twentieth century.[14]

The popularity of the signs was such that they appeared in the first block books of the mid-fifteenth century. Block books resulted from printed woodcuts containing images, writing, or both. One such text was the *Der Antichrist und die fünfzehn Zeichen* (The Antichrist and the Fifteen Signs), produced around the 1450s. The illustrations throughout the work depict the End of Days, including each of the fifteen signs.[15]

Regardless of its popularity, however, the unorthodox pedigree of *The Fifteen Signs* prompted the fifth-century Gelasian Decree, which determined the canon of the Church to condemn earlier versions of the work.[16] Despite the decree, the text's appearance in works throughout the Old and New Worlds and its consistent inclusion among Advent sermons indicates its overall popularity among ecclesiastics and laity.

The Fifteen Signs in the Maya Sermons Manuscript

Christian stories of creation and destruction, as well as period endings and beginnings, resonated with preexisting Maya worldviews. Today, many Maya continue world-renewal ceremonies of death and rebirth during Holy Week that herald back to a precontact era.[17] During the colonial period, the

Maya readily adopted Christian stories of creation and destruction and preserved such in their own texts.[18] In truth, ecclesiastical officials had prohibited Nahuas and Mayas from composing and keeping their own religious texts—they were concerned with the spread of unorthodox doctrine and pagan beliefs. Yet Indigenous writers largely disregarded the mandate and continued age-old cultural traditions of local record keeping and the preservation of religious texts. These forbidden manuscripts came to include Christian texts as well—often altered somewhat to accommodate an Indigenous audience and worldview and including texts relating the creation and end of the world. The Chilam Balam of Chumayel, for example, contains numerous references to the Final Judgment throughout its pages. In one instance, God ends the world with a flood (reminiscent of Chac Chel and the deluge in the Dresden Codex) before descending to the Valley of Jehoshaphat. In another is a Maya redaction of Matthew 25 relating the separation of the righteous and wicked as sheep and goats, positioned on the right and left hands of God, respectively.[19]

In addition to the Books of Chilam Balam, Maya Christian copybooks are rich mines from which to draw insights into those Christian teachings the Maya—at least those who were literate—most readily accepted and deemed important enough to record in their own texts. It is possible that some priests knew of, and even employed, such texts. Yet the Maya played the dominant role in their compilation and preservation. Short of a time machine allowing an interview with the colonial Maya to ask what they thought of Christianity, these copybooks provide some of the best insight available to researchers today. The following text is one such example.

As mentioned, the Maya Sermons copybook contains over seventy folios of Christian texts in Maya. Although the collection does not mention an author or town of origin, its orthography and content suggest its compilers and keepers as Maya. Indeed, portions of the manuscript also appear redacted in other Maya texts including the Chilam Balam of Tusik and the Teabo and Morley Manuscripts. Included in the manuscript is an edition of *The Fifteen Signs*. Not surprisingly, the signs and their role as markers of a period ending were popular, appearing in four Maya-preserved manuscripts. And as late as the 1980s, the town healer and historian of Tusik owned a written copy of the signs and could remember them when recited

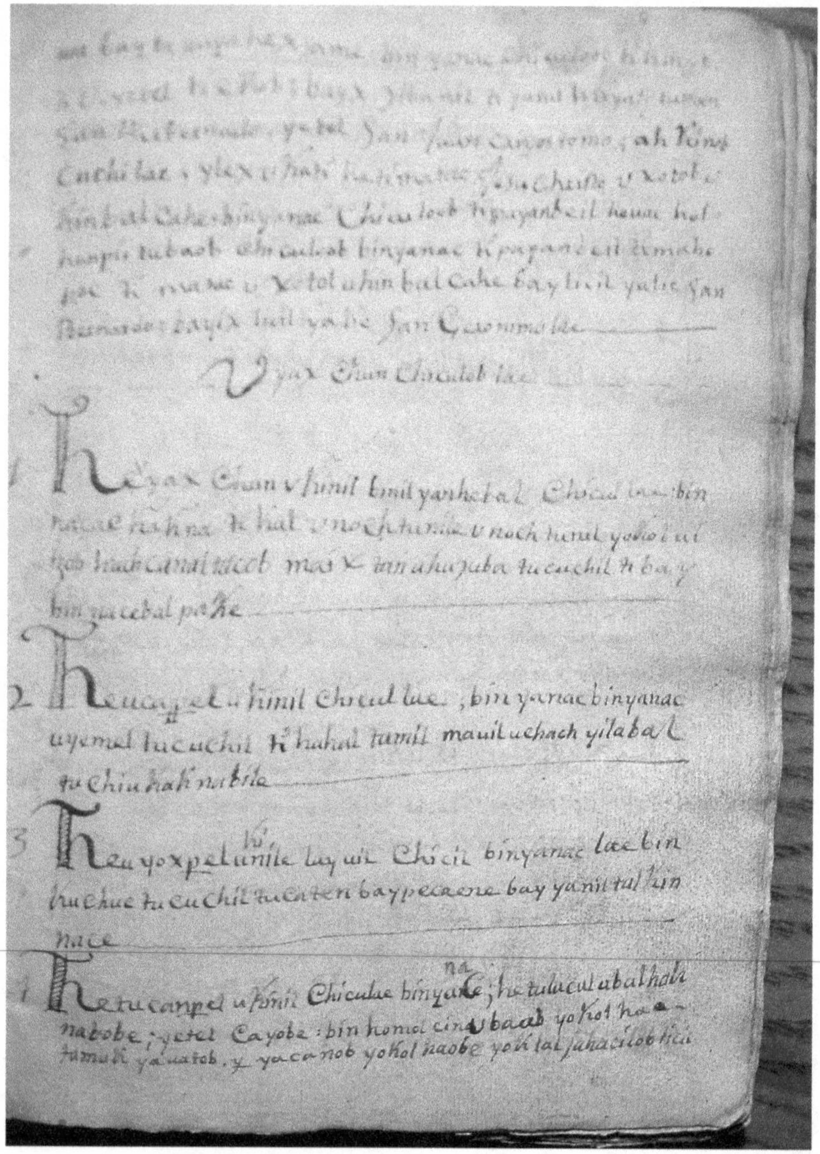

Figure 3.2 *The Fifteen Signs* in "Maya Sermons."
Courtesy of Princeton University Library.

orally.[20] The Maya Sermons text also includes a preface-like introduction likewise found in the Teabo Manuscript.[21] This preface makes clear the intention for the following signs to be read during Advent by either the priest or the Maya maestro of the town who probably also played a role in the copybook's compilation and preservation.

The similarities between the signs and preface in the Maya Sermons text with those of other Maya-preserved works illustrates their circulation among the Yucatec Maya. Here we can observe two important elements. First, none of the redactions is an exact copy of the other and each betrays modifications due to the text's transmission over time. Perhaps a maestro or escribano decided to pare down a phrase or augment, or perhaps words and sentences became lost or muddled in their redaction. Regardless, none of the redactions perfectly mirror the signs as recorded in European texts.

Second, the close similarities among the texts clearly betray a common source, whether it was textual, oral, or both. The signs in the Maya Sermons text mostly resemble those found in the works of Damian and Aquinas, although differences in content occur (see table 3.1). *The Fifteen Signs* and even its preface might have originated in the first schools employed to instruct the Maya nobility. From there, the texts could circulate in both written and oral mediums. The Apocalypse and its signs clearly made an impression on the Yucatec Maya as they made conscious decisions century after century to preserve the event in their local manuscripts.

The manuscript itself is likely an eighteenth-century copy of an earlier original and lists the signs concisely. The lack of additional commentary to the signs limits somewhat the amount of cultural modification to the signs themselves especially when compared to Bautista's Nahuatl text. That said, elements within the signs contain the fingerprints of Maya culture. For example, the text refers to Saints Bernard and John Chrysostom as *ah kinob*. The ah kinob[22] were traditional Maya priests who tended to the material and spiritual needs of townspeople. During the colonial period, many ah kinob resisted Christianity and became targets for ecclesiastical authorities, who arrested hundreds if not thousands of them. Yet despite this campaign against the ah kinob, ecclesiastics appropriated the term as a synonym for a Catholic priest, and here the ah kinob take on the persona of Catholic saints.[23] As the colonial Franciscan Bernardo de Lizana stated, "Today, the

TABLE 3.1. *The Fifteen Signs* in Peter Damian's *De novissimis et Antichristo*

1. Sea will rise fifteen cubits and stand like a wall.

2. Sea will sink and hardly be seen.

3. All seas will return to their original state.

4. Sea creatures will gather on the water and will cry out, and only God understands the sound.

5. Birds will assemble in the fields, and they will speak and cry together for fear of the Judge.

6. Fiery streams will rise from the west and flow across the face of the firmament to the east.

7. Planets and stars will have fiery tails, comets.

8. Earthquake. All living things are brought down to the ground.

9. Stones will split into 4 parts, each part hits the other, and only God understands the sound.

10. Trees and plants have a bloody dew.

11. Mountains and buildings turned to dust.

12. Beasts will emerge from the woods, mountains, and fields and roar but not eat or drink.

13. Tombs will lie open from sunrise to sunset while the corpses arise.

14. Men will leave their houses and places, running like madmen, not understanding or speaking.

15. Men will die that they may arise again with the dead.

Adapted from Heist, *Fifteen Signs before Doomsday*, 27–28; also in Christensen 2016. Reproduced with permission.

priests of Christ are called in their (the Maya) language, 'ah kin,' just as they called those [priests] of their false gods in ancient times."[24] One can only imagine the paradox created as Mayas heard decrees aimed at eliminating the evil ah kinob only to read about them as saintly figures in religious texts. In addition, the use of couplets for emphasis is present throughout the signs. Indeed, the first sign describes the sea rising to a height that "the great rocks, the great rock of the mountains, the very high ones, will not divide its place as it will rise as a wall."

Moreover, the signs in the Maya Sermons fail to follow any European text of which I am aware and include modifications to the Damian and Aquinas models. The sixth sign, for example, only mentions fire and does not designate it to the fiery streams typically associated with the sign. And the fifteenth sign focuses on the renewing of the earth through fire in preparation for the Final Judgment. Within such alterations we can see the impact of Maya colonial society. When discussing portentous comets and falling stars, sign seven includes lightning strikes. Although some European renditions, even poems, mention lightning, it is not surprising that the Maya elected to include it in their rendition, as lightning was closely associated with the rain god, Chac. Furthermore, sign fourteen relates how men will emerge from the caves in which they were hiding and makes specific reference to fornicators. Fornication and sexual deviancy among the Maya greatly concerned ecclesiastics and perhaps, aside from drunkenness, represents the most common complaint levied against their Indigenous fold. Thus, its particular mention here is not surprising given the colonial context of the manuscript.

Finally, the Maya Sermons text—and most other Maya renditions—inserts an element into the ninth sign not seen in European or Nahuatl texts, at least to my knowledge. In typical renditions of the sign, stones break into four parts from hitting each other. The Maya text, however, includes an additional part that has the stones reunite again by a miracle. The reason for this inclusion remains uncertain. However, the phrase used to describe the reunification that occurs, *yoklal mactzil* (because of a miracle), likewise appears in the thirteenth sign when describing the restoration of the bodies of humankind. The consistent pairing of the phrase *tumen mactzil* (through a miracle) or *yoklal mactzil* with extraordinary restorations is a unique element of the Maya text and reflects, again, the impact of cultural preference on *The Fifteen Signs*.[25]

The following is a translation of the signs and their preface as recorded in the Maya Sermons text. Although the Maya text does not include images, I have inserted illustrations of the signs found in the fifteenth-century German block book *Der Antichrist und die fünfzehn Zeichen* to illustrate the visual and literal European context from which the signs derived. However, because the order and content of the signs in the Maya text do not mirror a European antecedent with exactness, not all the signs included in the Maya text appear in the German block book, and vice versa.

Maya Sermons, pp. 16–19

Advent Sunday, when the Son of Man will have come.[26]

Here are the words that you hear here today; they have been written in the explanation of the Gospel that was said in Mass. Receive this speech that you hear from our Holy Mother Church as has been written in the explanation of the Gospel of Saint Luke Evangelist in the twenty-first chapter, the theme of this sermon today, the belief of us Christians.

My beloved people, it is necessary for you to listen carefully to my word for my sake as we are with you. When the child of the virgin comes in his great majesty with all the angels behind him, then he sits on his chair of majesty and they will quickly be seated in front of him, and they will gather themselves [the righteous] together in one place on the right, separated, as a shepherd gathers together his sheep.

But as you heard my saying, it is necessary that you believe, my beloved people, this here Sunday of Advent regarding the coming of the lord. It is important to know the book of his coming, of Final Judgment [book of Revelation]. However, as you heard earlier, there will be signs concerning the sun and the moon and the stars, thus it has been written in the book of wisdom by Saint Bernard and Saint John Chrysostom, ah kinob back then.

You see what was inquired of Jesus Christ about the last days of this world here. There will be signs preceding it, but among them there will be fifteen signs preceding, when it has not begun, when it is not yet the last days of this world here, so says Saint Bernard and so says Saint Jerome.

finis

Figure 3.3 Signs 1 and 2, *Der Antichrist*, 16r. Reproduction in *Der Antichrist*.

The first signs

1. Here is the first initial day, there will be this individual sign: the sea will rise, raise up; the great rocks, the great rock of the mountains, the very high ones, will not divide its place as it will rise as a wall.

2. Here is the second day, there will be this sign: it [the sea] descends to a place of great depth; it is not possible to see the seashore.

3. Here is the third day, thus will be the sign: it [the sea] will arrive flat in its place again, like the coming of the sun.

Figure 3.4 Signs 3 and 5, *Der Antichrist*, 16v–17r. Reproduction in *Der Antichrist*.

4. Here on the fourth day, this sign will occur: all creatures of the sea and fishes will gather themselves together on the waters while they cry and moan on the water because they fear that which comes, this Judgment Day.

5. And here on the fifth day, this sign: all birds will gather together, and the elevated [flying] creatures will gather together as one, they also cry because they fear that which comes, this Judgment Day.

6. And here on the sixth day, these signs: fire will come forth from the west where the sun sets and where the sun emerges in the east.

Figure 3.5 Signs 12 and 8, *Der Antichrist*, 18v, 17v. Reproduction in *Der Antichrist*.

7. Here on the seventh day of the signs, there will be very many comets and many great lightning strikes; likewise, stars fall to the earth, they will be seen coming from the sky.

8. And here on the eighth day, these signs: there will be an earthquake, so then the beasts cannot stand up; also, all will fall on the face of the earth, also.

Figure 3.6 Signs 7 and 5, *Der Antichrist*, 17v, 17r. Reproduction in *Der Antichrist*.

[9.] And here on the ninth day,[27] these signs: all the stones will fight each other while they rub together alone, and large ones and small ones will separate into things; and large ones and small ones will crack open, divide into four parts; then, the rocks will unite again through a miracle.

[10.] And here on the tenth day, these signs: blood will[28] fall from them [plants] just as dew descends.

Figure 3.7 Signs 9 and 11, *Der Antichrist*, 18r, 18v. Reproduction in *Der Antichrist*.

[11.] And here on the eleventh day, these signs: the stones, all mountains and hills, and the buildings of men and the high forests all will fall on the face of the whole earth.

[12.] And here on the twelfth day, these signs: all living creatures will gather together on the plain to fight among themselves; Judgment Day comes for all of them.

[13.] And here on the thirteenth day, these signs: here all graves will open; all of their entrances will open from the time the sun emerges in the east to when the sun sets in the west; and then the bodies of the people who are in them will rise to the openings, rise it seems to the very opening of the graves and these graves because of a miracle.

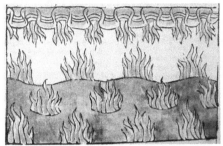

Figure 3.8 Signs 10, 14, and 15, *Der Antichrist*, 18r, 19r, 20v.
Reproduction in *Der Antichrist*.

[14.] And here on the fourteenth day, these signs: since all men will hide them-selves in caves, those that fornicated and sinned will emerge, come forth from caves or whatever cavern; also wherever they hide themselves, they will all come forth and speak words among themselves without under-standing them, nor hearing them also, thus because of their evil works, when they all emerge.

[15.] And here on the fifteenth day, these signs: fire descends again from the sky to finally make new the face of the earth and burn all things on the earth in fire, through the power of the fire, the pain, the final judgment of our great lord, Jesus Christ, when he finally comes in his power as the great ruler.

The Fifteen Signs in Bautista's 1606 *Sermonario*

As mentioned, Bautista taught and worked at the College of Tlatelolco, where he and his Nahua colleagues collaborated on a number of works—one of which was his 1606 *Sermonario*. The *Sermonario* contains sermons for the four Sun-days of Advent, feast days of Saint Andrew, and the Immaculate Conception.

The product of a collaborative effort that included eleven friars and eight Nahua assistants, the *Sermonario* was an incredible literary achievement.[29]

Unbelievable as it may be, the collection of sermons in the *Sermonario* was only part of what Bautista intended to publish, yet the work still reaches 709 printed pages of ecclesiastical treatises. Perhaps aware of the daunting length of the work, Bautista includes a brief caveat of sorts in his prologue stating that due to the elegance and abundance of Nahuatl, "scarcely a line of Castilian or Latin can be translated in it without it ending up twice as long."[30] Scholars have noted that this is not necessarily true for all Nahuatl texts—and, I would add, particularly for those produced in the mid-seventeenth and eighteenth centuries—and instead reflects the authors' general preference toward Nahuatl's use of metaphors and parallel constructions where expressions are reiterated in similar yet different ways to emphasize themes and points. In addition, the authors display a firm grasp of the *huehuetlahtolli* genre of oratorical speech.[31] Nahuas employed huehuetlahtolli, or "speech of the elders," in various settings including in discourses promoting moral behavior. Aspiring to make Christian texts and their teachings resonate with the Nahua, some of the early friars, including Bautista, adopted the genre.[32] After all, friars had seen parallelism used as a rhetorical device before in various biblical passages.[33]

The sheer size of the *Sermonario* is not its only distinctive feature; its prologue and its open acknowledgment of the work's Indigenous contributors is likewise uncommon to say the least. A variety of factors contributed to the reluctance to mention direct Indigenous influence on a text including ecclesiastical officials' increasing skepticism of translations deriving from Indigenous assistants and the suspicion surrounding the ability of the assistants themselves to accurately understand and translate Catholic doctrine—a tumultuous topic in general in the age of Reformation and one addressed by the First and Second Mexican Provincial Councils of 1555 and 1565, respectively.[34]

Nevertheless, Nahua collaborators played a vital role in translating the oftentimes arcane Catholic message into Nahuatl, including lengthy passages in Latin. Included among the eight Nahua collaborators mentioned in the *Sermonario* is don Antonio Valeriano who studied at the college and later became an instructor. In truth, so proficient were his abilities that Bautista lauded him as one of the most accomplished linguists the college ever produced and employed his expertise to compose the Spanish glosses in the text that reveal the definition and etymology of various Nahuatl words. It would seem that Bautista aimed to employ an elevated and refined version of Nahuatl in his sermonary; one that the general Nahua population did not use in their daily interactions, as "many of them use corrupt words."[35] Indeed, friars Pedro de Castañeda and Francisco de Solis stated in their approbation of the work that the *Sermonario* was composed in "very elegant Tetzcocan language."[36]

This "sophisticated" Nahuatl is evident in the work's redaction of *The Fifteen Signs*.[37] The signs appear in a sermon composed for the first Sunday of Advent. The Nahuatl, as Joe Campbell put it, is "very interesting and challenging," and it employs twenty pages of text to list, relate, and expand upon *The Fifteen Signs*.[38] This is the longest redaction of the signs of which I am aware in either Nahuatl or Yucatec Maya. It is well thought out, designed with purpose, and a wonderful example of an oratorical, eloquent form of Nahuatl already fading from texts (and certainly speech) by the seventeenth century, not to mention the eighteenth when Paredes would attempt its replication. Moreover, the text reflects the humanist training of Bautista, and that of the college overall, with its emphasis on the use of scripture. Indeed, nearly every sign is supported with biblical citations and explanations in what seems like an attempt to ground the apocryphal signs in scriptural validity. The following explores various aspects of the text to better illustrate these points mentioned above.

Regarding the overall structure of the text, the signs largely follow the order and type established by Peter Comestor's popular twelfth-century *Historia scholastica* (see table 3.2) and made even more popular by the *Flos sanctorum* in the fifteenth century.[39] Bautista's first sign, however, and its mention of the sea rising fifteen cubits, or *caxtolmolicpitl*,[40] reflects the type seen in Thomas Aquinas's *Summa theologiae* and Peter Damian's *De novissimis et Antichristo*. This mixed origin of the signs is not unique, however; in fact, a French illuminated manuscript from the mid-fifteenth century, *Livre de la vigne nostre seigneur*, follows the same pattern as do certainly many others.[41] Yet Bautista's text is different in one way from its European antecedents. In European texts, the seventh sign typically describes how stones will fight each other and break into four pieces. Bautista, however, has the stones break into eight pieces—again, something I have not seen in

TABLE 3.2. *The Fifteen Signs* in Peter Comestor's *Historia scholastica*

1. Sea will rise forty cubits and stand like a wall.
2. Sea will sink and hardly be seen.
3. Sea monsters appear and roar.
4. Sea and water will burn.
5. Trees and plants have a bloody dew.
6. Buildings will fall.
7. Stones will strike one another.
8. Earthquake occurs.
9. Earth will be leveled.
10. Men will come out of caves like madmen unable to speak to each other.
11. Bones of the dead will rise and stand on the tombs.
12. Stars will fall.
13. Living will die that they may rise with the dead.
14. Heavens and earth will burn.
15. New heaven and new earth and all will rise.

Adapted from Heist, *Fifteen Signs before Doomsday*, 26; also in Christensen 2016. Reproduced with permission.

any other text, from the Old or New Worlds, and likely illustrating personal modifications to the signs themselves.[42]

The signs' elucidation in Bautista's text is also unique among New World renditions of the signs. The text supports almost every sign with additional citations from the Bible and relates nearly each sign to a particular form of punishment for vice of the wicked (see table 3.3). For example, on the ninth day the sign concerns the leveling of the earth so that everything from the mountains to the canyons will be equal and flat. The text then states how:

> It is an instrument of fear that will occur especially to the nobles, the elite, the rulers, who greatly bragged about themselves, made themselves nobles, elevated themselves, and saw as nothing the others, the poor, the orphans. . . . At that time they [the poor, etc.] will understand, they will be content for all of us will simply be equal, we will all simply be commoners, we will not appear as separate individuals, but each one will be judged as thus is their reward.

Thus, as the world's geography will be made equal, so will the social divisions in Nahua society in preparation for God's judgment. Moreover, on the eleventh day, bones buried in graves will emerge, assemble themselves on top, and come to life. This is then compared to the wicked, whose hidden and buried sins will emerge and be made public at Judgment Day.

TABLE 3.3. Bautista's *Fifteen Signs* and Corresponding Punishments for the Wicked

Sign	Meteorological Effect	Comparison to the Wicked
1	Ocean will rise, become uneasy.	Self-aggrandizing, restless attitude of the proud.
2	Ocean will descend.	The prideful will be brought low, humbled.
3	Fish will gather and cry out.	The wicked will cry out of fear.
4	All water will burn.	Adulterers will burn.
5	God's anger causes all plants to sweat blood.	Murderers who spill blood will be punished.
6	Houses will crumble and fall.	Worldly possessions of the wicked will be destroyed.
7	Stones will knock, break.	Those with hearts of stone will be afraid.
8	Earthquake causes all living things to fall.	Hearts of sinners will collapse out of fear.
9	Earth will be leveled.	Nobles will be brought to the level of commoners.
10	Men will emerge from hiding in caves.	Wicked cannot hide, be saved from judgment.
11	Graves will open, bones will come alive on top of the graves.	The sins of the wicked will be revealed, placed in front of everyone.
12	Falling stars and flaming comets appear, and animals gather.	Wicked will be destroyed with flames; gluttonous will cry.
13	All people will die.	All people will die.
14	Heaven and earth will burn.	Heaven and earth will burn.
15	Heaven and earth made new; and resurrection occurs.	Heaven and earth are made new; resurrection occurs.

Certainly numerous medieval exegeses on the book of Revelation followed a similar formula, which expounded on the various signs and events described in the book with additional scripture, even relating them to contemporary events and sins. Concerning the influential commentary of the fourth-century Tyconius, Paula Fredriksen stated that he provided "a reading of John that affirmed its historical realism while liberating it from the embarrassments of a literal interpretation."[43] Tyconius also related specific signs found in the book to events in Africa where he lived. Thus, as Fredriksen explains, Tyconius saw the suffering Rome imposed upon him and his Donatist brothers reflected generally in the prophecies of Daniel and John, although not necessarily as indicators of an imminent Apocalypse.[44] The master of this genre was Christ himself who frequently likened the human condition and specific people to everyday examples found in his parables.

The book of Revelation states regarding the sinner that "to the measure of her boasting and wantonness repay her in torment and grief."[45] And the Book of Wisdom states that "one is punished by the very things through which one sins."[46] Likewise, the association of sinners with a particular punishment appeared in various medieval texts, including Dante Alighieri's popular fourteenth-century *Divine Comedy*. For example, Dante observed how those of the second circle of hell who were constantly driven by their lust find no rest as they are now carried and driven by "the hellish blast with ceaseless fury"; and "the souls of those, whom wrath has overcome" found in the fifth circle hit and bite each other in a muddy marsh.[47]

Such irony where the punishment fits the crime also occurs in *devotio moderna* works popular among many Franciscans in the College of Tlatelolco including the texts of Thomas à Kempis's *Imitation* and Granada's *Libro de la oración*. Kempis states, "For a man will be more grievously punished in the things in which he has sinned. There the lazy will be driven with burning prongs, and gluttons tormented with unspeakable hunger and thirst."[48] Granada agrees and adds, among other examples, that "the carnal and dishonest will be dressed in flames of stinking sulfur. The envious will howl with pains of longing as rabid dogs."[49]

Yet Bautista seems to have modeled his discourse on the signs on the sermonary of the fifteenth-century Dominican Johannes Herolt. His *Sermones discipuli de tempore* offered over two hundred sermons for the liturgical year and other subjects, and experienced incredible popularity, with over eighty-four editions in print.[50] Importantly, but not surprisingly, the College of Tlatelolco owned a copy.[51] Herolt's work included a treatise on *The Fifteen Signs* that associates each sign with a particular group of sinners—just like Bautista's text. Indeed, the close similarity—often verbatim translation—between Bautista and Herolt's work concerning the signs and the sinners they punish is striking.[52] Even the biblical citations match. For example, consider the fourth sign:[53]

Bautista

On the fourth day, here is what will occur with the fourth omen. The ocean, the sea, and all waters everywhere will burn, catch fire, ignite. This omen is the instrument of fear and fright that will occur to carnal people, adulterers, those having sex, that have engrossed themselves in licentiousness, lasciviousness here on earth, they wrap up in the water thoughtlessly with pleasure, with sexual pleasure, they satisfied their desire; because of this, they will burn in hell with fire and sulfur. As it says in the divine word (Rev. 21:8), *Their portion will be in a pool burning with fire and brimstone.* Which means: "The wicked, the spoilers of the divine commandment, they will be thrown down into a trough of fire water, there they will be bathed, scorched, roasted with fire, with sulfur." And it is true that however much they took pleasure with their bodies, they will be tormented, afflicted the same degree. Thus it says, *As much as she has glorified herself and lived in delicacies, so much torment and sorrow give ye to her* (Rev. 18:7). Which means: "However much they were happy, were licentious, pleased themselves, to the same degree you all torment them, cause them to cry, cause them pain!"

Herolt

The fourth sign is that the sea and all waters will burn, and this to the reproach of the wanton and the adulterers, who here swam in carnal delights, and who against God satisfied their lascivious cravings, so that it will come to pass that such as these will burn in fire and brimstone. [As we read in] Rev. 21, their portion will be in fire and brimstone. For each occasion, just as here and now they delighted in the satisfaction of some passion, so in the future they shall have the everlasting punishment that matches it. Rev. 18. In the measure she basked in voluptuousness, give her grief and torment in the same measure.

Certainly it is possible that Bautista and his Nahua associates employed some other unknown text or a combination of texts as various commentaries on *The Fifteen Signs* employed similar biblical citations.[54] Yet Herolt's sermon provides the closest match to Bautista's correlation of the signs with sinners that I have uncovered.

Like all apocalyptic and eschatological texts examined here, their New World authors clearly drew from Old World prototypes. That said, the texts necessarily adapted to their American surroundings. Here, as the authors crafted their discourse, they remembered their audience and, similar to the Maya text, altered the traditional apocalyptic narrative to accommodate an Indigenous worldview. The full translation of the fourth sign, below, shows the influence of Nahuatl parallelisms and oral discourse in elaborating and expanding the text. Also evident is the use of huehuetlahtolli to describe the human body as *intlallo, inzoquiyo* (their earth, their mud).

Indeed, Bautista and his aides present the entire discussion of these foreign signs within the familiar Nahua concept of *tetzahuitl*. Indeed, the phrase "fifteen signs" is translated in the text as *caxtollamantli tetzahuitl*. As Louise Burkhart explains, "The term tetzahuitl, often translated as 'omen,' applied to anything of a frighteningly extraordinary or unexpected character . . . it is an anomaly, a rupture of harmony, a little bit of chaos slipping into ordered reality."[55] Nahuas believed that those engaged in improper living invited such tetzahuitl into their lives. Sahagún recorded that hearing unexpected animal cries could herald death or misfortune.[56] Similarly, a question in Molina's *Confesionario mayor* asks the Nahua penitent, "Did you take as a tetzahuitl the barn-owl, the owl, the weasel, the black beetle, the big russet beetle, the skunk that made a stink in your home . . . ? Perhaps you took as a tezahuitl the fire loudly crackling and exploding?"[57] In his 1599 confessional manual, Bautista related an exemplum about a woman who failed to give a full confession as a tetzahuitl.[58] And the mid-eighteenth-century Nahuatl confessional manual of Carlos Celedonio Velázquez de Cárdenas y León and its concern over the Nahua belief in omens illustrates the continued significance of tetzahuitl throughout the colonial period.[59] Such concern appears in the Nahuatl Annals of Puebla particularly regarding eclipses, storms, and comets allowing some to see them as signs of the end of the world.[60] So ominous was tetzahuitl that it was an epithet for the important deity, Huitzilopochtli.[61] Perhaps most well known are the eight tetzahuitl, which heralded the arrival of the Spaniards.[62] Interestingly, six of the signs share close similarities to those of *The Fifteen Signs*.

Many passages in Bautista's text on *The Fifteen Signs* emphasize the extraordinary and unexpected, including the sound of fires crackling and exploding. Such becomes clear in the fourth sign compared above. In another instance, when the second sign describes the descending ocean the text states, "noisy crackling sounds will occur abruptly, so that the people of the earth will be very afraid, apprehensive, and dead tired."

Prior to the arrival of the Spaniards in Tenochtitlan, Montezuma supposedly was made aware of various tetzahuitl foreshadowing the end of one era and the beginning of another governed by the Spanish. Regardless of whether or not such signs occurred, for the Nahua Tlatelolcans composing the story of the conquest, it would make sense for there to be tetzahuitl to herald in a new age of Spanish rule.[63] Thus, it seems only fitting that tetzahuitl would proceed the end of the world itself and the beginning of its rule under Christ. For the Nahua, then, *The Fifteen Signs* as tetzahuitl, as unexpected and extraordinary events that usher in a new age, surely made sense.[64]

Throughout the text, many of the misdeeds and punishments of the wicked described in the signs directly engage Nahua culture while reflecting colonial concerns in New Spain. For example, many signs highlight the importance of moderation and balance in the worldview of the Nahua; extremes and peripheries were to be avoided, and those who upset the balance or failed to achieve such through improper living lived in danger of worldly repercussions.[65] Above all, moderation was key. During the twelfth sign, all the animals on earth gather together and cry out in fear of their impending deaths, not eating or drinking. The *Sermonario* then explains how the wicked will likewise be crying out of fear, particularly "the over-eater, the gluttons, the swallowers, and the heavy drinker, the very drunk, the drunks." The Nahua believed that those who ate excessively or even too quickly neglected important order and equilibrium; they were equated with animals of a gluttonous nature, including the puma and coati. Although intoxication was permitted at times for certain festivals and for certain people, the Nahua worldview, in general, discouraged drunkenness as an extreme.[66]

Both ideas resonated with Catholic doctrine that held gluttony among one of its seven deadly sins, and yet both are expressed in ways familiar to Nahua culture. Drunks are described as those who "never denied the request for a pulque jar."[67] Pulque was the Indigenous fermented drink produced from maguey sap. For such gluttons, the only relief mictlan has to offer is *chapopoatl* (bitumen or asphalt water), *tlequiquiztlalli* (sulfur), and innumerable *tletepuzxayocomitl* (fire-metal-pulque jars). As mentioned, although the Nahua underworld, mictlan, was not a nice place, it was not analogous to the torturous realm of the Christian hell. However, ecclesiastics and Indigenous collaborators made efforts early on to transform mictlan into a more dreadful place and here they employ water to do so. As Ben Leeming notes, water was used occasionally in the description of the Nahua concept of heaven, often called "the flower world," where jewels, butterflies, iridescent flora and fauna resided. For mictlan, the pure water of heaven becomes the foul, asphalt, sulfur-scented, fire-water of hell, thus certainly creating a stark contrast in the Nahua mind.[68]

The Nahua need for moderation and balance and the avoidance of extremes weaves its way into other parts of the signs. During the third sign, when the fish gather upon the waters and yell, the wicked will feel fear and cry out, particularly "those who celebrate, take pleasure with dancing, drums, rattles, flutes and still more did not celebrate with God; it was just frivolity, because of this at that time their shouting, their laughter will turn into weeping, sadness." Here, the sin is not in the dancing or music. Indeed, music formed an important part of the religious instruction of the Nahua.[69] The sin was in its improper and excessive use for personal pleasure that led to shouting and not for the veneration of God. In another instance and in the second sign when the ocean descends beyond view, "the everlasting all-powerful God will punish the rulers, the governors, the nobles, those who afflict their children, their subjects, that do not speak for them, do not help them, and do nothing for them." Again, the sin is not in being a ruler, but in being a ruler who is excessive in their own self-indulgence and neglects their reciprocal obligations to their subjects.

The *Sermonario* made other elements of the Christian discourse familiar through the Nahua worldview and the authors' expert use of huehuetlahtolli and metaphorical couplets. The text addresses commoners by their traditional diphrase or semantic couplet *in ancuitlapiltin, in amamatlapaltin* (you tails, you wings); *eztli, tlapalli* (blood, dye) represents "offspring"; and, as we have seen, the text refers to people's human body as *intlallo, inzoquiyo* (their earth, their mud). At times the use of such couplets can produce specious meanings. For example, when referencing the greatness of the humble and despised the sermon states that on such is found *teuhtli, tlaçolli* (dust, filth). Although such items would match the physical description of the humble, together the words can produce a meaning of "vice" or even "sin," thus contradicting the desired imagery.[70]

Parallelisms abound throughout the text, creating extra emphases and the impression of an oral performance common in Nahuatl texts. Describing the unrighteous desires of the prideful within the first sign, the text declares, "Wherefore, the proud greatly want, desire to become perhaps a principal person, a leader, a judge; that which they do is very little, a bit, is not great, not precious, not valued." During the twelfth sign describing falling stars, the text states that, "Truly a very great fire, very enormous hairs of fire really will come huffing and puffing, come raining down, come making flames, making tassels of fire, making tongues of fire here on earth." Combining both parallelism and culturally specific metaphors, the text describes the cry of the fish that gather together on the third day thus: "It will exceed all others, they will cry out in fear, it will be like leg bells worn by warriors, like the sound of water flies, really they will reply to heaven."

The mention of leg bells brings to mind the story of Coatlicue—a Nahua goddess. While sweeping a temple, Coatlicue becomes impregnated from touching some feathers. Her son-to-be was the prominent Huitzilopochtli. Coatlicue's children became enraged and prepared to attack their mother, dressing in their battle attire and donning bells to their legs. Nahua warriors mirrored the practice and likewise wore leg bells into battle.[71]

Yet perhaps most common is the lengthy strings of parallel descriptions awarded to the fear of the wicked. Some border on the humorous such as when the string includes the statement that the wicked will *mauhcaçonequizque* (wet themselves out of fear). But most simply use repetition and alternating description to convey an awful state of fear. One such passage speaks to the physically draining fear the wicked will experience when the plants begin to sweat blood and reads as follows:

> And the wicked will see it, because of which they will be very scared, startled, faint of heart, afflicted in spirit, they will pass out from fear so that no longer anywhere will they feel joy, be strengthened, no longer anywhere can they lean on something, salvage themselves, they will be dead tired, they will faint because of the frightful sign, the frightful affliction that will occur to them, so that they will be severely afflicted, suffer, because of their sinfulness.

Connected to tetzahuitl is the Nahua concept of *tlazolli*, or pollution that disrupts order with chaos. Nahuas frequently employed tlazolli and its association with dirt and filth to convey deviance and Bautista's text freely engages with this ideology.[72] Here, the fourth sign boldly accuses adulterers: "You take dirty pleasure, dirty satisfaction with your earth, your mud [bodies], you did not defend yourselves against the black, the dirty." Moreover, the fifth sign describes the wicked as "those who merely go along focused solely on the filthy pleasures of their bodies, their dirty pleasures so that they go about sick because they go about dirtying things."

The ecclesiastics and their Nahua collaborators likewise found various occasions to relate esoteric Christian concepts and words creatively into a Nahuatl vocabulary that would effectively resonate with an Indigenous audience. In Catholicism, confession serves a fundamental role whereby the penitent declares their sins to a priest and receives absolution; it is a purifying rite whose importance colonial ecclesiastics spent many pages trying to explain. Here, confession is described using a descriptive triplet, *yolcuitia, yolpetlahua, yolchipahua* (declare the heart, reveal the heart, clean the heart)—all fitting descriptions for confession. Repentance also receives a descriptive elaboration. Indeed, the text tells the sinner to "wake up, rise up, turn around quickly, for I awake, twist you." In Hebrew, the word often employed for repentance is *shube*, "to turn back."[73] Turning back toward God is a common concept in Christianity and is seen used here to describe the actions of the penitent. Indeed, Bautista's text describes the Final Judgment as a time "when there is no longer a means to turn around, a means to turn back."

Such beautifully descriptive Nahuatl words and phrases also appear to describe unfamiliar Christian jargon. The phrase *in inecehuilizquauhpet-lacaltzin Dios* (the wooden chest where God rests) appears for the Ark of the Covenant, which reportedly housed various sacred items including the tablets containing the Ten Commandments. And *mamaça intlaquayan* (the place where deer eat) appears for "manger" in reference to where Mary laid Christ after his birth. In sum, Nahuatl had the syntactic and metaphoric malleability to convey beautifully both the wonder and dread of the Final Judgment through *The Fifteen Signs.*

This, then, makes Bautista's text simultaneously common and uncommon. Common in the sense that it draws upon the genre of expository works that were abundant throughout the Middle Ages relating apocalyptic signs to historical, contemporary, and future individuals and events, even employing an existing work—perhaps that of Herolt—as a framewrok. It was uncommon because of its tailoring of the signs to a Nahua audience and its relation of the signs to the sins of their wicked. In short, Bautista's text on *The Fifteen Signs* continues an Old World tradition of expository apocalyptic writing beginning in the early years of Christianity while pioneering a new employment for the signs in a New World discourse directed to a Nahua audience.

The following is a translation of the *Sermonario* sermon containing *The Fifteen Signs* as composed by Bautista and his Nahua collaborators. After discussing *The Fifteen Signs,* the sermon continues for an additional twenty-nine pages to describe and expound upon other signs mentioned in the New Testament and the torments of sinners, and such is not included in the translation. Nor have I included the various Spanish glosses Valeriano inserted throughout the sermon to explain the etymology of certain Nahuatl words or the Spanish marginalia. Translations of the Latin, which appear in reference to biblical citations, are included and italicized as they form an important part of the sermon itself. Although Bautista's text does not include images of the signs themselves, I have inserted some here derived from the mid-fifteenth century French illuminated manuscript, *Livre de la vigne nostre seigneur.* The images not only add imagery but also illustrate the

European context of the signs that Bautista and his collaborators expertly modified to accommodate an Indigenous audience.

Fray Juan Bautista, *Sermonario*, pp. 158–78

Sermon II. Regarding the Gospel

Of other many and no less frightening and terrible signs that will precede the frightful and terrible Day of Judgment.[74]

Where it is mentioned other very frightening signs, frightening attestations that will come to precede the very startling, frightful, shiver-causing day of their eternal judgment.

And there shall be signs in the sun and in the moon and in the stars, and upon the earth distress of nations by reason of the confusion of the roaring of the sea and of the waves, men withering away for fear and expectation of what will come upon the whole world.[75] Which means: "When the world is about to end, a frightening sign will appear, in the sun and the moon and the stars; on earth will be great affliction, the ocean will no longer be quiet, calm; the people of the earth will grow thin with affliction, with fear, because of all the frightful things everywhere on earth that will befall them."

This is the divine speech, oh my precious children, that our lord Jesus Christ really declared in order to tell and mention to us first the frightful, dreadful, scary signs, attestations that will occur, appear before he comes to judge so that everyone will then turn themselves around, amend themselves; beware lest his very frightful judgment, punishment, and condemnation befalls your companion.

Our lord is about to say to them, "Before I come to judge, very scary attestations will occur, really scary things, things that cause cries of fear, screams of terror, things that cannot be resisted, are insufferable, that cause great affliction, torment. In heaven and within the whole earth, very many omens of death will occur, of ominous destruction, ominous attestations. The sun will no longer shine, night will fall on the earth, it will turn the darkness of night, it will be a very dark night, it will erase, hide, cover its light so that it will be made entirely dark, obscured. The moon will no longer shine, it will truly be red as if covered with blood, as if it will be sweating blood so that entirely everywhere on earth will be obscured with darkness. In addition, the stars no longer will shine, no longer will their light, their gleam really be seen, really appear. Everywhere on earth things will be greatly unsettled, there will really be no understanding, the earth will rush, will emerge red, dust will emerge, dust will boil. And when a roar will spread throughout the world, heaven will crackle, flaming comets will fall to the earth, stars will run and there will be comets that last a long time. Thereupon a roar will occur throughout the earth, there will be earthquakes, frequently, really often the earth will shake and really not just occasionally; there will be storms that arise in the ocean as though a small hill, as though mountains the waves will stretch out; these are all terrifying things. Still more a great omen will occur that exceeds all others, this type has never occurred; the heaven will shake, not without reason will it be this way, as though it rushes, goes back and forth; this really will cause fainting, be a really frightful thing. When such occurs, it will be a sign of my arrival when I will arrive, come to judge the people on earth."

It is very necessary for you, oh my precious children, that you understand what occurred before it comes to be fulfilled, before he comes, our lord Jesus Christ, to save us; in the beginning there were very large, many omens, signs that occurred on earth preceding his coming, his incarnation. Likewise, when he comes to judge us, many startling, faint-inducing, frightful signs, attestations will first occur. And although in the scriptures are seen, offered many things, frightful attestations, frightful signs that will appear, occur, when your just judge comes to judge, it really does not appear in them [the scriptures] the order, the arrangement, which one comes first, which one follows, or how distant they will appear from when the judgment occurs; it is not entirely known, as says Saint Augustine. However, I will list only a few omens that Saint Jerome and Saint Bonaventure list. Afterwards, I will list the frightful signs really taken, removed from the Holy Gospel written by the order of our lord Jesus Christ. In one of the books of Saint Jerome it says that he read in an ancient account of the Hebrews fifteen omens, very frightening, very shiver-causing signs, that will herald the coming of our lord, the manner of what will occur to his people at judgment; it is just not explained well if it will continue until the end, or each last one day, or if it will occur now and then, but every one, every day [every sign] will happen.

On the first day, here is what will occur. The ocean, the sea,[76] the divine water will rear up, rise up like a wall, thereby it will stand, in no part will it be divided. And it will ascend fifteen elbow lengths [cubits] so that it surpasses everywhere on earth the high mountains, as occurred when it [the earth] flooded when the water ascended fifteen elbows onto all the high mountains.[77] And by the will of God it will come to pass, he will not completely submerge the earth, [the water] will merely be standing there in its place, it will wall up around where our lord God marked the

Figure 3.9 Signs 1 and 2, *Livre de la vigne*, 41v, 42r. © Bodleian Libraries, University of Oxford.

boundaries. Thus, it will really prove to be true what David said, *awesome the swellings of the sea; awesome the Lord on high.*[78] Which means: "The rise, the increase of the ocean is very worthy of admiration, and very worthy of admiration is the sole divinity, God, and the many things he does there on the sea." Also, Isaiah wrote the word of God. He said, *I am the Lord, your God, who stirs up the sea, [and] its waves swell.*[79] Which means: "I am your divinity, I am your ruler, I disturb, froth the water; therefore I enlarge, make undulations in the water." In the holy scriptures it is said that when our lord took his children of Israel to the other side of the great river called Jordan, the priests carried the wooden chest where God rests [the Ark of the Covenant]; then, when they entered the river, a part of the river receded, ran away, and something else, the water returned, came back, it swelled, rose so that the nonbelievers became very fearful when they saw it. And it will be the same when the ocean rises, all the people of the earth will see it, because of it they will become very fearful and very scared, they will tremble greatly. But it is much more, greater still [than the river rising] so that the wicked, the bad, the villains will be scared, feel afflicted. This omen is the great fear, apprehension of the arrogant, the puffed up, the prideful. Wherefore to the hearts of the arrogant, prideful, the self-aggrandizing the ocean is equal to the waters of hell, always boiling, always turbulent, it is not calm, it swells, never ever does it sometimes rest, it never settles, it never is peaceful, safe. Likewise the haughty are always bothered, always self-aggrandizing, always wanting more rank or position, never ever do they settle down, never do they rest. Thus says Isaiah, *The hearts of the wicked are like the raging sea, which cannot rest*.[80] Which means: "Pride, haughtiness commence, begin, and create discord, conflict, contention." Thus says the Holy Spirit, *Among the proud there are always contentions*,[81] Which means: "The proud always quarrel among themselves, contend, make war on each other, and give discord, hatred to each other." Wherefore, the proud greatly want, desire to become perhaps a principal person, a leader, a judge, that which they do is very little, a bit, is not great, not precious, not valued. Thus, it is known that at the time of the very great, marvelous, they are presumptuous, they esteem themselves above others. And also it happens that the proud are not just, they suffer, struggle in vain, really without purpose. Moreover, it happens that to satisfy the heart of his poor servant, [the servant] will be revered, honored, raised up, and preferred.

Therefore, the wicked, proud are always turbulent, always they will rise up as if to make waves, swells, be really wild, restless, they never rest, settle, are peaceful; even though they are honored, their heart is not satisfied, settled. On the contrary the humble, respectful always live prudently, calmly; wherefore on the humble, respectful appears dust, filth, they are nobody for which reason they bow down, are subjected to all people. Concerning them, the chosen, selected words speak about them, *The servant of God does not attempt to appear greater than others, but seeks how to seem inferior to all*.[82] Which means: "God's servant does not wish, desire, seek how they will appear great, how to exceed others. But really they wish, seek, concern themselves with how to be seen, known as the younger sibling of others and never will they be established as much of anything." Oh, you Christian! Really, by the means of God, humble yourself, bow yourself low, prostrate yourself, so that you will not be counted among the proud, the arrogant, those who greatly esteem themselves.

On the first day, the ocean rises. But on the second day the ocean will descend, it will go inside very deep, it will fall in, because of which it will quickly diminish, it will retreat, sink, go underground quickly, no longer can it be seen, no longer will it appear, great thunder will occur quickly, noisy crackling sounds will occur abruptly, so that the people of the earth will be very afraid, apprehensive, and dead tired. Thus is the divine words [scripture], *The deep put forth its voice*.[83] Which means: "The watery caverns, wells, deep abysses broke very noisily at the coming, at the judgment of the sole divinity, God." In a statement about God by the great seer Nahum, he says concerning our lord, *He rebuketh the sea and drieth it up, and bringeth all the rivers to be a desert*.[84] Which means: "The sole, omnipotent God really will dry out the ocean, the waters, and all the rivers."

Because of this omen, oh my beloved children, the wicked sinners will be very scared, very frightened, especially the prideful, arrogant, the covetous, the desirers of nobility, because of which the lords, nobility were very proud, and they made every effort so that they saw it as, made it their property, found themselves worthy of rulership, fame, honor, and thus they greatly enlarged themselves, they esteemed themselves better than others. And their subjects, their governed people, they merely afflicted, tormented them and they placed them under their feet, because of which they will be cast down, shrunk, abased there in the abyss of hell. Thus says our Lord, *Everyone who exalts himself will be humbled.*[85] Which means: Whoever esteems themselves as great, desires to be a principal thing, the prideful, the arrogant, the merely haughty of their own accord, they will be abased, humiliated, finished, nowhere will they be considered as anything except only there in the abyss of hell. The wise man, Solomon, says it in this way, *Humiliation follows the proud.*[86] Which means: "The prideful, the arrogant, afterwards they will be humiliated, humbled, abased." You tails, you wings [commoners] may you not be very anxious, sad, unhappy because you are afflicted, you suffer, and you view yourselves as nothing. The everlasting, all-powerful God will punish the rulers, the governors, the nobles, those who afflict their children, their subjects, that do not speak for them, do not help them, and do nothing for them.

Figure 3.10 Signs 3 and 4, *Livre de la vigne*, 42v, 43r. © Bodleian Libraries, University of Oxford.

On the third day, the third wondrous portent will occur. Everything that dwells in the ocean, the fish and all living things, will assemble, herd together, gather themselves, come out on the water, they will really shout, growl, yell, make their animal sounds. Their cries, growls will reach heaven, really it will be as though they rip heaven; it is a very frightful, startling thing, they will quickly prick, they will puncture, they will stir the water, because of which the people of the earth will be very frightened and tremble, they will wet themselves out of fear, this is as the wise man says. The shouts of fear, strong yells, growls of the various fish at that time before the judgment—really they will growl, give sad cries of fear, yell from fear—will cause the people of the world to grow thin from great fear and really be fatigued and afflicted in spirit; they will faint from fear, pass out. Some people [will say], "We never saw, never had appear before us the fish, very large, like hills, like homes." Really all of them, all things will give sad cries of fear, really they will cry, they will cry in pain because they are about to die, perish. And all people will cry because of the creatures, given that living are about to die, perish forever, termi-nate forever.

Concerning the cries of the fish that will occur: it will exceed all others, they will cry out in fear, it will be like leg bells worn by warriors, like the sound of water flies, really they will reply to heaven. Because of this omen, they will feel fear, will be startled, those who celebrate, take pleasure with dancing, drums, rattles, flutes and still more did not celebrate with God; it was just frivolity, because of this at that time their shouting, their laughter will turn into weeping, sadness. Thus it says in the Gospel, *Woe to you that now laugh for you will mourn.*[87] Which means: "Woe to you, you who now go around laughing because then you will weep." They will never be peaceful, never be happy, never be a good thing because they laughed here [on earth]. But those who, with our lord Jesus Christ were sad, wept here on earth, as Christ wept, then they, at that time, will really laugh, be consoled. Thus are the words of the Gospel, *Blessed are you that weep now for you will laugh.*[88] Which means: "Fortunate you are, you blessed, that you weep now, because afterwards you will be happy, laugh, be consoled." Saint Gregory says, *Today's gladness follows [yesterday's] unrelenting sadness.*[89] Which means: "Eternal suffering follows current happiness on earth." Oh, you servants of God. May you do penance, do anguishing penance; may you cry with tears now while it is still a good time, a good hour, so that afterwards you can be eternally happy, eternally prosperous with the sole deity, God.

On the fourth day, here is what will occur with the fourth omen. The ocean, the sea, and all waters everywhere will burn, catch fire, ignite. This omen is the

instrument of fear and fright that will occur to carnal people, adulterers, those having sex, that have engrossed themselves in licentiousness, lasciviousness here on
earth; they wrap up in the water thoughtlessly with pleasure, with sexual pleasure,
they satisfied their desire; because of this, they will burn in hell with fire and sulfur
[brimstone]. As it says in the divine word, *Their portion will be in a pool burning
with fire and brimstone.*[90] Which means: "The wicked, the spoilers of the divine
commandment, they will be thrown down into a trough of fire water, there they
will be bathed, scorched, roasted with fire, with sulfur." And it is true that however
much they took pleasure with their bodies, they will be tormented, afflicted the
same degree. Thus it says, *As much as she has glorified herself and lived in delicacies, so much torment and sorrow give you to her.*[91] Which means: "However much
they were happy, were licentious, pleased themselves, to the same degree you all
torment them, cause them to cry, cause them pain!" Oh you sinners, carnal people, adulterers, you take dirty pleasure, dirty satisfaction with your earth, your mud
[bodies], you did not defend yourselves against the black, the dirty; may the thought
of eternal fire scare you, frighten you, may it cause you to refrain from sin, may it rid
you of sin, because you will be burned, scorched, bathed there in the abyss of hell; if
you do not turn your life around, if you do not weep over your sins, may the cracking
noise, the sound reach your ears, may your hearts really be penetrated inside by the
noise, the cracking sound, the whimper of the fire in hell; yes it is coming making a
loud noise, breaking noisily, it will sop you up, it will swallow you.

Figure 3.11 Signs 5 and 6, *Livre de la vigne*, 43v, 44r. © Bodleian Libraries,
University of Oxford.

On the fifth day, the fifth frightful sign will occur. All trees, all the various plants everywhere laid out on earth that are growing, sprouting, blossoming, germinating, all will sweat blood, will be covered with a bloody dew, will be trimmed with blood. The grasses, plants, willows, cypress trees, bushes, zapote trees, fruit trees, peach trees, quince trees, pear trees, avocado trees, flowering trees, nopals, magueys, tzihuactli cactus, all growing things; really all will sweat blood, be captured in blood, break out in blood, bleed; the trees really will bubble, run, drip with blood as though watered, drizzled with blood so that it will drip on the ground, so that blood will be leaked, poured. According to the divine words, *And I will show wonders in heaven and in earth, blood, and fire, and vapor of smoke. The sun will be turned into darkness, and the moon into blood before the great and dreadful day of the Lord comes*"[92] Which means, before the eternal Judgment Day—that very great, very terrible, very frightening, very scary, very alarming thing, that causes you to pass out, to faint—here is what our lord says to them that occur:

"I will give omens, wonders in heaven and on earth; the sun no longer will shine, it will simply become darkened, be made completely dark, it will be darkened. And the moon also will not shine, it will merely be red as if covered in blood, as if it will sweat blood, it will really be red everywhere in the world and on earth."

It means, however it occurs on earth, the sprouting, blossoming of blood as sweat and rising smoke; it means very great blazing coals on fire will really descend, come falling on fire, come emitting flames and much lightning striking, bolts of lightning; there the burning, scorching will begin to emerge, and there smoke will arise. This is joined by the words of Isaiah, he says to them, *Their land will be soaked in blood, for it is the day of the vengeance of the lord, the year of recompenses of the judgment of Zion.*[93] Which means: "Blood will flow on earth because God's Day of Judgment, day of vengeance comes quickly, his year of recompense where he will judge the bad, the corrupt, where he will forever curse them, forever condemn them, forever angrily causes them to arrive into the fire, but where he will forever pay back, reward the good, the righteous."

And for what reason will such occur that all grasses will sweat blood, that blood will flow? May you all understand that it is simply because of, in relation to the wicked, the bad, the corrupt, those who merely go along focused solely on the filthy pleasures of their bodies, their dirty pleasures so that they go about sick because they go about dirtying things, loving sex, committing adultery, so that they go about coveting people, desiring women so that they go about womanizing, putting their women, their mistresses in their houses so that with them they go about having filthy pleasures, and they go about getting drunk, stuffing themselves [with food], vomiting, rinsing their mouths out, and go about proud, arrogant, hating people, desiring the deaths of others, speaking bad of others, tricking others, really committing all types of sin, omitting nothing, if it is something doable, they simply go do it.

This omen especially is the instrument of fear, the apprehension, and the punishment of the murderers, those who took vengeance on people, afflicted others, deceived their companion. Wherefore, a deadly attack is the fourth of the great [deadly] sins, it shouts summoning and causes to hurry punishment from heaven. Thus said our lord, *The voice of your brother Abel's blood cries to me from the earth.*[94] Which means: "The blood, the dye of your younger sibling, Abel—caused, did nothing, it has no sin—cries to me and asks me, makes me hurry to do it, 'May you quickly punish him, may you quickly repay him!' because it [his blood] was spilled on the ground."[95]

The wrath, the rage of our lord, the sole deity, God, is excessively great for the wicked for he is getting angry with them, considering them with anger because of their sins, their wickedness, because they did not obey, did not believe in the true deity, the ruler, who made, created them, goes along sustaining their life; and they did not do all the good, right that the true God desired; instead they believed in the devil and committed all sins, their dirty pleasures with their bodies; thus he [God] will be excessively angry with them. And all plant life—the trees, grasses everything that is sprouting, blossoming—is colorless unto death so the wicked will be very startled, scared at this, they will regard them with fear, trepidation, how they did that which was very wicked, bad, they lived their life according to sin so that they offended our lord. Likewise, the trees will bleed, sweat blood so that it will startle and cause the wicked to regard them with fear, so our lord will cast them off into hell.

Likewise, because God will reveal, show his very great anger to them, because he will be angry with them, hate them, all creation will bleed, sweat blood. And the wicked will see it, because of which they will be very scared, startled, faint of heart, afflicted in spirit, they will pass out from fear so that no longer anywhere will they feel joy, be strengthened, no longer anywhere can they lean on something, salvage themselves, they will be dead tired, they will faint because of the frightful sign, the frightful affliction that will occur to them, so that they will be severely afflicted, suffer, because of their sinfulness. And if they do not turn their life around, if they do not now, here on earth, begin, start their suffering, affliction, then there in hell it will be excessive because the devils will torment them, afflict them in the midst of the fire. In this way will the frightful sign, frightful affliction affect the wicked so that really they will suffer. Because of this, my children, may you abhor all sinful things, all evildoing while it is still a proper time, a good time, so that you will not be placed eternally into the abyss of hell.

On the sixth day, the sixth frightful sign will occur. All houses, the tall houses, short houses, or the old thatched houses, the walls will fall, crumble, fall to the ground, roll, collapse, become divided; really on the people they will collapse, because of which they will be covered and die. Given that when Jerusalem was destroyed, razed to the ground, not even one stone remained standing, did not fall down, how much more will it be when our lord God comes to judge and punish all of the sinners?

This omen will cause them to be afraid, to be frightened, to be punished, the sinners, those who covet earthly things, really they desired to build their homes here on earth rather than in heaven; their home was to be in a really good place, really a place of enjoyment, of pleasure, if they had served God, if they had been obedient, and if they had kept, lived according to his mandate. Know, my precious children, that there in heaven there are many glorious places that our lord God will give to those who, while here on earth, deserve it, acquire it, make it their property, through good deeds and service. As is the statement of our lord, *In my father's house there are many mansions.*[96] Which means: "In the house of my precious father there are many places, many places to rest, that he will give to my servants." Oh how really many concern themselves with building houses, making houses, making palaces where to rest their bodies, their earth, their mud. But they think nothing of getting themselves ready, preparing themselves so that there our lord God will reside, there he will rest. These the prophet Isaiah really scolded by the order of God, *Woe to you that join house to house and lay field to field even to the end of the place.*[97] Which means: "Oh you cursed, you seek many houses and you build two-story houses[98] for yourselves with presumption and with boasting, and you establish boundaries so that you multiply, increase your land, your cultivated fields."

You Christian, you who built a house or that has a good home, a few times enter there and remember and say, "Oh, may I concern myself with my soul as I concerned myself with the home, resting place of my body." But if you are poor, if your home, your resting place is nothing, let it be that you are content through our savior Jesus Christ who was merely laid out in a manger. All of you, may you not really love earthly things, all that will end, be lost, destroyed; let it be that you seek, thirst for the heavenly things our lord God will give to the good, pure, that really keep, live by his divine commandments, his divine custom.

Figure 3.12 Signs 7 and 8, *Livre de la vigne*, 44v, 45r. © Bodleian Libraries, University of Oxford.

On the seventh day here is what will happen concerning the seventh omen. All stones will run into themselves, knock against themselves, throw themselves together so that each stone will split into eight parts. Additionally, the small stones again will knock together, crush together, grind together, crumble together, and this will make a sound that will frighten, startle, scare to death the sinners, the offenders. This is how it happened at the time of the death of God's true child, our lord Jesus Christ, many stones split apart. Likewise at the time of the destruction, the end of the people on earth, God's adopted children, the stones will crack.

Because of this omen all sinners will be very scared, they will faint from fear. What is more the obstinate, the stubborn, those that really surpass stone because of metal hearts, the fright of hell, the respect of hell, the fires of hell cannot soften their hearts, withdraw their sin, neither can the joy of heaven. Moreover, God's suffering did not soften their hearts although many stones broke together when our lord Jesus Christ suffered. Because of this, my precious children, may you not be stubborn, may you not be as obsidian, may you really quickly turn your lives around, may you really quickly do penance so that the sole deity, God, will have compassion on you, so that he does not throw you into the abyss of hell among the stubborn, the devils.

On the eighth day, here is what will happen concerning the eighth frightful sign. Everywhere the world will shake because there will be a very great earthquake, people will be scared because all the people of the earth will be beaten, all people will be silly [with fear]. Then, all living things, beasts, will fall down, roll, no one will be standing or sitting any longer. Thus are the divine words, *And there was a great earthquake, such an one as never had been since men were upon the earth, such an earthquake so great.*[99] Which means: "It happened when our lord will judge people, a very great earthquake, such that never occurred up until that time people had lived on the earth, a very great, very frightful earthquake that groans in pain, is distorted into another, is going crazy."

This omen is the instrument of fear, apprehension, and punishment that will happen to the sinners; really their hearts will collapse so that they cannot be transported, carried, because they offended their maker; and since the hearts of the sinners really collapse, there is no way to hide them, no way to conceal them, it is simply necessary that they go along appearing, standing, being placed before the great and very just judge, Jesus. Oh you sinners, you are very ashamed at that time you are about to confess, you do not go and stand before the confessor and discuss your sin, your fault. How can you stand, appear before God and all the people of earth who will see and be startled by your sins? Perhaps it will not be especially good now for you to declare the heart, reveal the heart, clean the heart before the

Figure 3.13 Signs 9 and 10, *Livre de la vigne*, 45v, 46r. © Bodleian Libraries, University of Oxford.

confessor so that you will not be ashamed before all the people of earth, before the devils, and before all the saints and angels? It is true. Because of this, wake up, rise up, turn around quickly, for I awake, twist you.

On the ninth day, here is what will happen concerning the ninth frightful sign. Everywhere on earth will be leveled, be made flat; the land, mountain, hillock, all the land will turn into a really large amount of sand; the mountain, the ravine, the precipice will become sand and the cave will really be filled up, overflow, leveled. Thus are the words of David, *The mountains melted like wax at the presence of the lord, at the presence of the lord of all the earth.*[100] Which means: "All the mountains melted, dissolved like wax in the presence of our lord, God." Which means, when he comes to judge, in the same way all the land before him will be as though it melted. Isaiah also speaks about it. *Every valley will be exalted and every mountain and hill will be made low, and the crooked will become straight and the rough ways plain.*[101] Which means: "When he comes, the judge Jesus, to judge the people on earth, everywhere the valleys will be made flat, be filled in; and the mountains everywhere will be knocked down, fall to the ground; and the crooked, rutted roads will be made straight; and at that time the elevated place and low place will be made good, ultimately the road will be level." And all people will see the salvation of God. Which means, really the precious son of God, Jesus Christ, came to become flesh.

The people on earth will really be afraid because of this sign, really because of it they will tremble, be afflicted of spirit, faint from fear; it is an instrument of fear that will occur especially to the nobles, the elite, the rulers, who greatly bragged about themselves, made themselves nobles, elevated themselves, and saw as nothing the others, the poor, the orphans. At that time they [the poor, etc.] will understand, they will be content for all of us will simply be equal, we will all simply be commoners, we will not appear as separate individuals, but each one will be judged as thus is their reward. Thus it says in the Holy Gospel, "*The Son of man will render to every man according to his works.*[102] Which means: "The son of God, child of the eternal virgin, when he judges he will repay, give in return; his recompense is according to what they did, made, according to their works."

May your hearts be content, my precious children, for our lord God is no respecter of persons but is one who omits no one, the nobles, the rulers, the great kings, the emperors, and the field workers, the soil-breakers, or the fishermen; he will judge them all that no one will remain that will not be examined, interrogated; but because of it they will be separated, divided, those that did, made, worked good and righteous things or bad, wicked things; and both groups will take, receive the reward of eternal magnificence, glorification or eternal scorn, condemnation and eternal punishment, torment. Because of this [the Final Judgment] simply by means of God, you should really see to, engross yourselves in, go along in good and righteous living, life, that [a life] which saves, so that afterwards God will give you everlasting joy, glory that will never end, be destroyed, finish there in *Glory*, in the place of eternal glory.

On the tenth day, here is what will happen concerning the tenth omen. All the people will emerge from underground caves where they had hidden themselves, but in vain, now in vain they go here and there, in vain they run every which way as if they are really drunk, as if they are really going about crazy, terrifying things will occur, they will tremble, no one any longer will speak. Thus is the prophecy of Isaiah, *The sinners in Zion are afraid, trembling has seized upon the hypocrites.*[103] Which means: "The sinners were very troubled, scared, apprehensive, and the terror, fear caused great pain on the deceivers, sinners because they did not completely turn their lives around."

Because of this omen the bad, wicked will understand that at that time there is nowhere to truly save themselves, and that no one can back out when we are to be judged, and that at that time no one holy will speak for them, no one will rise up before the judge to merely speak for them, offer to do some good deed for them,

Figure 3.14 Signs 11 and 12, *Livre de la vigne*, 46v, 47r. © Bodleian Libraries, University of Oxford.

bestow mercy on them. Oh, you Christian! How vain it is that you really, firmly guard, strongly keep your possessions. Let it be that today you give, distribute them to the very poor, for those same ones will serve as your intercessors before our lord at the eternal Day of Judgment.

On the eleventh day, here is what will happen concerning the eleventh omen. All graves, all cemeteries will open beginning in the east until reaching the west, and all the bones of the dead will gather, assemble, place themselves on top [of the graves] so that life will go on again, they will revive. Thus the words of the prophet Ezekiel, *Behold I will open your graves and will bring you out of your sepulchers.*[104] Which means: "Here it is for you to see, I will open your graves, burials, and I will bring you out of there and cause you to live again, come to life."

Because of this omen, sinners will be revealed, for all the secret sins they committed will appear, be placed on top, will surface, so that they will be ashamed, dumbfounded, as our lord says to them, *For nothing is covered that will not be revealed, nor hid that will not be known.*[105] Which means: "Truly nothing is being hidden, concealed, covered up such that will not appear on top, such that the sinner will not confess." Concerning this, you Christian that currently hides your sins, wickedness, may you declare and reveal it to the confessor, and if he absolves you, do not worry, be ashamed because of it even if all people will learn of it, but if now you still will hide, conceal it [your sins], truly I say to you that God will truly tell you your faults to your face in front of all the people on earth, and he will throw in your face something insufferable, irrefutable, so that you will be ashamed, speechless, embarrassed.

On the twelfth day, here is what will happen concerning the twelfth frightful sign. Stars in heaven will come throwing themselves to the ground, pulling themselves loose. Thus the sermon of our lord, *The stars will fall from heaven and the powers of heaven will be moved.*[106] Which means: "The stars will fall from heaven where they dwell, and the goodness, strength of the heavens will stir, shake." Wherefore, all the stars will go about moving and those fixed to something will cast hence comets, shooting stars, and many other comets of fire. Understand, my precious children, that the stars truly dwell in heaven just as a wood-eye [knot] dwells in a plank or wooden beam. It is said that stars will fall from heaven to here on earth, thereby it is heard, thereby it is explained. Which means, truly a very great fire, very enormous hairs of fire[107] really will come huffing and puffing, come raining down, come making flames, making tassels of fire, making tongues of fire here on earth; never once has such occurred. Heaven will really crackle, really bloom like many flowers when this great ember, comet of fire falls, throws itself on the wicked, the rebellious, the sinners so that the earth will catch fire.

Because of this the wicked will be scared, they will be very afflicted in spirit, faint from fear so that they are paralyzed, so that they are destroyed, crackle, disappear with fire because of their sins. It will be as an omen of death, omen of destruction for the wicked so that they will greatly suffer, be afflicted, especially those wrong believers, sideways believers[108] who did not believe in God, or did not really entirely believe in him, and also those with riches or with poverty who abandoned the sole deity, God, who no longer have confidence in him, they will suffer greatly.

During this day, all living things will gather themselves on the plains, they will howl, cry, no longer will they eat, drink. All living things, the four-footed animals, the wild beasts, the big brown wild cats, the mountain lions, the ocelot, the wolves, the bobcats, and the deer, the rabbits, the coyotes, and the rattlesnakes, the large, poisonous snakes, the black snakes, truly all will come, come down, come to gather, come completely, all come to assemble from everywhere on earth, the living things. And all that go along above, go along flying, the birds, the eagles, the quetzal birds, the red birds, the green parrots, the large parrots, the ducks, the herons, the hawks; yes all the birds truly come to assemble as a whole in the same place so that they will mix there in Tlalnepantla [the middle of the earth], on the plains. And when they have gathered, assembled, the wild beasts, the birds, really they will give one great cry of fear, they will cry from fear, they will be sad, they will cry concerning themselves, for themselves they will cry because they truly understand that they are about to die, about to be destroyed, that never again will they live on earth; because of this, they will really cry from fear, howl in fear, scream in fear. And also the wicked, those who have defects, will cry because of their sins and their ingratitude. Thus are the divine words [scriptures], *The lions have roared upon him and have made a noise.*[109] Which means: "The big brown wild cats and various living things roared and growled at the sinner." Because of this omen, the sinners will be very scared, the wicked will be really paralyzed, it will especially frighten the over-eater, the gluttons, the swallowers, and the heavy drinker, the very drunk, the drunks, they that really went about satisfying their appetites, getting drunk, giving edible things and drink to themselves.

And because of this omen they will be made to know, understand, be satisfied. But if they do not do penance for their sins, they will be very hungry, dying of starvation, will be anxious to eat, dying of thirst, have a dry mouth from hunger and thirst there in hell; not one thing will be used for them except it be merely the smell of sulfur, bitumen water, and all deadly mixtures. Oh, you who drinks too much, you drunks, you who never denied the request for a pulque jar, may you be content that an infinite amount of fire-metal-pulque jars, bitumen water, and sulfur is kept for you to be given to drink, at that time. And then you will desire it, may you turn your life around, may you curse the wine, the pulque, and all the drunks, those who get others drunk; it is powerless, it is not a place of salvation.

Figure 3.15 Signs 13 and 14, *Livre de la vigne*, 47v, 48r. © Bodleian Libraries, University of Oxford.

On the thirteenth day, here is what will happen concerning the thirteenth frightful sign. At that time, all the people of earth will die, pass away, be destroyed so that they will resurrect with those who had died long ago.

On the fourteenth day, here is what will happen concerning the fourteenth frightful sign. At that time heaven will burn, which means, the subtle breeze, the gentle breeze that begins on land reaches to heaven, and the land everywhere will burn on earth, and the wind will burn everything, all will burn with a loud noise.

On the fifteenth day, here is what will happen concerning the fifteenth frightful sign. Heaven and earth will be renewed, become clean. And at the time that it will resurrect, again there will be life; the dead will rise again. At that time our lord God will give them that which they deserve; then they will take, receive the due reward, recompense. Take heed therefore to the manifestations, signs that will occur; it is already hurrying, completed its time for the signs, for the very frightful, very great judgment, *sentence* to ultimately emerge when there is no longer a means to turn

Figure 3.16 Sign 15, *Livre de la vigne*, 50v. © Bodleian Libraries, University of Oxford.

around, a means to turn back. When God, our lord Jesus Christ will come, he will descend in order to judge; then all the people of the earth will see him come to appear among the clouds; truly he will come to appear, this great, very revered person.

$$\Longrightarrow\Longleftarrow$$

A sign occurred on June 23, 2016, that fulfilled biblical prophecy—at least according to the Seventh-day Adventist magazine *Signs of the Times*. On this day, British citizens decided to end the United Kingdom's involvement with the European Union thus hindering a united Europe. The magazine's article, "Brexit: When Dreams Collide," claimed that "the dream of a united Europe contradicts the dream God gave to Nebuchadnezzar." Interpreted by the prophet Daniel, the dream included a large image with limbs representing different kingdoms of the world that was shattered by a stone representing God's kingdom on earth. In the dream, no unity is permitted to exist. This, then, allowed the article to claim, "The European Union, whatever its lofty goals may be, was doomed from the beginning . . . and it appears that Brexit was the beginning of the EU's demise."[110]

The season of Advent certainly focused the gaze of Christians on the pending Second Coming of Christ and Apocalypse. Serendipitously, *The Fifteen Signs* often engaged simultaneously ancient beliefs and traditions from the Old and New Worlds that valued period beginnings and endings and the calamitous events associated with both. Modified in Maya- and Nahua-specific ways, the signs made sense of the world's inevitable chaos while making relevant an Apocalypse that can appear in almost any calamitous event. These events serve as constant reminders (like a text alert on our phones) that the Apocalypse is never too far away. Yet other eschatological reminders are likewise woven into the very fabric of Catholic belief, including the Apostles' Creed and its resulting Articles of Faith—the subject of the next chapter.

— 4 —

The Apocalypse of the Body: Resurrection

It's the end of the world as we know it, and I feel fine.

Michael Stipe, REM

In 1987, the American band REM released their album, *Document*, on which was the song, "It's the End of the World as We Know It (and I Feel Fine)." I recall hearing the song on the radio constantly, and subsequent movies, TV shows, apocalyptic events (2012), and even pandemics (COVID-19) granted it additional relevance over the years.[1] Yet perhaps an overlooked reason for the song's continued popularity resides in the truth of its title: "It's the End of the World *as We Know It*" (emphasis mine). In truth, the world *as we know it* is always ending. Consider the world in 1987, the year of the song's release. The public had no internet access, the TSA did not yet exist, a gallon of gasoline cost around $0.85, movie nights included not only renting a VHS tape but also the VCR that played it, and the Berlin Wall still stood strong.[2] But with every ending is a renewal. New technologies, social norms, geopolitical events, and people themselves cause a continual rebirth and renewal, not an end, of the world as we know it.

This is perhaps the most misunderstood aspect of the Christian Apocalypse: the world and its people do not end, they are simply renewed. The Bible speaks of such a renewal. In one instance, Saint John declares that in a vision, "Then I saw a new heaven and a new earth. The former heaven and the former earth had passed away."[3] In the original Greek text of this passage, instead of employing *neos* for "new," the text uses *kainos*, which carries a meaning of "renewed."[4] Thus the world will not end but be renewed, albeit through catastrophe. Or, as Pope Francis stated, the Apocalypse is not the "annihilation of the cosmos and of everything around us"; instead God will "bring everything to its fullness of being, truth and beauty."[5]

According to the *Lumen Gentium*, a product of the Second Vatican Council, "Already the final age of the world has come upon us and the renovation of the world is irrevocably decreed and is already anticipated in some kind of a real way; for the Church already on this earth is signed with a sanctity which is real although imperfect."[6] Moreover, the *Catechism of the Catholic Church* likewise affirms this belief in renewal declaring that God will "transform humanity and the world" and that "the world itself, restored to its original state, facing no further obstacles, should be at the service of the just."[7] Thus, along with the renewal of the heaven and earth is the renewal of humankind's bodies, and it is this doctrine that the Nahuatl and Maya sermons on the seventh Articles of Faith found in this chapter emphasize.

After a brief overview of the Articles of Faith, the following presents two examples of Indigenous-language discourses on the seventh Articles of Faith. The texts themselves reveal insights into their authorship; the utility of such eschatological discourses in teaching various Christian doctrines, particularly that of the resurrection; and the influence such texts received from both the Old and New Worlds. On this last point, the texts expose, again, the importance of understanding Old World doctrine in order to accurately view New World contributions. In the end, the overarching message of the Nahuatl and Maya texts discussed here revolves around the renewal of one's body upon resurrection and its glory or damnation as determined by the Final Judgment. Certainly the message of REM's 1987 song would have rung true in the colonial period, as the Apocalypse brought both an end to the world (and bodies) of Nahuas and Mayas as they knew it and a renewed world and body as taught by the seventh Articles of Faith.

The Articles of Faith

According to the *Catechism of the Catholic Church*, four pillars support the catechesis of the Church. One of those pillars is the Apostles' Creed. In

TABLE 4.1. The Apostles' Creed

I believe in God, the Father almighty, Creator of heaven and earth,

and in Jesus Christ, his only Son, our Lord,

who was conceived by the Holy Spirit, born of the Virgin Mary.

Suffered under Pontius Pilate, was crucified, died, and was buried;

he descended into hell; on the third day he rose again from the dead;

he ascended into heaven, and is seated at the right hand of God the Father almighty;

from there he will come again to judge the living and the dead.

I believe in the Holy Spirit,

the holy catholic Church, the communion of saints,

the forgiveness of sins,

the resurrection of the body,

and life everlasting. Amen.

Source: Catholic Church, *Catechism*, pt. 1, sec. 1.

its early years, the nascent Christian church needed to form and define its essential doctrines, and it is likely that congregations possessed individual creeds accomplishing as much. By 180 A.D., Rome had established a creed likely used by baptismal candidates to testify of their Christian belief.[8] The various creeds, or statements of faith, combated and accommodated one another until the current state of the Apostles' Creed appeared in the eighth century.[9] Today, the Creed contains the fundamental doctrines of the Catholic Church as held by the Twelve Apostles and provides believers the knowledge of essential teachings without having to become biblical scholars (see table 4.1).

The Apostles' Creed gave form to the Articles of Faith, which contain the teachings of the Creed. The articles were commonly parsed into either twelve or the fourteen articles typically used by colonial authors—six or seven concerning the godhead or Christ's divinity and six or seven concerning Christ's humanity.[10] Both the Apostles' Creed and the Articles of Faith were useful and effective tools in evangelization. Indeed, the Creed and its articles cover all the doctrinal basics of Christianity including the Trinity, Creation, Passion, role of Mary, resurrection, and Apocalypse. Because the Creed and its articles provided effective ways to present essential Christian dogma, such appear in the first texts produced in New Spain by friars and their Nahua and Maya collaborators. As Louise Burkhart aptly noted, knowledge of certain prayers and doctrine, including the Creed—and thus the contents of the Articles of Faith—became required, standard knowledge for the Indigenous population, and their recitation might be required prior to confession or Communion. Indeed, "to be Christian meant that one participated in group and individual recitations of a small set of sanctioned texts."[11] And the doctrine within this small set of sanctioned texts included the raising of the dead.

In his thirteenth-century *Summa theologiae*, Thomas Aquinas refers to the seventh Articles of Faith belonging to Christ's divinity (or "the majesty of the Godhead") as "concerning the resurrection of the dead and life everlasting," and the seventh article speaking to Christ's humanity as "his coming for the judgment."[12] Many ecclesiastical texts composed in Nahuatl and Maya—from sermons to *doctrinas* to confessional manuals—employ these particular articles as a springboard of sorts to begin a broader discussion on the Apocalypse and its eschatology, Works of Mercy, and the just rewards and punishments of the righteous and wicked. The Creed and discussions of the seventh Articles of Faith, then, not only allowed the Apocalypse to enter into the basic canon of doctrine required of the Indigenous population but also illustrate the utility of the Apocalypse in shoring up other Christian doctrines such as the resurrection.

The Seventh Articles of Faith in León's *Camino del cielo*

Although published Dominican texts in Nahuatl fall a distant third to the volume of Franciscan and Augustinian publications, Martín de León is undoubtedly the most prolific of his order's colonial authors.[13] Like others of the early colonial period, León sought to compose a sermonary for the entire year. And, like others, he only succeeded in publishing the first portion of it, in 1614, which contains sermons from Advent to Holy Week. Also in 1614, he published a manual on how to administer the sacraments, which experienced multiple reprintings throughout the seventeenth century.[14] However, his first published work, and the one examined here, appeared in 1611 and is the devotional manual *Camino del cielo*. The manual is extensive and eclectic in its attempt to provide the necessary doctrinal instruction for salvation. The work includes a catechism, small and large confessional manuals, a guide on how to die well, prayers, expositions on idolatry and the Mexican calendar, and many other texts including a discussion on the fourteen Articles of Faith.

As previously indicated, in central Mexico the Dominican order generally lacked the optimism of the early Franciscans regarding the potential of the Indigenous population. Indeed, the Dominican archbishop, Alonso de Montúfar, consistently expressed his concern about the use of Indigenous people in translating and even possessing religious texts during the First and Second Mexican Provincial Councils of 1555 and 1565, respectively, over which he presided. One particularly illustrative example concerns answers given by Franciscans and Dominicans to a 1570s questionnaire from the Mexican Inquisition regarding the translation of biblical scripture into Indigenous languages. In general, the Franciscan respondents said the translation of scripture should be allowed as it would benefit the Indigenous people; the Dominicans argued against such translations.[15] This suspicion and even pessimism regarding the Indigenous population appears in León's work. Although many, if not most, ecclesiastics employed Nahua collaborators when composing their religious texts, León declared, "They are the ones that have to learn from us, not us from them."[16] And when writing his sermons for his 1614 work he stated, "I agreed to work and compose them myself, and I do not trust the Indians to do them."[17] For León, Nahuas could never form or lead a perfected, renewed church that would usher in the Apocalypse as some Franciscans believed (is it a wonder many desired Nahuatl translations of scripture?). Instead, "it is the duty of the ministers to carry them [the Nahua] on their shoulders and remove them from the claws of the enemy with designed plans, examples, doctrine, admonitions, and corrections."[18]

Certainly ecclesiastics could openly take credit for their works while secretly employing Indigenous ghostwriters. Yet the Nahuatl text of the *Camino* itself does seem to support León's claim that he worked alone, although it is always possible he benefited from the cursory assistance of some Nahua speakers. However knowledgeable in the language, León was not a native speaker and his text favors clarity and simplicity over the poetry, imagery, and smoothness evident in Bautista's text, which employed numerous Nahua assistants. As Barry Sell put it, "he wrote in a very down-to-earth, direct style."[19] At times, León's Nahuatl text feels more like a translation of a Spanish prototype than a naturally forming discourse. In short, from a philological standpoint, León's fingerprints appear throughout the text and suggest him as the primary author.[20] Similar to his Nahuatl, León's apocalyptic discourses on the seventh Articles of Faith concerning Christ's divinity and humanity are direct and straight to the point: the world will end, and all will resurrect and await Christ's judgment, whereupon the wicked will go to hell and the righteous to heaven. However, within his apocalyptic texts, León emphasizes certain themes and doctrines more than others.

León begins reiterating the medieval idea that heaven is filled with vacant thrones left by those angels who, along with Satan, were cast out into hell before the world began. Theologians believed that upon their favorable judgment, the righteous inherit such vacant thrones and enjoy eternal glory.[21] As mentioned previously, in the Nahua worldview, mictlan was neither a good nor a bad place and often described as cold. To instruct the reader, León uses the uncommon parallel construction *tleoztocalco in mictlan* (fire-cave-house, mictlan). The idea of mictlan being a fiery cave housing the wicked is vivid, yet, again, ultimately foreign to a traditional Nahua worldview.

León then addresses the terrible fires destined to destroy the earth and its inhabitants, going into some detail with regard to their all-consuming power. Second Peter 3:10–12 describes the Apocalypse and how "the heavens will be dissolved in flames and the elements melted by fire." León likely had this scripture in mind as he described his doomsday inferno, which consumes all living things, even the heavens. Indeed, the end of the world and apocalyptic fire share a close relationship as fire is the Bible's medium of choice when describing Doomsday. Yet it is possible that Nahua recipients of this sermon had something else in mind. As mentioned, the Nahua worldview included a belief in four previous eras of the world, which ended in catastrophe only to be renewed (think Noah and the Flood). The era of the third sun, 4 Rain, ended in a torrential rain of fire that engulfed the earth and its inhabitants, necessitating its renewal. Recently, Stephanie Schmidt noted how although Bautista's *Sermonario* declares this Indigenous worldview as *iztlacatlahtolli*, or "false words," with the Spanish glosses of *patrañas, y mentiras* (tall tales and lies), the work reflects aspects of this worldview in its discussion of the Apocalypse. Perhaps a cleansing fire from the heavens purifying the world for its renewed role as the kingdom of God was not as strange to Nahua ears as we might think.[22]

Then comes what appears to be a central concern of the text: the resurrection, and the pleasures and torments associated with the resurrected bodies of the righteous and wicked respectively—a topic familiar among European texts.[23] Yet, as Devorah Dimant observed, "The doctrine of bodily resurrection at the End of Days was one of the most controversial teachings within ancient Judaism"[24] (and I daresay is today!). Indeed, at the time of Christ, the doctrine divided the two main branches of Judaism's ecclesiastical leaders, with the Pharisees believing in the resurrection and the Sadducees denying its existence. Moreover, many of the Pauline epistles in the Bible repeatedly addressed the resurrection in attempts to encourage an accurate belief among early Christians.[25] Perhaps Augustine attempted to set the record straight when he said, "The faith of Christians is in Christ's resurrection."[26] The Nahua, however, lacked a belief of anything similar to the Christian resurrection. Thus, perhaps it should come as no surprise that León devotes a hefty portion of his discussion to the resurrection and the resurrected body.

First, León instructs the Nahua audience on the immortality of the soul and how it rejoins and "sticks together with" the body during this event. Here, León emphasizes that each person reclaims his or her own body, not a different one: "Then, just as when God created all his works with his power, then again will he quickly bring them to life, all bodies, flesh, truly what we now go along carrying that is a part of us, and each person and their body that had been made, then he [God] will place it inside them, each one will take their soul."

To an audience unfamiliar with the resurrection, this clarification is an important one to distinguish it from reincarnation. León continues to describe the bodies of the righteous and their abilities to never tire, be agile, shine, and even fly through mountains and walls if they desire. Such bodies enable them to join Christ as he and his angels descend through the air to judge the world and then ascend again, accompanied by music, to heaven after the Final Judgment.

At first glance, such descriptions of the resurrected bodies of the righteous might be seen as the inflated fancies and modifications of New World

Nahua amanuenses. Yet all have Old World roots of which León would have been aware. Biblical passages discussing the resurrection allowed for speculation. For example, 1 Thessalonians 4:13–18 states that the righteous will rise at the trumpet of God and "will be caught up together with them in the clouds to meet the Lord in the air," thus indicating that the resurrected body can fly. Philippians 3:21 states that the resurrected body will "conform with his [Christ's] glorified body." The resurrected Christ spontaneously appeared and disappeared, even in rooms with closed doors, thus so too can the resurrected bodies of the righteous.[27] And various scriptures describe the ability of such bodies to shine as the sun.[28]

Although the Fourth Lateran Council of 1215 confirmed that at the Final Judgment "all will rise with their own bodies which they now wear," these biblical passages provided fodder for theologians to develop "qualities" for resurrected bodies.[29] The supplement in Thomas Aquinas's thirteenth-century *Summa theologiae* listed four, and Caroline Bynum describes such gifts theologians frequently associated with the resurrected body as "agility (a sort of weightlessness that enabled it [the body] to move with the speed of light), subtlety (a sort of incorporeality . . .), clarity (which seems to have meant beauty), and impassibility (an inability to suffer)."[30] Aquinas's *Summa* was common among the New World libraries of the friars and certainly influenced the seventeenth-century discussion of his fellow Dominican, León, which embellished Aquinas's qualities with Nahuatl couplets and strings of synonyms.[31]

León then moves on to discuss the bodies of "idolaters and the wicked," who when they resurrect "will be very sluggish, sick, rotten, become wormy, be peeled, will stink, be something dirty, something frightening, something nauseating, will be full of various torments, agonies, afflictions; and very many painful, injurious things will happen to them, they will know it, really greatly they will tremble, will cry out of fear, not be able to lift themselves on top of the wind [into the sky], they will merely flop to the ground as they are waiting for their judgment." Scholars, such as Louise Burkhart, have provided valuable insights on the Nahua worldview's association of malodorous objects with misfortune, filth, and even death.[32] Indeed, those considered "bad" in Nahua society were frequently referenced as dirty or smelly in book 10 of the *Florentine Codex*. For example, the harlot is "a filthy one; a filthy old dog who brings herself to ruin like a dog"; the traitor is "excrement, dung"; and the lewd youth is "revolting, filthy."[33]

The negative connotations associated with sluggishness and heaviness likewise appear in the *Florentine Codex* regarding those lacking in Nahua society. For example, in a series of discourses from a noble father to his son instructing him on proper living, revered Nahua forefathers are described as those who "came not as fools, they came not panting as they walked, out of breath as they walked." Moreover, elderly women criticized for desiring young men responded to their impotent, elderly male accusers, "Ye men, ye are sluggish, ye are depleted . . . we who are women, we are not the sluggish ones." Later, the father admonishes his son to "in no wise be sluggish" or lazy or a "constant sleeper."[34] To be fair, the *Florentine Codex* was authored by a Franciscan and various Nahua authors steeped in Christianity. The negative descriptors of filth and sluggishness could accurately reflect precontact beliefs or the effect of Christianity supporting or emphasizing similarities, or simply inserting itself into the discourse.[35] Yet the order-disorder framework that encompassed the Nahua worldview makes the preexisting negative associations of filth and sluggishness plausible, if not likely, and surely facilitated the transmission of the intended message on the resurrection.

Although León's descriptors of the wicked's resurrected body likely resonated with a Nahua audience, and although we might be tempted to see such as examples of the influence of Indigenous culture on the Christian message, we must be cautious. They did not originate in the New World. Like the qualities of the resurrected bodies of the righteous, those of the wicked also derived from Old World antecedents. The stench of the damned was a common theme circulated in medieval and early modern Europe. The thirteenth-century Saint Bonaventure certainly equated sin with stench. For example, when preaching against lasciviousness in marriage, Bonaventure declares, "Those who, namely, receive matrimony with libidinal love, shut out God from themselves, by the stench of fornication."[36] In Luis de Granada's explanation of the torments of hell, he comments how the smells will punish the nose terribly.[37] And the early modern fray Martin von Cochem stated, "The very bodies of the reprobate are so foul and disgusting that they emit a most offensive odor, worse than any stench in this world. According to Saint Bonaventure, the body of a single reprobate would so taint the air on earth as to cause the death of all living beings coming near it."[38] On the other hand, in 1571 upon the death of one of the first missionaries among the Nahua, fray Andrés de Olmos, the ornaments with which he used to say Mass reportedly emitted a fragrant and beautiful smell that "surpassed the smells of the earth."[39]

Moreover, the sluggish and heavy nature of the damned body was seen as a logical opposite to the agile bodies of the righteous. In his *Summa contra gentiles*, Aquinas notes that the bodies of the wicked will be "rather ponderous and heavy and insupportable to the soul."[40] Certainly, at times colonial authors intentionally engaged Indigenous culture to familiarize Christian concepts. Yet at other times, Christian concepts aligned with those of the Indigenous.[41] The negative descriptors of the bodies of the wicked appear to be an example of the latter.

Following the resurrection, León, like many authors, engages Matthew 25:31–46 to describe the Final Judgment. Those who performed works of mercy on earth will go to heaven to sit in thrones and live in palaces; those who failed to do so are destined for hell and eternal torment. One final note on a slight León inserts in his text. Nahuatl contains a reverential form used when speaking to respectable people or when desiring an honorific tone. Interestingly, when Christ speaks to the righteous, he employs the reverential but fails to do so when addressing the wicked, providing, as one scholar puts it, an "insult by omission."[42] Overall, the text presents a vivid image intended to both motivate and instruct on the Apocalypse and the glorious and harrowing destinies of the renewed Nahua bodies.

Fray Martín de León, 1611 *Camino del cielo*, fols. 26v–28v, 39v–40r

The seventh *article*,[43] Article of Faith that is to be believed: God will resurrect the dead and he will glorify the righteous and cast the wicked down to hell where they will be tormented forever.

I really will declare to you all these divine words; it is necessary for you to understand that the earth will end, finish, once the time actually has arrived that God determined, when he judged that it will end; then all the seats, palaces, thrones in heaven will be filled up, those that the angels left behind when they were exiled from heaven, they were thrown down to hell, they turned into devils, there they were forever locked up in the fire-cave-house, mictlan. And when the palaces, thrones in heaven that were vacant are filled up, then God will send from heaven exceedingly great and many fires; the earth, the world, the ocean, the various springs, rivers, the wind, and all that goes about on top of the wind [the atmosphere] will burn, catch fire, and then they will die, be destroyed, the various people on earth and the various living things—those that go about on four feet, flying, in the water—all will entirely end, be completely destroyed; and all the various trees, grass, plants of the world will burn inasmuch not even one root will survive, everything will burn with, be destroyed by fire, and all homes and mountains, all hills will be razed to the ground.[44]

Afterwards, when everything on the earth has burned, all living creatures have died, all has turned into ashes, then God will send angels from heaven, they will come to declare, say, *Arise, dead one, and come to your judgment*.[45] Which means: "All of you dead, stand up, rise up and come to the place of God's judgment!" Then, just as when God created all his works with his power, then again will he quickly bring them to life, all bodies, flesh, truly what we now go along carrying that is a part of us, and each person and their body that had been made, then he [God] will place it inside them, each one will take their soul. Those [the dead] that went to heaven, God will cause to emerge, and those that went to hell also will emerge, all come to assemble, to present themselves before God, they will discover, there they will hear their judgment; we all who are living today, and all those who died, all those through the beginning of the world, of the earth,[46] to as many as will die while the world ends.

Therefore, may you remember what we have already said to you, that the soul is not mortal, perishable; only our bodies are mortal, but our souls live and exist forever; therefore, all souls left their bodies until again they grasp, again they close together, stick together with their bodies that they belong to, they will be put inside, unite within them as we are now. Although all people will resurrect, each one separately will get their body, the bodies of the righteous and the wicked will not be the same; for which reason when the righteous resurrect, they will be forever entirely happy, content, they will rest, no longer will they suffer, worry, be afflicted, be unsettled; their bodies will be really agile, they will run, no longer will they be sluggish. And when they enter inside heaven, the bodies of the righteous, the Christians, will become really very clean, their bodies are as if like heaven's light which really, greatly will surpass, exceed the sun. And really they will fly, go to anywhere its heart will desire, really they will traverse among, through mountains, walls; no longer will they be tired, and each one of the good Christians, the inside of the body, really each one of our bodies will change in the blink of an eye so that they will go to heaven and then again descend on earth; thus will be our understanding.

But the bodies of idolaters and the wicked, who neither desired baptism nor had faith in God, and all the bad Christians that did not really keep the commandments of God, who did not honor their deity, their ruler, when their bodies resurrect they will be very sluggish, sick, rotten, become wormy, be peeled, will stink, be something dirty, something frightening, something nauseating, will be full of various torments, agonies, afflictions; and very many painful, injurious things will happen to them, they will know it, really greatly they will tremble, will cry out of fear, not be able to lift themselves on top of the wind [into the sky], they will merely flop to the ground as they are waiting for their judgment.

Our savior, our lord Jesus Christ, the precious child of God, then will come descending from heaven with all his power; he will come really shining, and they will come gathering, all the angels and all the saints that reside in heaven and the good Christians. And these saints will resurrect, take up their bodies, and when they have resurrected, they will rise up high on the wind next to our lord Jesus Christ who goes to sit among the angels. But the bad Christians and the various idolaters will remain on the ground next to, in the company of devils because they are very heavy. Then, our lord Jesus Christ will judge them [the risen], the righteous will be placed on his right hand side, and the bad, the wicked will stand up and be placed on his left hand side. And then our lord Jesus Christ will say to the righteous, *Come you who are blessed of my Father, inherit the kingdom prepared for you, etc.*[47] [Which means:] "You all are my friends, you labored on earth and truly loved me, served me, entirely kept my commandments, and you performed all the Works of Mercy. Come, you are the blessed, the elect, of my honored father! Take possession, inherit my kingdom in heaven that I entirely left to you since the beginning of the world, the earth!" Then, our lord Jesus Christ will take all the righteous, he will gather them together with him and the angels.

Afterwards he will say to the bad people, "You idolaters, nonbelievers, disobedient, and you that did not keep my commandments and did not perform good works, Works of Mercy, *go thou, accursed of my father into the eternal fire, etc.*"[48] [Which means:] "Go you cursed of my precious, honored father, to hell where forever you will be scorched entirely; for a long time you were on the side of the devils." Then the earth will open and completely swallow the bad people and all the devils so that there [in hell] their bodies and their souls are forever burned, forever afflicted. Then the angels and various saints will depart; one thing, very marvelous music, various wind instruments will be audible from very far away. Thereupon everyone will join together and take our lord Jesus Christ, our savior, God's precious child, to heaven. And then he will give seats to all of those newly ascended to heaven, he will place in a row their thrones, their royal homes; because of which all the thrones that had been vacated after the devils were forced to leave, when they were cast out of there, will be filled. And forever there with God they will preside, unified with the body and their souls, their living flesh forever among eternal riches; there, nothing will torment them, upset them, afflict them, but forever they will be healthy, there they will see everything, they will behold all that the heart desires, and they will be consoled through their sight of the precious face of God, forever they will be looking at it with their eyes; each one, all will be consoled through his great energy because they served God here on earth.

This is the seventh Article of Faith that is to be believed that our lord God will resurrect the dead and give the righteous eternal riches as their reward for they really kept his divine commandments, but for the bad people, he will afflict them with eternal torments for they badly kept his divine commandments. Oh, know the seventh Article of Faith associated with the worship of God, his divinity, because of which you know God, and because of which you know he is the only one all-powerful God, three divine persons, *persons*, as has already been said, God the Father, God the Son, God the Holy Spirit, and because of which it is believed, it is known that God the Son, our lord Jesus Christ, will come to judge here on earth at the end, the conclusion of the world. . . .

The seventh Article of Faith that is to be believed pertaining to our lord Jesus Christ as a man, that when the world comes to an end he will come from there to judge the living and the dead; the righteous he will take them to his royal palace because they really kept his divine commandments, but the wicked he will entirely cast down to hell for they did not keep his commandments.

As I already told you, our lord God as a divine being [*teotl*] does not go to some place, it is really everywhere in heaven and on earth. But when the world comes to an end, and he comes to judge people on earth, he will descend as a man just like when he was first seen; wherefore, he will judge them all, the good and the bad, really the righteous will see him, but the wicked will be cast to hell, they will not be able to see our lord God as a divinity. And he will come there to the plains of Jehoshaphat, and he will take the righteous to his royal palace in heaven, an eternal place of supreme happiness where they will rejoice forever with our lord God, they will be sent with their bodies and their souls. But the wicked, those that did not obey, completely keep his divine commandments, will be entirely cast down to the abyss of hell. And also their bodies and their souls will be sent there, and there they will be rejected, tormented forever, never ever will they once come out as was already seen in the seventh *article*, article of faith pertaining to our lord God as divinity.

This last one, this seventh Article of Faith, this honored thing to be believed that God's precious son, our lord Jesus Christ, will come here to judge on earth when the world is over, he will give the righteous supreme happiness in heaven, but he will cast down forever the wicked to the abyss of hell where they will be tormented forever because they did not obey God completely. Here it is seen how really the fourteen *articles* are to be believed: seven pertaining to God as divinity and also seven pertaining to the only deity, our lord Jesus Christ as man.

The Seventh Articles of Faith in Coronel's 1620 *Discursos predicables*

The most extensive extant example of a Maya text discussing the Articles of Faith is Coronel's 1620 *Discursos predicables*. Coronel structures the first part of his *Discursos* around the fourteen Articles of Faith, with separate sections discussing the seven articles on the humanity of God and the seven pertaining to his divinity. The texts translated here derive from these two sections.

For the most part, Coronel's discussion of the seventh Articles of Faith reflects an older style of colonial Maya that employs terms and phrases not commonly seen in later texts. For example, he employs the term *ah tanal* for "sinners," which the Motul dictionary designates as a *vocablo antiguo* (old word).[49] The term makes two appearances in Coronel's *Discursos* and rarely is seen in later works authored by either Spaniard or Maya. Other more obvious influences exist in the sermon that betray its colonial context. The text is didactic, with basic explanations on what happens during the resurrection and Final Judgment. Biblical locations familiar to most Christian readers, such as the Valley of Jehoshaphat, are explained and concepts of particular concern for ecclesiastics are reemphasized. The sermon takes the opportunity, for example, to reinforce the doctrine of the Trinity. Teaching the traditionally polytheistic Maya that the Christian god is one but three but one surely raised some eyebrows—as it does for many Christians today. Is it surprising that the current *Catechism of the Catholic Church* states that "the mystery of the Most Holy Trinity is the central mystery of the Christian faith and life."[50]

To reaffirm the monotheism so central to Christianity, Coronel's sermon states that after gathering in the Valley of Jehoshaphat, Christ will come to judge humankind. But to emphasize both the reality and singularity of God, the text states, "Soon, without delay, the son of God, Jesus Christ, will descend in the flesh because, as was already said to you, it is all God. But when he is in the flesh, there is nobody else in heaven." Thus, since the son of God is God, when he descends, heaven is lacking its god. The conclusion of the sermon again makes clear that it is God the Son, not the other members of the godhead, who will descend in the flesh to the earth and conduct the Final Judgment.

Similar to León's treatise, Coronel spends significant space explaining the resurrection and the difference between the resurrected bodies of the righteous and the wicked. The sermon explains how the soul reenters the same body to appear "as we are today," but then explains how the righteous will never suffer pain or injury and their bodies will shine brighter than the sun. Such bodies are light, able to fly and travel great distances at speed, and "they will be able to slide through the middle of mountains and the earth or inside stones without being dented. Also, they will be able to enter into all parts of a house with a closed door as they pass through walls." Coronel then describes the four qualities gifted to the resurrected body calling them a *can tzuc tuba çijl*, or "four-part gift," from God.[51]

Subsequently, Coronel explains that the bodies of the wicked lack such a gift and thus abilities. Indeed, the wicked will complain, saying, "These bodies are really sick, really smelly, terrible, really ugly also, also they are filled with great pain and I did not imagine such affliction and pain could be in earthly bodies." Likewise employing Matthew 25, the righteous and wicked are judged according to their performed Works of Mercy. While the righteous meet God high in the air because "really they are light without burdens," the wicked bodies again are described as heavy. Such heavy bodies seem to have no choice but to roll and stumble into a grim fate:

Quickly and without delay the earth will open and then devour in one blink of an eye all the non- and bad Christians, and then they will go rolling and stumbling head over heels behind the devils and they will go together, balled up they arrive in hell; and then they are poured in the middle of the fire where their souls and bodies burn forever, and then the earth closes over them, caves in the escape, never will they come out.

The similarities between León and Coronel's descriptions of resurrected bodies in their treatment of the seventh Articles of Faith are striking. Although Nahuatl and Maya religious texts typically share broad Christian themes, the overlap of such specifics here is uncommon, particularly when considering that one is a text derived from a Dominican in central Mexico and written in Nahuatl, while the other is from a Franciscan in Yucatan and written in Maya. Both texts describe the bodies of the righteous as light, luminous, and able to fly through mountains and walls; and both relate the bodies of the wicked as smelly, susceptible to pain, and heavy. The abilities of the righteous to fly through mountains and walls, particularly, appears unique to these two texts.

Yet understanding dawns when considering the Old World roots of such descriptors in texts surely well known to both authors. Indeed, discourses on the qualities of resurrected bodies can be found in other colonial texts, such as fray Juan de Anunciación's 1577 *Sermonario*, Manuel Pérez's 1723 *Cathecismo*, and Ignacio de Paredes's 1759 *Promptuario*.[52] Yet even these fall short of the details found in León and Coronel's works. The nearest runner-up, Paredes, discusses the abilities of the resurrected bodies of the righteous to go anywhere they want with speed and without being impeded and how the bodies of the wicked will be like drained sores and drop and lie burning on the ground like a *mictlan tecolli, mictlan tlequahuitl* (hell-charcoal, fire stick from hell), but no more.[53]

This is not to say that Coronel's sermon is without its own nuances. Indeed, the text emphasizes the inquisitorial aspect of the Final Judgment and repeatedly affirms how no one will be able to hide his or her sins from the scrutiny of Christ during Judgment Day: "Then it begins with the rulers, governors, lords, and all principal men, nobles, and all the elders, as well as Spaniards and Indigenous people and all men and women who are on the earth today, who once existed, and who will exist; each one will be interrogated by the words of God." The text also adds "bishops and all the rest of the men of the Church" to those interrogated. In this inclusion and general emphasis on the examination of rulers, perhaps, we see the subtle influence of Coronel's training as an Observant Franciscan. As mentioned, the Observants' philosophy owed a debt to their Spiritual predecessors who criticized their ecclesiastical leaders, even the pope, believing that they were the ones to govern the Church in a new age.[54] Moreover, the Franciscans rarely placed any faith in the secular clergy or, at times, members of other orders. In 1555, fray Toribio de Benavente Motolinía made the case for the Franciscan presence in the New World by reminding authorities what happened when the order was removed from converting the Moors in Granada: "And after greed appointed clergymen, the religious relinquished their care of them [the Moors], and your Highness already knows how they have made good use of Christianity, for they are as Moorish as they were on the first day. . . . The same thing has occurred in all of Peru, Panama, Nombre de Dios, and other parts where the religious have lacked the favor of the viceroys, courts, and bishops."[55]

Despite abundant European and Spanish influences—including such details as a hellmouth and the empty seats in heaven abandoned by the devil's followers—Maya culture certainly influenced the text itself. As we have seen, religious texts composed in Indigenous languages frequently borrow preexisting ideas from Indigenous culture to help convey Christian concepts. The process of associating Indigenous words and phrases with Spanish concepts was a necessary one and can be effective in familiarizing foreign characters and concepts.[56] That said, the tying of the Christian worldview to an Indigenous one can produce altered meanings.

For example, Coronel's text awards Christ the title of *ah cambeçah*, or "teacher," which holds deep roots in Maya society. As mentioned earlier, many of the early friars, particularly the Franciscans, sought to create a new, more perfect Christian society worthy of the Second Coming of Christ. To do so, education became paramount. Indigenous people educated in reading, writing, and in a Spanish-Christian worldview and culture would not only form the foundation for such a perfected society but also its messengers as they assisted the vastly outnumbered friars in their educational and pastoral efforts—such were the Maya ah cambeçahob or maestros.

Yet Mayas trained in education, religion, and writing who maintained the community's material and spiritual health were certainly not a Spanish introduction. The ah kin (traditional Maya priest), *ah dzib cah* (town scribe) and the ah cambeçah all made valuable contributions to precontact Maya society, and all three positions continued in their importance during the colonial period, albeit more commonly as maestros and escribanos.[57] The shaping of future Maya Christian rulers, teachers, and assistants—the Maya maestros—required the Maya nobility to send their sons to the friars' schools. Although many did so, likely seeing the benefit of such schools in allowing their posterity to maintain their positions of power in colonial society, others resisted. Cogolludo comments on those *sacerdotes Gentiles* (lit. "Gentile priests," by which was meant Maya priests) who resisted the Franciscans and were inspired by the devil to persuade many "that they [the friars] were witches, that during the day they appear in the form that everyone usually sees, and at night they transform into foxes, owls, and other animals."[58]

To be sure, many of these ah kinob continued to make things difficult for the friars throughout the colonial period, oftentimes resisting Christianity outright.[59] However, at other times ah kinob found a middle ground and appropriated aspects of the Christian worldview to incorporate into their own ritual practices. In fact, evidence exists to suggest a connection between the roles of the precontact ah kin, the colonial ah cambeçah, and the modern h-men.[60] In 1610, the secular priest, Pedro Sánchez de Aguilar, reported that two Maya trained in both Maya and Christian worldviews claiming to be a pope and a bishop performed Mass at midnight, baptized children, heard confession while ordaining priests to serve Maya deities and honoring them with incense upon an altar, among other things.[61] Overall, then, the colonial Maya maestro derives from a complex precolonial past that included the ah kin, ah cambeçah, and ah dzib cah.

Coronel's discussion of the seventh Articles of Faith employs the precontact position of ah cambeçah to represent Christ on two separate occasions. Both instances pair the title of teacher with another: *cah lohil, cah cambeçahul ti Iesu Christo* (our redeemer, our teacher Jesus Christ) and *ca cilich yumil cah cambeçahul ti Iesu Christo* (our holy lord, our teacher Jesus Christ). Certainly this served to reference Christ's esteemed position and calling as a master teacher of the Christian doctrine. Yet, knowingly or unknowingly, Christ as an ah cambeçah also connects him to a precolonial past that included the ah kin and ah dzib cah. At the very least, the term places Christ among the ubiquitous colonial ah cambeçahob serving as maestros in their respective towns. Any maestro reading from Coronel's work surely would have felt honored to share the same title as Christ.

In another instance, Coronel uses *ah tepal* (ruler) to reference the Spanish *Dios* (God). Ah tepal has precontact roots and could be used to reference a variety of Maya rulers. Sergio Quezada relates that in the late twelfth or early thirteenth century, the ruler of the Itza was an ah tepal after having subjugated other rulers, "and there was no one above him."[62] In the colonial period, however, it became part of fixed phrases to reference both the Spanish king and Spanish God.[63] Throughout the colonial period, the phrase *ca yumil ti dios ah tepal* (our lord God, Ruler) is commonly seen in religious texts. Uncommon, however, is the sole appearance of ah tepal without the accompanying "Dios," yet Coronel does so in two occasions during his discussion of the seventh Articles of Faith, referring to God as simply "ah tepal." Today, modern h-men pray to the deity *ah tepaloob* (the rulers) in their rituals suggesting the possibility that the term continued to possess some precontact significance throughout the colonial period and beyond.[64]

Other influences reflect the colonial realities of the Maya and include slight changes to the traditional biblical text. Both the Nahuatl and Maya sermons employ Matthew 25 as the litmus test for salvation, with the righteous performing charitable works. Here, the list includes feeding the hungry and thirsty, taking in strangers, clothing the naked, tending the sick, and visiting those in prison. The Maya text exchanges visiting those in prison with freeing captives and slaves. Spaniards certainly did not introduce the practice of slavery to the New World. Indeed, along with multiple wives or mistresses, slaves were a mark of nobility among the Nahua and Maya. Yet ecclesiastics strove to eradicate all such practices from the nobility—an effort that frequently spilled into sermons.[65]

One final, noteworthy example regarding the influence of Maya culture includes the phrase employed to translate the Christian concept of "blessed" with regard to saints, *ah/ix bolon pixan*. Typically, the Maya term appears in conjunction with a saint name, as in Ah bolon pixan San Miguel, and carries the literal meaning of "he/she of the nine souls" or the "nine souled." The Motul dictionary likewise associates the same meaning of "blessed" to *oxlahun pixan,* or "thirteen-souled," but the term is seldom used in colonial texts.[66] In fact, the only instance of which I am aware appears in Coronel's present discussion in reference to those who will claim the heavenly homes and seats vacated by the wicked. Coronel refers to them as *ah bolon pixan oxlahun pixan* (the nine-souled, the thirteen-souled). The numbers nine and thirteen hold significant meaning to the Maya and are frequently associated with deities and even the underworld.[67] Oxlahun ti Ku appears in various Maya codices and texts at times as a singular deity or as representing multiple deities.[68] Moreover, thirteen is also important in the Maya Long Count and the Calendar Round. Both numbers, nine and thirteen, appear to also have conveyed a figurative meaning of "many," "forever," or "supreme," which likely contributes to their association with the saints, or those with great or superior souls. Either way, the terms tap into a deep well of Maya cosmology.[69]

Like León's and his Nahuatl discourse, Coronel's discussion on the seventh Articles of Faith intended to motivate and instruct with a particular emphasis on the eternal fate of the resurrected body. Yet that did not prevent the Maya worldview from affecting the prose and content and thus the meaning of the sermon itself however subtlety. This mercurial amalgam of worldviews is seen in the following translation of Coronel's treatment of the seventh Articles of Faith concerning first the divinity of Christ and then his humanity.

Fray Juan Coronel, 1620 *Discursos predicables*, fols. 30r–34r, 58r–61v

How we all have to resurrect on Judgment Day

In my flesh I shall see my God, my savior. Job 19.[70]

And then we will live again, all we people here on the earth, as will all people who were here on the earth when God began humanity back then, and also those that will exist until the arrival of the day of the destruction of this world; as was said to you, our souls are eternal and infinite, only our bodies are perishable. But these, our souls, continually live for they are not able to die, they are nearby you also, our souls all live when our bodies are dead, and they will enter again a second time into our bodies, and will resurrect, our souls and our flesh both together as we are today. Yet truly there will be a difference among the righteous and wicked people, because when the righteous resurrect, they will not suffer, nor perish because it is impossible to torment their bodies, nor will they have pain or sores over them, nor is it possible to burn them with fire or injure them by some means of eternal suffering. Likewise, the bodies of the righteous will shine really greatly and also the resplendence of each one of them will surpass the brilliance of the sun. Likewise, the bodies of the righteous will be really light, they will really walk lightly and fly and travel as much as they desire without tiring, without suffering also, for in the blink of an eye we will go to heaven and return to where we came from, and so we go to where we desire. Although really far away, it [the distance to heaven] is in vain, as the journey, the travel is really as fast as our thoughts and sight are actually today, nor is the arrival to where you desired delayed. Likewise, our bodies will really end, when finished they will be filled with *glory*,[71] because of which they will be able to slide through the middle of mountains and the earth or inside stones without being dented. Also, they will be able to enter into all parts of a house with a closed door as they pass through walls. Nothing will be able to truly prevent this four-part gift, which is the impassibility and brightness and [agility] and subtlety that God will give to our bodies when we live [again], and these are the names of the four-part gift from God.

But these things are impossible for the wicked, because they are lacking this four-part gift, because these [the wicked] are bad Christians, they were not baptized nor will they be twice born [baptized] and thus become Christians.[72] They did not keep the commandments of God. Truly they will say when they live [again], "These bodies are really sick, really smelly, terrible, really ugly also, also they are filled with great pain and I did not imagine such affliction and pain could be in earthly bodies," this will be said by the sinners, truly, but as for the righteous, they will be high in the air, really they are light without burdens.

And then our great lord, Jesus Christ, the son of God, comes quickly from heaven, the Almighty, and very resplendent, also with him will come all heavenly people, and all the angels and archangels that are in heaven, and all his companions and the chosen people, the *male and female saints*,[73] and also the living [resurrected] righteous who walked virtuously here on the earth, they really are beautiful and good also, and they will also be in the air surrounding our lord Jesus Christ, on his right, together with the angels and the great heavenly army. As for the wicked, they will fall, really they are heavy and deformed; really they are horrible things in the company of devils on the face of the earth on the left hand of our lord Jesus

Christ. Then begins the judgment of our lord Jesus Christ of the righteous and the wicked alike, and thus will be said to the righteous:

"You who are my beloved people, you loved me and obeyed me, back then for you kept and completed the commandments. You who took care and were careful that charity was performed and carried out, for you gave food to the hungry and drink to the thirsty, for you clothed the naked and helped the poor and afflicted, and for you took in the stranger also you freed the slave. You usually performed many other [acts of] charity, to these you were devoted. Let us go, blessed of my father. You will receive, take, possess the kingdom prepared for you by me since the beginning of the world." And then our lord Jesus Christ will gather all saints and angels close, near to him, and so it will be for the first of those all gathered together.

Then our lord Jesus Christ will bring around near to him the wicked, they will be on the left, and thus it will be said to them:

"You who are without faith, you despiser, you never wanted to believe in me, you did not want to obey me. How did you honor me? Nor did you desire to do it. What works of charity did you perform? Nor did you care for me—you gave me nothing, neither food when I was hungry nor drink when I was thirsty. And when I was naked and I was dying as a traveler on the road, you did not care for me nor did you show me mercy. For this reason, then, I will not show you mercy today."

Then the wicked will say, "Oh, we are miserable, wretched! Lord, when were you hungry and afflicted or sick and we did not care for these things nor show you mercy?"

Then our lord Jesus Christ will say to them:

"Oh, you miserable, bad, wretched ones! When you did not care for my miserable children, back then, nor show them mercy, you also did not care for me and show me mercy. Thus, for this reason, I eternally condemn you now by expelling you far away forever. Come, follow behind the devils you serve and obey there to your suffering and to the endless fires of hell forever."

Quickly and without delay the earth will open and then devour in one blink of an eye all the non- and bad Christians, and then they will go rolling and stumbling head over heels behind the devils and they will go together, balled up they arrive in hell; and then they are poured in the middle of the fire where their souls and bodies burn forever, and then the earth closes over them, caves in the escape, never will they come out.

And then sweet singing, flutes, and music will begin from the righteous angels, and in the company of God and also all the saints, they will immediately go behind our lord Jesus Christ. These will rise to his royal home there in heaven, then immediately will be given to them eternal royal homes and the seats abandoned, lost by the wicked angels, so then the abandoned homes are filled up by the saints, the blessed [the nine-souled, the thirteen-souled]. There their bodies and souls are eternally happy and have much happiness with our great ruler God and all his companions. Never will remorse come to them, nor will annoyance or danger befall them. But always they will have infinite happiness and will be given everything, all that they desire, they will not want something else, because they are truly satisfied.

And this is the reason for which you say the seventh Article of Faith, so that the one God, giver of eternal glory, is placed with them. For it has been said to you that all the dead will live and forever the righteous will be given endless blessings and eternal happiness, *glory* because they kept his commandments, and the wicked will be given eternal torment there in hell because they did not keep his commandments. Here is the seventh Article of Faith: that our lord God will cause all the dead to live again, and he will reward his beloved people for all the virtuous, good, and worthy works they did while here on the earth, for which they will be taken care of. And also he will severely punish and greatly afflict the wicked because of their evil works. These seven Articles of Faith you have been commanded and given to understand them. These pertain to the divinity of our lord God, with which we say the merits of the divinity of our lord God pertaining to these seven Articles of Faith through which we come to understand the divinity of our great ruler, God.

How he is to come to judge the living and the dead.

He will judge the people with justice. Psalms 95.[74]

Here is the seventh Article of Faith, something to know also: the son of God who is in the flesh, this we will firmly believe, will come again from heaven to judge the living and the dead. Really be attentive, you my beloved person. When the world finishes and when the world ends in the future, then all people that are in all parts of the world will die; there is not one male or female alive but all are dead. When we all live again, we also will create our bodies for the second time as we are today, thus it will happen when God commands it.

Then, when they all live again, then they all gather in a valley called Jehoshaphat, it is there with Jerusalem where our redeemer died, this is the reason they are going to gather themselves together [there], this so that all the people of the earth can be judged, as was said to you, and I declared for you to hear in the other seven articles. Soon, without delay, the son of God, Jesus Christ, will descend in the flesh because, as was already said to you, it is all God. But when he is in the flesh, there is nobody else in heaven, he is alone. And this is the reason he will descend himself in the flesh, to judge those good and bad. These he will interrogate and scrutinize one by one, that which they did, performed, said, thought, and coveted, what they desired here on earth. And not only this alone, but he will ask about the good things they did not do while they lived here in life because of laziness. The prominent people, governors, and bishops, and all the rest of the men of the Church, each one will be asked regarding the manner of their works; to all people (and before the Ruler) it [the works] become apparent. Then it begins with the rulers, governors, lords, and all principal men, nobles, and all the elders, as well as Spaniards and Indigenous people and all men and women who are on the earth today, who once existed, and who will exist; each one will be interrogated by the words of God. Then he begins to ask regarding the manner of the works of his subjects, all of which are the people on the earth everywhere. And as for us, each one of us will confess and know all of our sins and errors before the Ruler; it is impossible for us to quickly hide them or conceal them because these, our works, will be known and also place themselves before us, and it will be said to us before God, "Did you not serve me, did you not do good works for me? It is impossible that I abandon you, but I will always be with you and stay with you."[75]

Thus, in this way our sins will become manifest and revealed and made public before us all, before our lord God. And because of this, it will not happen that we deny them, for we see our good works with which we serve our lord God here in life and with which we fulfill and keep his commandments, and they will be manifest, revealed, and also made public all our good works, good thoughts, good words, and also our good desires, all of them. And then they come to know us and they say to us all, "I am your work, your speech, your thought, I am ready to help you, I will never ever forget you."

Like this it will be declared, announced, and be made public the work of each one before our lord Jesus Christ when he inquires after the manner of our works.

These good people will be taken to their home, to their celestial temple, in heaven. The bodies and souls of these, then, will live forever because they keep and obey and fulfill his commandments while they live here on earth and because they hate sins here in this life. But as for the wicked people, their bodies and souls will be cast and thrown down to hell and very, severely punished forever without end; never will they leave because they did not keep his commandments as is told to you in the seven Articles of Faith regarding the holy divinity of our lord God, that you are to be punished.

You see, then, my beloved son, the seventh Article of Faith and something to know, the son of God in the flesh, who was sent when the world concludes, when the world ends, truly he will come in the flesh to judge all the people on earth, the righteous and the wicked alike. As for the righteous, he will take them to his holy, celestial temple, his home in heaven with their bodies. To these he will give eternal happiness and glory, never will it end because they kept his holy commandments. But the wicked, he will give them eternal suffering and eternal torment there in hell when he casts them down because they never kept his commandments. . . .

My beloved son, you heard these things of faith called the *Articles of Faith*;[76] [there are] fourteen parts: the first seven pertain to the divinity of God, the last seven pertain to the humanity of God.

Understand you, my beloved person, it is very necessary for you to firmly believe and declare them with all your heart, for thus do all good Christians firmly believe and rightfully say, in which, therefore, is salvation and they are saved. And thus it says in the holy *Gospel*,[77] it was taught to you, *He that believeth and is baptized, etc.*[78] Which means: "Whoever will believe and be baptized is one who is saved." Oh that our holy lord, our teacher, Jesus Christ, takes us there to heaven! Amen.

⇒⇐

Grove Street Cemetery in New Haven, Connecticut, was the first graveyard chartered in the United States, in 1797. Its 1845 gateway boldly displays an engraved inscription reflecting 1 Corinthians 15:52, "The Dead Shall Be Raised" (see figure 4.1).[79] In truth, the inscription is missing an important word at the end included in the biblical passage: "incorruptible." Saint Paul, like León and Coronel, apparently wanted to emphasize the immortal state of the resurrected body.

In reciting the Apostles' Creed, Christians testify of their confidence "in the resurrection of the body and life everlasting."[80] Yet, just as in the colonial period, reciting is not believing. Although fundamental to Christianity, the resurrection is finding fewer believers among Christians today. According to a 2017 BBC-sponsored survey, only 31 percent of British Christians

Figure 4.1 Gateway to Grove Street Cemetery. Author photo.

believe in the biblical version of the resurrection of Christ, with a little over 40 percent stating a belief in some sort of resurrection.[81] Interestingly, a Pew survey in 2018 reported that 36 percent of Catholics in the United States believed not in the resurrection but in reincarnation.[82] The advanced and increasing public awareness of science and competing worldviews continues to chip away at such traditional declarations, or articles, of faith held by Christianity leaving both pastor and parishioner to negotiate their faith. Certainly, the version of Christianity and its doctrines held by many Christians today differs from of those four hundred years ago or even ten years ago.

Perhaps a modern priest could empathize better than most with the efforts to instruct on the resurrection and other basic Christian doctrines found in the sermons of León and Coronel. The Nahuatl and Maya texts allow European Christian narratives regarding seats in heaven, charitable works, and the state of resurrected bodies to dominate the sermons. Yet, similar to modern influences that affect a Christian's understanding of the Apocalypse's resurrection and Final Judgment, Indigenous worldviews, creation myths, and even social structures affected the sermons themselves to produce various possible interpretations and understandings. Today, many Christians in Mexico (and I daresay the world) do not concern themselves with the details of the qualities of the resurrected body—glorified, damned, or otherwise. For many, a modified version of REM's song would seem to apply: "It's the end of the resurrection as Aquinas knew it, and I feel fine."

⫸ 5 ⫷

Heaven, but Mostly Hell

Each of us finds the world of death fitted to himself.

Virgil

This is hell. It is telling God, 'You take care of yourself because I'll take care of myself.' They don't send you to hell, you go there because you choose to be there. Hell is wanting to be distant from God . . . This is hell.

Pope Francis

Dying man couldn't make up his mind which place to go to—both have their advantages, "heaven for climate, hell for company!"

Mark Twain

While venturing through Wonderland, Alice encounters the wise and enigmatic Cheshire Cat. She asks the cat which way she should go, to which the cat responds, "That depends a good deal on where you want to get to."

"I don't much care where—" said Alice.

"Then it doesn't matter which way you go," said the Cat.

"—so long as I get *somewhere*," Alice added as an explanation.

"Oh, you're sure to do that," said the Cat, "if you only walk long enough."[1]

Figure 5.1 Cheshire Cat, Arthur Rackham. In Carroll's
Adventures in Wonderland (1907).

Christian theology believes that, like Alice, all will eventually end up somewhere—either heaven or hell. Yet without knowing the destination, humankind would wander aimlessly, choosing incorrect paths. Thus, understanding heaven and hell, and the pleasures and pain offered by each, became essential in educating (and motivating) Christians to choose the correct path and follow the commandments and instructions of the Church. Heaven and hell served as the outcome of the Apocalypse and justified both Doomsday and Catholicism in general. After all, without heaven and hell, what is the point?

This chapter provides four examples of texts discussing heaven or hell or both. Not surprisingly, hell and its horrific torments seemed more popular and occupied more space in religious texts than heaven and its rewards. After a brief overview of the development of heaven and hell in Christianity, the following examines their elucidation in two Indigenous-language printed texts and two unofficial, Indigenous-authored texts. In new and important ways, these illustrate the heavy influence European worldviews, theology, and works played on such texts. Yet the texts also expose how Nahuas and Mayas incorporated and made sense of the foreign destinations within their own worldviews. To be sure, ecclesiastics and Indigenous authors desired their audience to, unlike Alice, care very much where they were going.

Developing the Afterlife

As J. Harold Ellens succinctly put it, "There is no developed concept of heaven or hell in the Bible."[2] The evolution of the afterlife derived from the Greek Hades and the early Hebrew tradition of Sheol, both representing a place of residence for the dead, among others. Like the Nahua mictlan and the Maya metnal, all such places represented the abode of the righteous and wicked alike, almost neutral and devoid of penitential afflictions, although various levels existed.[3] And also like mictlan and metnal, Sheol and Hades were used to represent the Christian hell, in this case in the Old and New Testaments, respectively.

Over time, and influenced by the duality of good and evil inherent in Zoroastrianism, the Judeo-Christian afterlife began to diversify and take on different forms for the good and the bad. Divisions in Sheol and Hades centered upon actions and choices on earth appeared with more frequency. This allowed for some New Testament authors to suggest a punitive after-life. Certainly Christ taught of a separation between the righteous and wicked during the Final Judgment and even, at times, referred to an outer darkness for the wicked as Gehenna. And in the New Testament, a rich man in Hades "where he was in torment, raised his eyes" to see Lazarus. Yet, "Gehenna meant the city dump outside the southeast corner of the wall of Jerusalem," and outer darkness was the symbolic spiritual separa-tion from God, while the rich man simply regretted his state in Hades, as was normal.[4] The specific and gory torments often associated with hell today would not come until later. Like mictlan and metnal, Sheol and Hades needed modifying to meet the eventual definition of a Christian hell.

As Christianity continued to redefine itself amid war, death, and the influence of other cultures due to expansion, the modification of the afterlife was constant in the early Church. The *Gospel of Nicodemus*, the Apocalypse of Peter, and the Apocalypse of Paul all provided more specif-ics on the types of sinners and the punishments they experienced in an ever-increasingly dismal afterlife simply known as "hell."[5] Although some contended that God's love would prohibit eternal damnation and suffering,

Augustine firmly defended the eternity of hell and its torments in the fifth century—and his voice clearly echoed within later Nahuatl and Maya texts.[6]

What of heaven? Speaking of ancient Jewish beliefs in the afterlife, one work asserted, "Far from being static, belief in the nature of Sheol and eventually heaven changed considerably during the pre-Christian period."[7] Thus, diversity in the belief of the afterlife was not all doom and gloom. It also made room for heaven. Judaism in the Greco-Roman period increasingly made room for the doctrines of the immortal soul and the resurrection.[8] And by the first century A.D., Christianity's afterlife included an eternal life in the next world beyond the gloom of Sheol to include heavenly compensation for the faithful. Regardless of the shortcomings, unfairness, and difficulties of this life, the righteous would experience a fullness of glory in heaven. Such a belief not only helped assuage any sociopolitical subjugation or oppression Christianity experienced but also encouraged a belief in its tenets by all, especially the downtrodden.[9]

Augustine, Aquinas, and other authors and artists continued to develop the details of heaven and its rewards and hell and its punishments throughout the ages, but their overall characteristic as eternal compensation for those who either chose or denied God over the world remained to be detailed in Nahuatl and Maya texts. In fact, heaven and hell represent some of the first Christian concepts friars labored to convey to Indigenous audiences. To assist his missionary efforts beginning in 1530 in Oaxaca, the Dominican Gonzalo Lucero employed *lienzos*, or "canvas paintings," depicting Christian images to accompany his preaching. These lienzos included images portraying the joys of heaven and the torments of hell.[10] Furthermore, in the supposed dialogue between the Twelve Franciscans and Nahua priests in 1524—claimed by Sahagún as the beginning event of evangelization—heaven, hell, and their inhabitants receive ample attention.[11]

Images and theatricality are agents oft employed in message transmission, and hell and its tortures typically dominate the narrative.[12] After all, fear has always been an important tool of the preacher. Andrés Pérez de Ribas recounts how priests administering to the Yaqui in northern Mexico employed a retablo of the Final Judgment that "portrayed the people whom the angels take to heaven as well as the condemned that the demons drag off to hell." According to Pérez de Ribas, the retablo was effective and scared the Yaqui away from sin.[13] Furthermore, fray Gerónimo de Mendieta mentioned a play on the Final Judgment in Nahuatl performed sometime between 1535 and 1548. Fray Bartolomé de Las Casas likewise wrote of a play on the Final Judgment performed by eight hundred Nahuas.[14] And both Sahagún and the Indigenous historian Chimalpahin referenced a play on the end of the world performed in Tlatelolco in the 1530s.[15] All such performances engaged the Final Judgment and the reward and fear associated with heaven and hell to encourage moral behavior among the Nahua.

One such play on the Final Judgment survives today as a seventeenth-century copy of an earlier original. In the play, Lucía engages in illicit sexual behavior and fails to confess before the end of the world. Upon her final judgment, Christ delivers her to the demons of hell with instructions to "take her into the sweat bath of fire" and to "torment her miserably there."[16] And perhaps mental images created by such plays occupied the thoughts of the Indigenous artists composing the murals of the Augustinians' open chapel at Actopan. Here the Final Judgment is illustrated with vivid depictions of torture, where sinners are flayed, burned, boiled, and hacked and pieced apart (see figure 5.2).[17] Similar artistic scenes of torture appear in churches throughout Mesoamerica.[18] And such violent scenes certainly mirrored the violence threatened and conducted by Spanish priests against sinners.[19]

Figure 5.2 Mural at San Nicolás de Tolentino, Actopan, Hidalgo.
Photograph by RubeHM. Courtesy Wikimedia Commons.

Religious texts discussing heaven and hell join such didactic mediums. The following texts provide examples of how ecclesiastics and Nahua and Maya authors alike interpreted and conveyed the rewards of heaven and the punishments of hell, with an emphasis on the latter as texts typically gave it more attention.[20] As we have seen throughout the book, European and Indigenous worldviews negotiated to produce a New World stage in the evolution and diversity of such eschatological topics—an evolution that began long before the birth of Christianity.

The Torments of Hell in Paredes's 1759 *Promputario*

European texts on the punishments of hell abounded, and Paredes certainly did not create his Nahuatl discourse in an intellectual vacuum. The text emphasizes that imagining the torments of hell helps to prevent experiencing them personally. It also includes the two ways hell punishes the damned: pain of loss for not being in the presence of God and pain of the senses. As such, Paredes's discourse is in step with various theologians and preachers, including Augustine, Aquinas, Luis de Granada, Alonso Rodriguez, and Giovanni Pietro Pinamonti.[21] Certainly, the lengthy descriptions of torments and pain found in Paredes's text reflect Nahuatl's use of parallelism and synonym or quasi-synonym strings. Yet the text strikes a familiar tone when compared with European texts, particularly Granada's *Libro de la oración* and the Spanish version of the Italian Jesuit Giovanni Pietro Pinamonti's seventeenth-century *L'Inferno aperto*, which appeared in the early eighteenth century under the name of his missionary companion, Paolo Segneri, as *El infierno abierto*.[22] For example, to describe the pain of loss, Paredes employs the example of a distraught child separated from his mother to relate the sadness sinners feel upon their eternal separation from God. Granada and *El infierno abierto* use the same example, although situated in the context of warfare when children are separated from their mothers.[23] Indeed, the similarities between the subject matter and format of Paredes's text and that of *El infierno abierto* is unmistakable (see table 5.1). Granada's text likewise shares many of these similarities.

As mentioned, the second way hell torments sinners concerns their senses. Here, Paredes conducts an assault on the senses as he describes pain, smoke, fire, sound, and other elements designed to afflict the sinner

TABLE 5.1. Comparison of *El infierno abierto* and Paredes

Topic	El infierno abierto (1701)	Paredes (1759)
1	The Prison of Hell	X
	-Its tightness	–
	-Its darkness	X
	-The stench	X
2	The Fire	X
	-Its quality	X
	-The quantity	X
	-Its intensity	X
3	The Company	X
	-Of the condemned	X
	-Of the demons	X
	-Of the accomplices in sin	X
4	The Pain of Damage	X
	-The infinite loss	X
	-The most painful loss	X
	-The loss is because of sin	X
5	The Worm of Conscience	X
	-Memory of past pleasures	X
	-The delayed repentance for sins committed	X
	-The good opportunities missed	X
6	The Desperation	X
	-The duration of the pains	X
	-The intensity	X
	-A comparison with the glory (of the saved)	–
7	The Eternity of the Pains	X
	-Its endlessness	X
	-Its consistency	–
	-Its fairness	–

Note: This table was inspired by a similar comparison of Pinamonti's work with a sermon in English by Doherty in his "Hell Opened to Christians."

according to their sin. Remember, Thomas à Kempis's taught in his *Imitation of Christ*, "Every vice will have its own proper punishment."[24] Interestingly, and as David Tavárez notes, a Nahuatl manuscript acting as an expanded translation of Kempis's work survives today in the John Carter Brown Library. This late sixteenth- or early seventeenth-century product of Nahua-friar collaboration elaborates Kempis's text with strings of parallelisms and metaphors.[25]

Thus, similar to Bautista's elucidation of the *Fifteen Signs* in chapter 3, and according to doctrinal belief at the time, Paredes assigns each abused sense a particular punishment elucidated by a string of parallelisms and synonyms. For example, in hell the ears of sinners "will be hearing strong shouting, moaning, crying, howling, hitting from all of the eternally condemned who will always be screaming, moaning, crying, howling, because the devils will be hitting them with stones, hammering them as is done in the residence of metalworkers [a forge]." Such pageantry and exaggeration likewise existed in European texts, particularly those of the *devotio moderna*, and again we see some parallels in Granada's text. Here, Granada contrasts the beautiful singing and shouts of praise in heaven to the wailing and blasphemes uttered in hell along with "a chaotic melody of infinite off-key voices that will be sung there to the sound of the hammers and blows of the tormentors."[26] And *El infierno abierto* states how the endless cries and howls of the damned are "intolerable."[27]

To describe the pain of hell's fire, Paredes states, "Let us consider since no one is able to bear on their finger one small fire although for only a small amount of time, how can they stand to be there in hell in their entirety burning forever?" Or as Granada would have it in reference to putting one's hand over a flame, "If I cannot endure this small amount of heat for a short time, how will I endure the fire of hell for a long time?"[28] Or *El infierno abierto*, "If we cannot tolerate the tip of a candle flame, how will we be able to be buried forever in a fire more violent than anything imaginable?"[29]

Whether Paredes directly employed Granada, the Spanish version of Pinamonti's work, or a similar work during the composition of his Nahuatl text is uncertain. After all, the example of the finger in the candle derives from a medieval exemplum of a monk burning his finger in a candle to ward off sexual temptation, asking himself, "If you cannot endure this slight fire, how can you bear the flames of hell?"[30] Regardless, once again the impact of Old World discourse on that of the New becomes apparent.[31]

As mentioned previously, Paredes's Nahuatl is an attempted imitation of an earlier form of the language and explains his heavy use of parallelisms and synonym strings. Yet other aspects of his text could have resonated with his colonial Nahua audience. Paredes employs a variety of creative phrases to align mictlan with the Christian hell, describing it as a *huei tlacomolli* (large pit); *huel temamauhtican Oztotol* (really frightening cave); *huel temauhcamictican Tlacoyoctli* (really deathly frightening hole). Nahuas viewed caves as entrances to the otherworld, and they frequently appeared in creation stories, served as ceremonial sites, and were associated with underworld deities.[32] Europeans likewise employed the imagery of a cave and dark hole for hell, allowing both worldviews to coincide in description, although not necessarily meaning. Paredes explains that this cave is mictlan and later refers to it as *mictlancalco*, or generally "the house of hell." This phrase is less common in colonial texts but does appear in Sahagún's *Florentine Codex* as a place built by the deity Quetzalcoatl.[33] Admittedly, it is uncertain whether an eighteenth-century Nahua parishioner would have made the connection between mictlancalco and Quetzalcoatl. Or even the relationship between the epithet Ipalnemohuani—used by Paredes in reference to God—and its traditional use for the deities Tezcatlipoca or Quetzalcoatl. Yet the sermon's extensive use of caves and such phrases demonstrate the effects of the Nahua worldview on the sermon and hell itself and even, perhaps, Paredes's attempt to engage that worldview.

Another effect appears as the text discusses the torment of realizing the endlessness of hell's suffering. "Truly, my children, it would console the eternally damned if they would know that after a year ended, or however many four hundreds or however many counts of eight thousand years, they would emerge from hell." Nahuatl numeration is vigesimal with counts, or *pohualli*, of twenty. Numbers like four hundred and eight thousand also hold the figurative meaning of "a lot," or the present colloquialism "a million," as in, "I have a million things to do today." True, the statement is not wholly original, as Granada asserts, "If the condemned believed that after one hundred billion years, their pain would end, they would have this alone as a great comfort."[34] Yet the literal and figurative meaning of the

Nahuatl counts and numerals as years in hell was certainly clear to the Nahua audience.

Ignacio de Paredes, 1759 *Promputario,* Sermon Quinto, pp. li–lix

Therefore, you hear them not, because you are not of God. [John 8:47][35]

Which of you can dwell with the devouring fire? Which of you shall dwell with everlasting burnings? [Isaiah 33:14][36]

Whosoever does not want to fall to hell, my children, may they always want to remember, ponder that same hell. Because truly the remembrance of hell, the consideration of hell will be to our advantage so that we do not sin. And truly, my children, if we will not sin, then never ever will we fall to hell, but we will save ourselves and go to enter the kingdom of heaven, the place of glory in heaven. Concerning this, the scriptural wise man, Saint Bernard, says to us, counsels us, *Let them descend alive into the hell* [of this life], *lest they descend dead into the hell* [of the afterlife].[37] Which means: "While they go about living on earth, let their memory, their spirit come descend to the abyss of hell so that they will not descend when they have died." Thus the saint, the hermit,[38] truly said to them when he was already very sick, he was only a very little, very short bit away from dying; thus at his time of death he said to his fellow hermits, *Whoever will have given serious thought to death, gateway to everlasting life or death, will neither sin* [his way] *into eternity nor will he perish* [forever].[39] Which means: "Whosoever will consider and go along pondering about death, the entrance to eternal life or eternal torment, they will never ever sin nor fall into hell." Concerning this, my children, let us enter hell with our spirits, our imagination. Let us consider, discern the many things that are there that frighten people, torment people, give pain to people, *let them descend alive into the hell* [of this life],[40] so that we will not fall to hell when we die, when we are ended: *lest they descend dead into the hell* [of afterlife].[41]

In this way we will know, my children, that there in the center of the earth, located inside the earth is a really great, really large pit, a really frightening cave, a really deathly frightening hole. And he, the all-powerful deity God, made and prepared it so that it would be a jail, a place of punishment, a place of torment where God can lock them up, make them suffer, and punish the various devils and other eternally damned, the sinners with hardened hearts, those that died in their sins: *which was prepared for the devil and his angels.*[42] And this cave is called mictlan, *hell*, and truly this house of hell is a place of great darkness, very foggy, dark. Because there at no time does day break, dawn come, never is God's light, candlelight, torch seen, but simply night falls there continuously, it becomes dark. And the cave of hell became the home, quarters, residence of the devils and those others eternally damned. Regarding those there, my children, it cannot be numbered nor comprehended how the all-powerful God punishes them and the various torments with which he torments them, causes them pain because of their sins.

Concerning this, we must know, my children, that there [in hell] there are many various torments, various sufferings; there is sadness, weeping, shouting, groaning, slicing, affliction, hunger, starvation, thirst, stiffening from cold, stabbing, bleeding, flames, intense heat, smoke, darkness, blindness, blasphemous words, great despair, great hopelessness, and still many other pains, tortures, various afflictions that are uncountable, unmeasurable, never ending. Since there are many torments together there in the house of hell, and still many more [unknown] afflictions, it is really impossible for us to declare, completely explain, or fully comprehend them. Thus, there is not one who can speak or understand. Oh my children, the frightening cave, this deathly frightening pit, this deathly scary hole, it is made the eternal home, eternal place of residence, the palace, the eternal city, the ending place, the resting place, and finishing place of the frivolous, drunkards, idiots, wicked, and the many other sinners who offended and with their sins opposed the great ruler, he by whom one lives, the all-powerful God; he will take revenge on them and give all of their inheritance, their wage, their recompense, their due reward to them. Oh my children, may we immediately today open our eyes and have remorse for our sins so that we do not cast ourselves into the abyss of the cave of hell, since we do not know if later we will have time to fix our lives, and when it [death] actually will occur or if we will die without warning.

After the all-powerful God threw the sinner to hell, we know, my children, that their very frightful torment, very sorrowful pain is divided into two kinds. The first kind of torment, affliction of the eternally damned, the sinner is this: their loss of God, their departure from God, their loss from negligence of the entirely beautiful God. This means, my children, that the eternally damned, eternally condemned sinner will never ever at any time see, marvel at, enjoy, look at the face, the head of God their creator, God their divine father, God their precious savior, their compassionate and loving God. Because of this, the eternally damned has forever lost, is eternally distanced from God. Forever the eternally condemned has moved away from and placed at a distance their divinity, their ruler God: *I am cast away from before thy eyes.*[43]

Ah, ah, my children, how very great, how very torturous, afflicting, and frightening is this torment, this pain! Concerning this, when our souls have left their bodies, they very greatly desire, hunger for, thirst for our father, our creator, and our savior God. And because of this, the anguish of our souls when they are forever taken away from God is immeasurable; never ever will he [God] see them, go to appear to them, be happy with them. Tell me, my children! If at times a small child loses their precious mother, how very much do they go about yelling, anguishing, crying, and never at all are placated, consoled if their precious mother, their instructor, one who loves them, has not appeared. But, my children, more, still much more, very much more the eternally damned will forever be anguishing, sobbing, and crying when they are forever lost and never again will appear to their deity, their ruler, their creator, and their precious father God. May it be that you live, my children, so that you will never offend and lose God for truly this, God's banishment, is something painful, hurtful above all other of the many torments of hell.

The second torment of hell, pain of hell concerns the destruction of our bodies, because we offended God, and it is called the punishment, torment of our senses. And concerning this, we must know, my children, that in the hell house, hell cave is always, eternally full of very great, strong, powerful fire, embers, flames, blazes, tongues of fire, smoke and many other unspeakable, uncountable torments. And this fire, my children, it will never end, cool, lessen, but it will forever exist, forever be burning, because of which it will always be something painful, throwing flames.

Oh my children, let us consider since no one is able to bear on their finger one small fire although for only a small amount of time, how can they stand to be there in hell in their entirety burning forever? Let us awake ourselves, my children! Let us open our eyes, let us amend our lives! And also we must know, my children, that the eternally damned that are there in hell, forever will be, forever will live in vain with their enemies, their adversaries, the poisonous vipers, the hell devils, and with the many other eternally damned people. And truly all of these will be absolutely hating each other, going along against each other, going along cutting each other into pieces, will be gnawing on each other even though they be parents or children or relatives, because there in the frightful place, hell, there are no longer parents, children, relatives, friends for there the roles of fathers, mothers, relatives, friends have finished, disappeared. And if truly, my children, it is impossible to live inside a home where there is a person who hates you, how is it possible that you will be, will live there in hell where everyone hates, goes against, mistreats, is disgusted with each other?

Furthermore, my children, you must know that there in hell each sense of the eternally damned, the sinners, will feel its very own torment, pain. Because of the diverse manner in which sinners offend God, similarly sinners will be afflicted, tormented, punished in a diverse manner: *by what things a man sinneth, by the same also he is tormented.*[44] In this way, the viewer, the eye of the eternally damned will feel its own torment by their sight of the eternally condemned and hell devils because always, forever they will be seeing them there in hell. And the devils that the eternally condemned will be seeing are very frightening wild beasts, very startling things such as fierce beasts, mountain lions, jaguars, snakes, scorpions, toads, and they [the beasts] will lash out at them, eat them, bite them, strike them, and cut them up: *the terrible ones shall come upon him.*[45] Also, our hearing, our ears will feel their own torment because of which the eternally condemned will be forever punished, forever caused to feel pain, because there in hell, forever, always it [the ears] will be hearing strong shouting, moaning, crying, howling, hitting from all of the eternally condemned who will always be screaming, moaning, crying, howling, because the devils will be hitting them with stones, hammering them as is done in the residence of metalworkers [a forge].

Still more our hearing will always, continually hear the despair, the desperation, the cursing of the eternally damned—these will simply despair, curse their parents, their relatives, their friends, their life, their joy, their sins; and especially those who will speak evil of and damn their creator, their father, he by whom one lives, lord of the near, lord of the close, God, his precious, honored mother, Holy Mary, and all the saints and all the creations of the all-powerful God. Oh my children, who can hear it and not ever be depressed? Oh the intense misery of the damned, the sinners!

And what is more, our sense of smell, our nose is important because of which it will be afflicted by the stench of death, stench of rottenness; the rotting, the stench that the condemned, the sinners will emit. And truly, they will stink, smell bad, reek; thus it is in hell because it is going to be full of countless dead dogs, the stench of dogs, the reek of dogs. So it will also be with the taste of our mouth as there in hell it will be punished. Regarding the eternally damned, forever they will go about hungry, starving, famished, thirsty and absolutely never will they achieve, get even a mouthful of a small tortilla, even a drop of water. And the cruel people, the devils will feed the eternally condemned poisonous food, harmful drinks. This, my children, will be made the food and the drink of the drunks, the gluttons, those who have abundant pleasures, lovers of illicit sex,[46] and other fools, wicked sinners.

In addition, it is impossible to end the payment, the return that will torment the sense of touch of the eternally damned because it is impossible to count the number of sins that they greatly sin through thoughts, abundant pleasures, greed, words, and through deeds. And our the torment of our touch will be the very strong hell fire, the powerful embers, the very frightening flames, sparks, tongues of fire; always, forever, and not merely on the surface, on top, but completely on the inside will it be burning, making into embers, and scorching the body, and the spirit, soul of the eternally damned, the sinner.

Thus in this way, my children, there are three ways that our spirit, our soul is able to know its very own torment. Because our memory will always, forever be remembering how it [the soul] was cursed by its own choice, because of its sins, because of its abundant pleasures. And that in many ways it was finished, ended, quickly destroyed. Also, it [the memory] will consider that it was possible to have been saved, that God counseled it, but that the appropriate time, day, already passed by quickly and no longer will return, come back. For that reason in no small way will it be hurt, distressed, burst. Also, our mind always, forever will be considering how immeasurable, endless, is the very great pain, torment it will suffer that never will end, finish, lessen, but forever will exist, be there, forever will torment. Truly, my children, it would console the eternally damned if they would know that after a year ended, or however many four hundreds, or however many counts of eight thousand years, they would emerge from hell. But truly, so much time and many more uncountable years will pass by quickly, finish, pass by in a moment and the torment of the eternally damned will not end, not lessen; but from there it will begin, commence so that it will exist and be there forever. Ah, ah, it very greatly scares people to death, my children. Finally, our will forever will be tormented because always it will be wanting, desiring that which it will never get, obtain, achieve, and forever will be abhorring, hating that which it never can leave, depart from.

And thus, my children, the cave of hell, the furnace of hell is a very frightening place, a terrible place, a deathly frightening place; truly although we would know just one person that would be eternally condemned, just one person that would fall into hell, truly all of us people would really go about in fear, go about disturbed, because of which each one of us would say,

"Maybe it is I, perhaps I will be cast down to hell?"

How can we not live in fear, my children, when we know not just a few people, but countless that are being cast, hurled, falling into hell? Oh, my children, let us revive ourselves, quickly turn ourselves around, and today open our eyes so that we will not fall into hell! If you have sinned, my children, understand that you are still able to be forgiven of your sins, still able to be saved so that you will not fall into hell. Regarding this, entirely all of your sins—although very great, although really frightening, although uncountable—truly all are remissible, releasable, removable while you are living here on earth. But after you have died, no longer is there time for a pardon, no longer is there time for mercy. Thus, my children, may you right now here in the church correct your life, right away have remorse for what you have done concerning your sins, may you forever forsake them so that you will sin no longer and may you at that moment with great truth, with all of your spirit, your soul call out to our precious savior Jesus Christ and thus say,

"Oh my deity, Oh my savior, etc.!"[47]

The Torments of Hell in Aquino's Sixteenth-Century Copybook

Although colonial authorities prohibited Nahuas and Mayas from producing their own religious texts, examples exist today to prove that the restriction was not always heeded.

Such manuscripts are invaluable for their insight into what Indigenous people chose to record regarding Catholicism and how the Faith was interpreted in their own texts. And, not surprisingly, these texts frequently speak of the Apocalypse, heaven, and hell. Years ago, I translated one such manuscript from Nahuatl, which provided a loose redaction of the *Apocalypse of Paul* heavily influenced by the Nahua worldview.[48] More recently, Ben Leeming uncovered a notebook containing a variety of religious texts, including two plays, authored by the sixteenth-century Nahua, Fabián de Aquino.[49] Among such texts is a treatise detailing the torments of hell that demonstrates both common European and less common Nahua influences.

The passages mentioning the cave-like darkness of hell, fire, torments, fear, emotional grief, crowded nature of hell, eternity of punishments, frightful devils, hell mouth closing to forever trap the wicked, and even worms draw from Old World authors and biblical descriptions. At first glance, Aquino's explanation of how hellfire fails to emit light to validate the darkness of hell may seem a creative workaround. However, John Milton's seventeenth-century description of hell in *Paradise Lost* poetically demonstrates the European antecedents of this idea:

> A dungeon horrible, on all sides round
> As one great furnace flamed, yet from those flames
> No light, but rather darkness visible
> Served only to discover sights of woe.[50]

Some descriptions, particularly those of filth and putrid smells, certainly touched both Old and New World traditions, thus making them especially efficacious. However, others seem more connected to a Nahua worldview. In his sermon, Aquino intentionally goes after those who believe in other gods besides the Spanish Dios, or idolaters, as ecclesiastics would have it—an everyday reality in the sixteenth century: "Great woe is you, very unfortunate are you, you who do not desire to believe in our lord God but you go about worshiping them as gods here on earth, when you die, they [the gods] will torment you in hell." This, perhaps, hearkens back to some early friars' association of Nahua deities with manifestations of the devil.[51] For Aquino, the ironic twist of worshiped false gods now torturing the worshipers seemed fitting.

Moreover, Aquino often enhances his description of the cave-like hell of mictlan with wind.[52] True, winds do appear in Dante's second circle of hell to punish the lustful by blowing them incessantly.[53] Yet the use of wind to describe hell and its torments is not overly common in European literature. On the contrary, winds were a common element of the Nahua and, as we have seen, Maya worldviews. They brought life-giving rains, but also sickness, death, misfortune, and fear. For example, the Nahuatl Annals of Puebla record how in 1683, "there arose a strong wind. It grew very dark." The next day, "a bad cough broke out."[54] Associated with the rain deity, Tlaloc, and the caves he so frequently inhabited, the connection between caves and wind was, and remains for many today, well known.[55] Put simply, Nahuas certainly would not have found it strange for winds to be blowing in the hell-cave of mictlan.

Fabián de Aquino, Sixteenth-Century Copybook, fols. 49r–51r

Oh, woe to them who will be very afflicted, very great will be their punishment, etc.[56] And here is what hell is like: hell is a very great cave, a place of great darkness;

this cave is like a very great pool of liquefied metal that greatly burns and boils. And the smoke greatly stinks; when the people here smell it, they will die immediately. And there in hell it is very windy, thus the fire greatly burns because it is blown by this wind that never ceases. And this hell fire is a great torment, the torment really surpasses the fire here [on earth]. And this fire never will be extinguished, and these, the devils, blow on the fire so that it will really burn; this fire, although it burns, it does not emit light; this fire burns the bodies and souls of the wicked. And although it burns, never will it disappear, because of which always, forever the bodies of all the wicked will be tormented; they will be counted as a great forest so that the fire will go along very greatly. This, then, is what it is like in hell.

And here is how they that go to hell will be greatly tormented. May you understand that fire will torment the souls, the bodies of the wicked so that they will greatly burn. And their torment, their pain from the burning is very great, it resembles no torment here on earth. And the second thing by which the wicked will be tormented is grief because always they will go about in extreme pain because of their sins. And they will greatly be tormented by the worms that eat their bodies, their souls. The [third] way that they will be tormented is fear, for the devils will really frighten them, and they will be very frightened of the darkness. And they will frighten each other, although there are a great many of them, they will not console each other, but will torment each other. And really they are squeezed together because there are a great many of them. And always they go about trembling greatly and really chattering their teeth because they are greatly afflicted.

And the fourth thing that the wicked suffer is the wind that greatly blows there in hell. And the fifth thing that will greatly torment is to really know that their affliction will never disappear, never end, never a mere drop of water to cool them off, but always, forever they will be tormented. So many things will torment the wicked that absolutely no one can really relate them.

Oh, great woe is you, very unfortunate are you, you who do not desire to believe in our lord God but you go about worshiping them as gods here on earth, when you die, they [the gods] will torment you in hell. And you who did not desire to obey our lord, who did not want to abandon sin, oh my children, great woe to you, very unfortunate are you, you will be tormented severely there in hell, never again will you emerge, never again will you be happy, never again will you drink, eat, but you will be engulfed entirely by torment. And when all of these hell people, the wicked are finally locked up, the earth will be closed forever so that the wicked will never come out.

The Pains of Hell in Coronel's 1620 *Discursos*

Although nearly all extant Maya religious texts mention the pains of hell to some degree, once again Coronel provides the most extensive discussion. While the text does mention the reward of the righteous as enjoying eternal life with God, the majority concerns the torments of the damned. In many ways, the texts of Coronel and Paredes are structurally similar. Like Paredes and various Old World texts, Coronel urges his audience to think of the pains of hell in life to avoid sin and experiencing them in death; the text employs the same exemplum as Paredes of the monk burning his finger in the candle to avoid temptation, sinners are meted punishments according to their particular sins, and the text even employs the simile of life or wealth "passing as a shadow" to describe its brevity. The simile appears in biblical passages and various popular works including Kempis's *Imitation of Christ*, and Granada's *Libro de la oración*, which, in the same context as Coronel, states that the wealth of the world gives only "a small shadow of fleeting pleasure" not worth the price of eternal torment.[57]

Despite its intimate connections to Old World archetypes, the text betrays many influences from the surrounding colonial realities and Maya worldview. When discussing the eternal pain in hell, the text describes a person afflicted with buboes and how—although extremely painful—it is but temporary. Buboes and similar ailments were common among Indigenous people during Spanish-introduced epidemics, and their inclusion here certainly would have resonated with the colonial Maya.[58] The sermon provides another example of the intertextuality evident among Maya texts. A similar variant of the phrase *hun uay ca kinili çinlic u numyatabal* (the suffering lasts for one or two days) appears in the San Francisco dictionary, and the popular Old World phrase *bay manci booy tulacale* (all passes as a shadow) makes similar—sometimes verbatim—appearances in the Motul dictionary and the Morley Manuscript.[59]

Maya orality and rhetoric abound throughout the sermon. In one instance, the author employs the diphrase *num kin, num haab* (all day, all year) for "always" or "endless." In another, the text employs numerical units familiar to the Maya to emphasize the eternity of hell. Like the Nahua's, the Maya's number system was based on twenty. As mentioned earlier, the number thirteen held importance in the calendar and, perhaps, the cosmos, as some posit that the Maya upper world consists of thirteen levels, although there is increasing reason to believe that a layered universe model resulted from European and Dantean worldviews.[60] Regardless, such numbers are put to good use in the sermon where although a Maya sinner believed 10 katuns (c. 200 years, as one katun is 7,200 days or roughly 20 years) or 13 katuns (c. 260 years) had passed in suffering, it would be as if no time had passed at all.

As mentioned, Coronel's text urges the audience to think of the pains of hell in life to avoid sin and experiencing them in death. But it does so in a way relatable to the colonial Maya. Engaging those familiar with day labor, the text states, "The person who carries for their labor, who is rented out to carry burdens to some place, first lifts their load so it is seen if they are able to endure it or if they are unable to carry the burden." Thus, if one "lifts" the load now by imagining the torments of hell, they will avoid being the *ah con muk* (wage laborer) of the devil for eternity.

One last example of the influence of Maya culture comes from the text's use of the biblical story of Joseph and the famine to relate the grief of sinners in hell. In the story, Joseph interprets an ominous dream of the pharaoh to mean that Egypt will have seven years of good harvests followed by seven years of famine. During the seven years of plenty, Joseph suggested that pharaoh save one-fifth of the harvest to use during the years of famine. Joseph, in fact, was put in charge of accumulating and managing such a store and became a powerful ruler in Egypt.[61]

The Maya text describes the wicked Egyptians pleading for food as they cannot find maize anywhere. Then, through poetic and witty dialogue characteristic of Maya prose, the text compares those starving Egyptians who failed to store food because they did not think ahead to the wicked in hell who failed to spiritually prepare and think ahead regarding their eternal abode. The condemned are forced to eat "the miserable tortilla of his justice, the judgment of God." Here, the Egyptians spoke and ate as Maya, and even suffered similar famines.[62]

Fray Juan Coronel, 1620 *Discursos predicables*, fols. 85v–93r

How great the pains of hell are.[63]

The sorrows of hell encompassed me. Psalm. 17.[64]

Although we want to relate and tell of the great pain and great suffering there in hell, the explanation is not sufficient regarding the fire that is there, which is not accustomed to going out, the horrible frightening visions, the stench, and the loud screams and loud cries that are there; finally all the suffering and torment that is there is greater than, above what can be thought and said.

What would your opinion be when you see a person who is hurting from buboes, has pain on their body, their head, hurting in their chest, their stomach, there is nothing in their body that does not hurt? Pain in the head, pain in the teeth, pain everywhere—is the person not really miserable, in your opinion, that is suffering like this? You think that their suffering is really miserable, really the greatest? But although you believe that their afflictions are really great and many, there is no such suffering and pain similar and comparable to the suffering in that hell. Because the suffering that is here on earth is all temporary and also lasts one or two days then it will cease. Likewise, nobody's suffering and misery here on earth is endless, for it ends, the suffering is alleviated a little, and others soothe what humbles this person. Likewise, there is other help by which they take heart from the strength of martyrs[65] here on earth. But in the fire of that hell, nothing will give people confidence, all is suffering, things that torment, all that they will see and realize is nothing that will not afflict them and bother them also.

Oh miserable, unfortunate is the person that goes to hell because forever it will be night and very dark. Who will help and have pity on them? No one, forever. Not even the devils nor those similarly damned also. Then says the person in the written word of the book of wisdom:

"Oh, we really kept and endured on the path of sin, no dawn and rising sun for us while we are living. How did obeying the will of our bodies benefit us? What did wealth and the things of this world bring us? Did it not all pass by as a shadow? Did it not immediately pass and end the excess that we enjoyed back then?"

Thus say the wicked who are there in the fires of hell in no little rage and hatred; they are like and similar to a stupid person, a debtor, which ceases to work while owing, including the interest of the debt that must be given of what is owed. They do not consider the hour of payment and some future moment to give payment of the debt. When the day of payment arrives, then it begins that the debt is asked for, then they are cast into jail, and their belongings are sold. They have fallen into suffering by which they remember and begin to say,

"Oh! Was my debt back then worth it?"

Thus are the works of the stupid people that are in the fires of hell; they have now fallen into suffering, now they remember and now they confess that they didn't know the good thing of considering at the beginning the remediation of their sins, back then. Therefore, they are cast into suffering. What benefit is it to them to now open their mouths or confess shamelessly? Just ask Judas and Cain how many tears they were caused to shed for being there in hell. They will say truly that they shed many tears. And it is said to them again,

"What benefit did you receive from your tears shed and your suffering endured?"

And they say, "In no way for eternity, because I bought and I received the praise of man that is here in this place, this suffering," so they speak.

Listen to an example of the works of the wicked that is written in the book of Genesis. The Egyptians had really abundant food for seven years' time. Although it was said to them that there was going to come a time of drought for many years and very great hunger from that time forward, they did not believe nor desire to keep some of the food for the future. When finally the great hunger began, their suffering started, and they began to sell their belongings in order to buy a little ration of maize. Then their belongings finally came to an end and then their suffering was the most extreme, back then. Then, they arrived in the company of Joseph, the servant of God, while they said,

"Lord, our lives and our health are in your hands. See us, because nowhere is there maize although searched for, there is nothing for us in order to buy it also," thus they spoke.

Well, what would the Egyptians have said as the memory came to them of their abundant food back then, and that they were able to keep some ration of their food for the time of hunger and suffering, back then? Perhaps they said,

"Oh, we are miserable! It is deserved that we die of hunger and our suffering because we did not desire to think of the time of hunger and suffering," thus they spoke.

Likewise, what will the wicked that are in hell say when they remember that they abandoned the word and the deadline that was given to them by God for their lives on earth, back then, so that they benefit from eternal life? Nor did they wish to hear the word of God and the preachers. They will say, "Oh misery! We wasted away the time. We eat the miserable tortilla of his justice, the judgment of God, because of which today we die of hunger, because we did not plant nor labor in the time for work, also," so they speak.

How the righteous will be rewarded and the wicked punished.[66]

They that do good things shall go into eternal life. John 5[67]

Therefore, the virtuous go to eternal life, then the wicked go to the fires of hell; each person is assigned their burden. First, think and consider about how what was said to you about the place and the misery to be endured, it ceased [the discourse] because my strength was not sufficient. Likewise, that path along which the devil guides you in sin, think if you are enough to carry and endure the suffering of hell, or if in vain you are the little peon of the devil.

You sons, perhaps this is not how the suffering of hell will be? However, the suffering is very great, really painful. Also, there is fire that does not go out, there are horrible sights, there are sorrowful moans and weeping, there is great hunger and thirst. Finally, there is all the suffering able to be spoken and thought of.

As for this suffering, the time of suffering is not only for two days, it is not only for two years nor ten years or thirteen years, but the suffering lasts as long as God says. As soon as two hundred years or two hundred and sixty years will pass, it will be as the beginning again. Oh! How miserable, wretched, unfortunate are those that are in the fires of hell in the center of the earth, because originally they were created by God for the purpose of heaven and eternal life. But voluntarily and because of their lack of discretion and stupidity they have thrown themselves into the fire of hell. This is the reason that they say the words written by Solomon, *We have erred and have strayed.*[68] Which means: "Oh! We erred, we are truly disgraced, we truly sinned in our deeds and there was no light in our souls when we lived our lives on earth, back then. What benefit was pride and vainglory to us? What good did earthly riches or the pleasures of life bring us? Nothing. It all passed as a shadow. Was not the false happiness for [only] one or two days?" thus they will speak.

The person without discretion does not consider something in the beginning while desiring the good way, but already falls into suffering since to make amends perhaps it will be given whatever debt is owed at their pleasure and they ask without remembering the day to pay. So then it arrives, the disregarded day of payment. There is nothing sufficient to pay the debt, then their belongings are sold at a low price, they are sold into slavery, locked in jail, and really tormented.

"Oh, oh, if I had not been in debt back then! Oh! How did I not consider in the beginning, before the day of payment arrived and I whiled away the time?" one says.

Thus it is similar to the works of wicked people and sinners to whom are given something, a sinful debt, by the devil—an easy thing with which he tests all—and the wicked did not consider the fires of hell. But since then they remember, they open their eyes while they say the words that were said, *We err, etc.*[69] Perhaps the wicked people hope that their suffering is going to finish and abate some day in the future, that they will be consoled a little in their suffering, that they will say, "We are content because we will not sit among our suffering forever, some day we will be saved people," thus their words seem.

But they will know that at no time their suffering and misery will finish, end. It is for this reason that they curse themselves and murmur as a child that says, "Oh, I am miserable! Cursed are my father and mother, they did not teach my life with theirs, back then; cursed are the people who persuaded me to sin and they that caused my loss and my coming here to suffer," thus they will say among all these wicked people that speak audaciously. And they wish to die and convert into nothingness; however in no way does the soul die, but will continually dwell in this suffering.

Thus, as a sick person with pain throughout the body and intense suffering who desires daybreak; but daybreak is useless for when the day is passed and it becomes night again they are still in pain, and they suffer all day while suffering the next. Likewise are those people that are in the fires of hell, their suffering is continuous. They will see, think of all the suffering, the suffering reminds them of their ability back then to serve God and redeem themselves from the fire of hell; the suffering reminds them that at no time will their suffering end. Well, think of the suffering of hell now, so that you guard yourself from sin. Perhaps you cannot endure the pain of this here little fire? How really great does your headache feel and pain throughout your body for one or two days? How will you endure your eternal life of pain and misery in hell? Perhaps it annoys you to reside together with wicked people? How will you endure living together with devils and wicked people? Finally, if one night of pain is really long for you now, how will you endure your eternal life in the darkness of hell, where in no way will you see light and daybreak?

It has been written, the deeds of a servant of God who had been tempted by sin and worried that he would fall, so he went to be burned with fire, back then. When he burned the fingers of his hand and felt the strong pain, he said, "Ay! If I am not sufficient to endure the pain from this little fire, how will I endure eternity in the fires of hell?"[70] thus he speaks.

So thus he had defeated the devil and that temptation.

Know that no one will get second portions of happiness and prosperity; if you desire to pleasure your body now, in the other world you will be tormented as was spoken of the rich man recorded in the Gospel, to whom when he begged clemency from Abraham and the descended [Lazarus], back then, it was said, "*Remember*,[71] remember, son, you received blessings and pleasure during your life on earth," it was said.

Thus will be said to you. If you desire prosperity and happiness in the other world, end your pleasure during your life on earth today.

The differences in the torments of hell.[72]

Our bones are scattered by the side of hell.[73] Psalms 140

There is not only great pain and horrors, suffering in hell, you child, but there are other torments by which those that do not honor the word of God are punished,[74] according to how they sinned against God. Those who are arrogant and prideful, such are humbled and subdued by God; the gluttons, greedy, and they that throw banquets here on earth are punished with great hunger and great thirst, and they will desire to be given one drop of water to quench their thirst and satisfy their hunger. Nor will it [relief] ever be given for some lecherous and lustful person whose body and soul really suffer torments and burning, because as their body burned and scorched in sinful lust here on earth, so will it be burned and scorched in the fires of hell also.

It is frightful to hear what happens to a rich one, one who enjoyed the pleasures of life, back then. As soon as the soul departs from its body, it is seized by the devils and brought to the fires of hell; it is brought tied up and is pushed also into the presence of its companions in life, the devils, there in hell. The devils are seated on benches of infinite fire while they say, "Sit lord, for you are a person that should be reverenced, it is not fitting for you to stand on your feet; sit already."

As he was crying loudly, a fellow devil with a large glass full of really stinking bile in his hand came and said to the lord, "Drink it, this drink, drink all that is here."

Then he forced it in his mouth; as soon as he was finished drinking, fierce snakes and wild beasts are spewed out from the earth while it is said, "These are the women you will carry in your arms and the virgins you will spoil here."

So thus he began to be tortured by these various sufferings; mocking and teasing words were also said by the devils. When they finally finished they said, "Lord, perhaps there is music you know, you greatly enjoy?"

Then the rich man said, "Alas, I am ruined, truly disgraced! What song can I sing? Here I would sing bellowing and wicked words also; there is nothing else that can come from my mouth while I am here with you," he says.

How the pains of hell are without end.[75]

Because in hell, there is no redemption.[76]

The greatest consolation for the person in suffering is that it is said to them that their suffering is finite and tomorrow or another day it ceases. But the people that are in hell, what will be said to them? They rightly consider, they know soon in no way will their suffering and misery end because when 4,000, or 144,000, or 6,000 years pass, it begins as it is today.

How does it seem to you? There is a person with a debt of twenty *tostones*,[77] but tomorrow they pay some of it. After days had passed, then they said to him who gave the debt, "Lord, how much of my debt remains?" Then he responds, "It is perpetual."

Likewise are those that are in hell. Each day it seems they perform their penance but in no way does their paying end. If they will say, "How much of my suffering and my penance remains?" Then the response will be, "Eternal suffering remains," thus it is said.

The person's sin against another is punished by some type of [temporal] suffering. But for the sin against God, the punishment with which they will be punished is without end.

So who will really harden and make like a stone their heart and not be disturbed and take fear when they hear this and return from the path of hell? Who will really be deaf so that this does not enter their ears? Where are their eyes, where are their nose? Where is this not heard, seen? Where is this prudence not heeded? What of the soul of the sinner who never hears this harsh thunder and loud cry? If, in your opinion, a headache, backache, and the other sufferings of your body are very painful, even though the time of the suffering lasts one day, how will you endure the various torments that are in the fires of hell? If a sick person thinks one night is long, how will you endure your eternal banishment among the pain and suffering of hell? Thus, consider how really severe the penance is so that because of this you will really hate it.

The person who carries for their labor, who is rented out to carry burdens to some place, first lifts their load so it is seen if they are able to endure it or if they are unable to carry the burden. And so it is said do not desire to be a wage laborer for or be rented by the devil so that he persuades you to take sin as the load you will carry. This is eternal suffering in hell.

The Torments of Hell in the Teabo Manuscript

The Apocalypse and the afterlife clearly made an impression on the Maya as they recorded these doctrines frequently in their own Books of Chilam Balam and Maya Christian copybooks. A collection of religious texts rooted in the early colonial period yet redacted and compiled in the early nineteenth century by the Maya of the town of Teabo provides an excellent example of what the Maya chose to record regarding Christianity and its doctrines on the end of the world and afterlife. Indeed, the vast majority of the Teabo Manuscript speaks of period beginnings and endings: the Christian creation of the world and its end. Not only does its pages contain *The Fifteen Signs*, but also various sermons on the Apocalypse, heaven, and hell. The example below derives from the manuscript's redaction of Christ's parable of the sheep and goats. Here, the righteous are equated with sheep, docile and easily led, that appear on the right hand of Christ, while the wicked, equated with the more stubborn and incorrigible goat, appear on the left. The righteous accompany Christ to heaven, but the wicked are sent to hell.[78]

Commonly employed in Old World texts, the parable, not surprisingly, frequently appears in New World eschatological texts including those of an unofficial nature. Indeed, the Chilam Balams of Tusik and Chumayel contain versions of the story.[79] Although the Teabo Manuscript provides a full redaction of the parable, the passage below begins with the separation of the wicked to hell and the righteous to heaven. Aside from the thematic structure provided by the biblical parable, other European influences are evident. The smell and torments of the damned body are all familiar, as are the rewards for the righteous who, with shining souls and faces, follow singing angels to heaven to receive their reward of eternal happiness.

More subtle examples include the description of the wicked placed head-first into the fire. The position served both figurative and literal meanings of shame. After his betrayal of Christ, Judas Iscariot hung himself and "falling headlong, he burst open in the middle and all his insides spilled out."[80] And while moving through the center of hell, past Lucifer, Dante questions, "how is Lucifer thus fastened upside down?" to which his guide, Virgil, explains that he remains in the position in which he was cast from heaven. Moreover, Dante placed Judas, "the archtraitor," headfirst in Lucifer's mouth while describing Simonists as stuck headfirst into the ground with their exposed legs and feet tormented with fire (see figure 5.3).[81]

Another Old World influence includes the contentious nature of the damned. Children in the Teabo Manuscript—and in other texts including the above passage from Coronel's *Discursos*—berate their parents for allowing them to sin and setting a poor example. Granda's *Libro de la oración* contains a similar instance.[82]

Teabo Manuscript

You mothers here are cursed, as is the breast that I nursed, which you gave to me. As for you, I saw your adultery and your concubinage so I learned also . . . And you did not chastise me nor admonish me back then. Now then cursed are those breasts that you gave them to nurse.

Granada, Libro de la oración

Cursed be the one who deceived me, and cursed whoever did not punish me, and cursed the father who indulged me, cursed the milk I sucked and the bread I ate, the life I lived. Cursed be my creation and my birth and all that helped and served so that I had to be.

Although not a direct translation, the inspiration for the passage in the Teabo Manuscript derived from somewhere across the Atlantic.

Of course, the Maya and colonial society likewise contributed their own elements to the passage.[83] In the biblical parable, whether or not someone engaged in charitable acts separated the righteous and wicked. Here, the text downplays charity to emphasize sexual morality. The Church struggled throughout the colonial period—indeed throughout its existence!—to regulate the sexual practices of its fold with attempts to do so frequently appearing in religious texts. Moreover, parallel constructions abound to describe the torments of hell allowing, for example, to compare the burning bodies of the wicked "as burns a hollow tree trunk, a hollow tree trunk that contains fire."

The text continues to describe the bodies of the wicked who misused their time on earth not only as being malodorous, but also having "horrible eyes, they have horns on their heads and really big claws on their feet and hands, and horrible faces." The appearance of the wicked's damned companions only frightens everyone that much more as they congregate in

Figure 5.3 Gustave Doré, *Dante and Nicholas III*. Reproduction in Dante Alighieri, *The Divine Comedy*.

Figure 5.4 The Pain of the Damned in Hell, *Le miroir de l'humaine salvation*, The Hunterian Museum Library, Glasgow, MS. 60, fol. 59r. Reproduction in *A Medieval Mirror*.

hell. Chapter 4 discussed the differences between the resurrected bodies of the righteous and wicked, and although the wicked do not have the glory and attributes of the righteous, their bodies are not transformed into devils. True, medieval and early modern paintings of hell include demons with horns and claws (see figure 5.4), but these are the fallen angels from heaven who accompanied Lucifer, not the resurrected wicked.[84] The worldviews of the Maya and other Mesoamerican cultures, however, allowed for the transformation of humans into animals as *nahuallis*. As Lisa Sousa explains, "A nahualli was both the person who possessed supernatural abilities and his or her assumed form.[85] In the end, the transformation of bodies into creatures with horns and claws, although unorthodox, accorded with a Maya worldview.

Finally, the text sends the wicked to the *tukil metnal,* or "corner of hell." The Maya worldview included a terrestrial plane with four corners and a center to create a quincunx of the cosmos. This perception of the cosmos persisted into the colonial period and beyond as colonial authors described plots of land by their four corners and modern-day rain ceremonies recognize such corners in their rituals.[86] Thus, it is not surprising that the Maya of the Teabo Manuscript assign hell its own corner.

Teabo Manuscript, pp. 28–33

Then they began to flay their bodies among themselves, and they are gnashing their teeth and biting each other. Then they are really tormented by devils in the great fire which they really stoked with the ravenous fire on the bodies of men and women. For their torment, their bodies and flesh are peeled; very miserable things also happen to them so that they scream and moan from their great suffering in hell. They repeatedly say, "Oh, I am ruined, I am miserable! When will it end, my suffering, my outcries from being beaten, and my screams here in hell? Because I have discerned that I wasted my time on earth. I am ruined, I am miserable," they say while they burn, and their pupils and ears burn as a hollow tree trunk, a hollow tree trunk that contains fire.

All the people have really foul-smelling bodies and horrible eyes; they have horns on their heads and really big claws on their feet and hands and horrible faces; they are in the presence of themselves also, they see the faces of each other only. Then the devil says to them, "You here are my servants. You fulfilled my commandments because of how you lived back then. I guided you into licentiousness. I showed you the way for me to be desired by you. I told you to be ashamed so that you were ashamed to confess to the priest, and you did not recount all of your sins; you were strengthened by me, so that you ceased to abandon your sin and your concubine. So then it begins that they are hurried along to burn in the fire of hell,

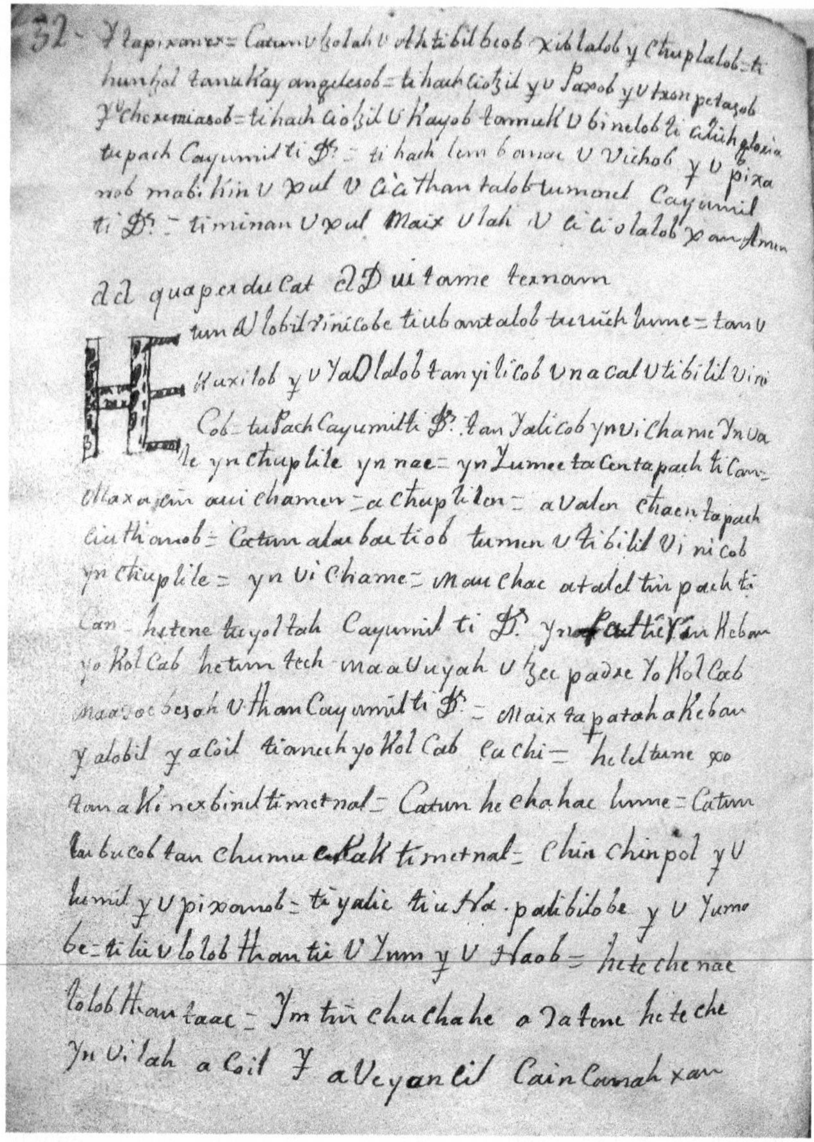

32 - Ylapixoner = Catun v tzolah v Ahtzibil bcob xiblalob y Chuplalob ti
hunzal tanukay angelesob = ti hach ciozil y v Paxob y v tzonpetazob
y v Cheremiasob = ti hach ciozil v Kayob tamuk v binelob ti cilich gloria
tu pach Cayumil ti Ds. = ti hach lem bonac v Vichob y v pixa
nob mabikin v xul v cia than talob tumenel Cayumil
ti Ds. = timinan v xul Maix v lah v ci ciolalob xan Amen

Ad quaperdu Cat ad Dui tame tenam

Hetun v lobil vinicobe ti u bantalob tu ruich lume = tan v
kuxilob y v yaDlalob tan yilicob v nacal v tibilil vini
cob tu pach Cayumil ti Ds. tan yalicob yn v ichamé yn v a
le yn chuplile yn nae = yn lumee ta centapach ti Cam =
Max a ayn auichamen = a chuplilen = a valen chacen tapach
ciuthanob = Catun alae bae ti ob tumen v tibilil vinicob
yn chuplile = yn v ichame = maac chae atalel tu pach ti
can = hetene tu yoltah Cayumil ti Ds. yn ...
yo kol cab hetun tech maa v uyah v zec padre yo kol cab
maazoc besah v than Cayumil ti Ds. = Maix ta patah a kebau
y alobil y a coil tiameh yo kol cab ca chi = heleltune xo
tan a kinex binel ti metnal = Catun he chahac lume = Catun
tu bucob tan chumuc kak ti metnal = chin chinpol y v
kimil y v pixanob = ti yalic tiu Ha. palibilobe y v Yumo
be = ti lu v lolob than ti v Yum y v Haob = hete che nae
lolob than taac = Ym tu chuchahe a yatone hete che
yn v ilah a coil y a veyancil cain canah xan

Figure 5.5 The Teabo Manuscript, LTPSC, MSS 279, box 74, folder 3, p. 32.
Courtesy of L. Tom Perry Special Collections, Harold B. Lee Library,
Brigham Young University, Provo, Utah.

but now no one can free you from my hand; never will I release you also, and never will your torment end here in hell, for the carnal sinners of the concubine women and men also, endless will be the crying and the tears that will be drunk."

See, then, Christian, you will drink and eat fire, thus your joy here on earth will be small when you live your life in hell.

Likewise, our lord God says to all men born here on the earth, "If you give gold to women, to your concubine, then you buy the fire of hell for your soul. If you receive gold for your body, you women, then you sell your soul to the devil and your body to the really severe fire of hell, to the endless fiery torment where Lucifer resides, and then the destruction of each of your hairs and flesh, all of your body will go to the fire of hell."

. . . But the righteous gather in front of our lord God while it is said to them by our lord God, "You here, I created your bodies; you heard my word; you fulfilled all my commandments I left on earth when I finished redeeming the world; you heard the words of my servants, my priests; they were among you on the earth. Now then, come you blessed of my holy father; you fulfilled my commandments. I was thirsty, you gave water to me; I was hungry also . . . and I was naked in jail, you were sad so you came and visited me."

Then the response of the righteous: "My father, when did we see you thirsty and hungry and imprisoned in jail, and you were a stranger and we took you in?"

Then our lord God said to them, "These were my suffering servants on earth, [when] you gave them compassion, you did it for me, back then. Come, receive that reward in the kingdom of holy glory where there is no end nor conclusion."

Then he said to the wicked people, "You here, you scorners, you will go there to the fires of hell forever where there are devils; you will carry this out. I remember, back then, that I was naked, and you did not have compassion on me. Go now forever to the fires of hell where there are devils. You will carry this out endlessly on your body and your soul."

Then the righteous men and women are arranged in a line before the singing angels of great beauty and they play trumpets and chirimías of great beauty. They sing while they go to holy glory with our lord God; their faces are really shining and their souls will never cease being blessed by our lord God. There is no end or termination of their happiness also. Amen. *Bring us to everlasting life.*[87]

However, the wicked people are gathered on the face of the earth among the embittered and guilty; in front of them they see the ascension of the righteous behind our lord God. They say, "My husband, my child, my wife, my mother, my father, take me with you to heaven. Perhaps you are not my husband, my wife, my child to take me with you?" thus they speak.

Then, it will be said to them by the righteous, "My wife, my husband, it is impossible for you to come with me to heaven. As for me, according to the desire of our lord God, I abandoned my sins on earth, but as for you, you did not listen to the sermons of the priest on earth, you did not carry out the commands of our lord God, nor did you abandon your sin, your evil, your adultery while you were on earth. Now, you are condemned to go to hell."

Then the earth opens up, then they are placed in the middle of the fire in hell head first, into the earth and its souls. The children say to their mothers and fathers as they curse their fathers and mothers, "You mothers here are cursed, as is the breast that I nursed, which you gave to me. As for you, I saw your adultery and your concubinage so I learned also. As for you, you saw my adultery and my concubinage, I abandoned my husband and I wandered with my sin. And you did not chastise me nor admonish me back then. Now then cursed are those breasts that you gave them to nurse. Now I will take revenge on you my wicked father, likewise you wicked mother also, likewise you wicked men also. Because of you I am lost to hell."

Then they begin to fight among themselves and tear the bodies of their mothers and fathers, and then underneath the devils they are tormented with fire while they [the devils] burn their bodies with fire as burns a hollow tree trunk, a hollow tree trunk that contains fire, with much gnashing of teeth and screams with no end or termination; they scream from the corner of hell.

In 2014, 72 percent of Americans believed in heaven and only 58 percent believed in hell.[88] Whereas a belief in heaven remains strong, hell struggles to keep up. Indeed, it seems that fewer and fewer today believe sinners will end up in a fiery, demon-run chasm. The lack of belief caused Pope Benedict XVI to comment recently, "Today, society does not talk about hell. It's as if it did not exist, but it does. There is eternal punishment for those who sin and do not repent."[89]

Although belief in hell as a place may have waned in popularity, its torments have not. Indeed, some of the torments described in the texts above horrify while simultaneously drawing in the reader. Many people seem to have a capricious attitude toward violence. In recent years, schools across America have made great strides in decreasing bullying and violence in general. Even nonphysical acts such as cyber-bullying are met with severe consequences. So, on one hand, America abhors violence—from police brutality to domestic violence to verbal violence to elementary school bullying. Yet on the other, we can't get enough of it.

In 2004, the horror film, *Saw*, was released. The plot was simple enough. A deranged killer puts his victims in a variety of traps that will kill them unless they endure or perform acts of mutilation, torture, and murder. The result provided scenes of blood, gore, and agony that likely would have caused even Virgil to look away. Although produced on a paltry budget of a little over a million dollars, the film went on to bring in a worldwide revenue of over one hundred million dollars. Eight sequels—the last appearing in 2021—would earn one billion dollars of worldwide revenue as people all over the world elected to spend their time and money to watch others engage in violence and torture.[90]

These modern trends are useful in examining the past, albeit with limitations. Ecclesiastics and their Nahua and Maya collaborators seemed to have agreed with Pope Benedict and others who noticed that while most believe in a heaven of sorts, hell, at least the Christian hell, requires further convincing. Perhaps this is why most colonial texts spent the majority of time detailing hell rather than heaven. Or perhaps colonial authors took advantage of the *Saw* effect and used violence, gore, and fear to engage and motivate their audience. When choosing between *pan o palo* (akin to the English "carrot or stick"), colonial authors often choose the latter. The Christian hell, in the end, was a foreign concept to Nahuas and Mayas thus likely explaining why their texts so heavily drew upon European models to frame their discussions. That said, elements of Indigenous worldviews continually penetrated the texts to create a new stage in the evolution of the Christian afterlife, one that could allow hell to become a windy cave, Quetzalcoatl's mictlancalco, or a corner of the universe.

Conclusion

A Final Wor(l)d

Anticipating the end of the world is humanity's oldest pastime.

David Mitchell

The probability of "apocalypse soon" cannot be realistically estimated, but it is surely too high for any sane person to contemplate with equanimity.

Noam Chomsky

In 2018 and 2019, *Fortune* magazine published various articles and posts describing the "Retail Apocalypse," referring to the closing of many thousands of retail stores throughout the United States.[1] Department stores including Macy's, Sears, and JCPenney closed hundreds of locations, while others, such as Toys "R" Us, shut their doors for the foreseeable future. Malls once bustling with shoppers and aimlessly roaming teenage youth are often ghost towns today. And many shoppers who do enter stores often do so with the intent of finding an item they like and then purchasing that same product online for a lower price. Innovation will certainly "update" such stores and malls—I personally have seen an increase in virtual reality stores in the local malls—but for many, the threat and doom of the Retail Apocalypse lingers dangerously close with an unknown arrival date.

Nearly five hundred years earlier, a different apocalyptic event devastated the Americas: disease. It was not hard for millennial-thinking fray Toribio de Benavente, known to the New World as Motolinía, to see the hand of God in the disaster. He placed the epidemics among ten plagues with which "God struck down and punished this land."[2] Motolinía often employed symmetry between biblical and contemporary events as evidence of a sort of eschatological foreordination, this time the ten plagues in New Spain with the ten God used against the Egyptians in the Old Testament.[3] Indigenous priests and their potential to delay the New Church were a problem "which God solved by killing many of them with the plagues and diseases."[4]

The Retail Apocalypse, colonial disease, and many other examples testify to the longevity and malleability of the Apocalypse. Those in business and retail have appropriated the concept to explain a changing market. It works, because it is applicable and relatable to them and their audience. Similarly, Motolinía employed the impending event to explain the rapid loss of innumerable Indigenous lives due to disease in a way that made sense to him and his audience. And, as we have seen, other ecclesiastics, Nahuas, and Mayas were no less astute and adapted and applied the Apocalypse in myriad ways to the worldviews of their audience in central Mexico and Yucatan.

Despite being referenced in the singular, the Apocalypse never existed as such. What the Apocalypse meant differed greatly among European Christians, the various religious orders, and theologians. Like many aspects of Christianity, there never was one Apocalypse but rather various Apocalypses, which evolved over time absorbing the beliefs and characteristics of its present environment. Although this book's exploration of Nahuatl and Maya religious, eschatological texts is in no way exhaustive and in many ways only scratches the surface of possible insights, it serves to illustrate an important, New World phase in this ongoing evolution.

Although imported from the Old World, the Apocalypse in central Mexico and Yucatan retained its importance in conveying the doctrines of Catholicism, and official and unofficial Nahuatl and Maya texts reveal the strong presence of eschatological themes and their popularity among Indigenous people themselves. Authors drew heavily from European theologies, sermons, works, and doctrines when composing their treatises, offering scholars today a better appreciation for the theological impact of the Old World on the New. Yet, like in all aspects of colonialism, such foreign novelties did not overrun preexisting beliefs and culture. Various aspects of the Nahua and Maya worldviews blended with Christian eschatology to make their own impact on the Apocalypse, as they do today, and created a negotiated and fluid Apocalypse acceptable to its adherents.

As a result, Apocalypses existed for both the Nahua and Maya. As Louise Burkhart noted, "Christian stories did become different when they were told in Nahuatl."[5] The same can be said of the Apocalypse and also applied to the Maya. When translating Old World, medieval concepts regarding Doomsday into Nahuatl and Yucatec Maya, preexisting cultural preferences created Nahua and Maya versions of the Apocalypse, which resonated with distinct worldviews. To be sure, foundational commonalities existed, and in many ways it is all Christianity. However, similar to Europe, distinct interpretations and renditions of the last days and the Final Judgment existed among the Nahua and Maya as they refashioned and negotiated existing worldviews. Often, the cultural impact of Indigenous worldviews is subtle. Yet it is this subtlety—the small, personalized adaptations—that makes Christianity conducive to various cultures and lifestyles and has allowed it to survive these millennia.

This process of forming a negotiated Apocalypse and eschatology should not be romanticized, as it did not occur on neutral ground outside colonial power relations. In truth, various peoples throughout history have been forced to reconcile with Christianity as it became forced upon them through expansion, conquest, and colonization. Consider Charlemagne's conquest and evangelization of Saxony, the northern crusades against the Baltics, and the *Reconquista*, to name a few.[6] A variety of immediate punishments and consequences awaited those who opposed Catholicism in addition to postmortem torments. And the apocalyptic doctrine contained in the texts discussed here could not only empower the Church and its leaders, but also those—Spanish and Indigenous—who wielded the texts and teachings over their congregations. Yet, in the end, Indigenous culture survived. Speaking of the Maya, Matthew Restall and Amara Solari aptly stated, "Maya history is not only a broad tale of victimization, with the Maya subjected to a series of colonizations, but also a continuation of the precolonial Maya story of adaptability, survival strategies, and local variations."[7] Such sentiment can easily be expanded to include the Nahua and myriad other Indigenous cultures. As shown throughout this book regarding the

Christian Apocalypse, Nahua and Maya culture and authors maintained a voice and influence within the texts themselves to construct New World discourses intended to resonate with their audience. And these discourses created additional steps in the evolution of the Apocalypse and its doctrine—an evolution that continues to make the modern understandings of the Apocalypse differ greatly from its nascent form in the pre-Christian Old World.

This malleability of Christianity and its Apocalypse endowed it with viability, not just in didactic religious texts but also in everyday life throughout the colonial period and beyond as people employed the Apocalypse for individual purposes that could or could not align with colonial and Catholic policy. In central Mexico, for example, the sixteenth-century Andrés Mixcoatl promoted a millennial age devoid of Christians to gain followers, while the image of the Virgin of Guadalupe reflected the apocalyptic woman appearing in Revelation 12:1 "clothed with the sun, with the moon under her feet, and on her head a crown of twelve stars," which artists commonly placed upon her cloak.[8] Later, the Nahua author of the Annals of Puebla connected natural phenomena to sins and even the end of the world: in 1682 a strong earthquake occurred because two homosexuals had been married; in 1686, "a fireball fell," which caused the people to lament, "Now is the time that we shall perish. Its omen [tetzahuitl] has occurred"; and in 1689 a storm with heavy rains, hail and strong winds caused people to believe the end was nigh.[9] In 1574, a nine-year-old Nahua girl named Ana prophesied during an epidemic that the end of the world had begun.[10] Furthermore, by 1816, Nahua testators still left donations to Jerusalem as they had throughout the colonial period, continuing—knowingly or unknowingly—the apocalyptic prophecy held by Columbus and others of the reconquest of Jerusalem and the final spread of Christianity.[11]

The Apocalypse likewise thrived in everyday Yucatan. In 1761, the Maya revolutionary Jacinto Canek declared himself as "the image of Christ," and "a king of liberation."[12] In addition, both the cyclical nature of the Maya worldview and Catholicism allowed for the birth of a new era, and indeed the Chilam Balam of Chumayel seemed to predict as much heralding the return of Christ as the end, or at least reduction, of tribute payments.[13] Later, the revolutionary leader Juan de la Cruz, of the Caste War (1847–1901), directly engaged the Second Coming of Christ and the Apocalypse in

Figure 6.1 2012 Restaurant. Author photo.

his attempt to usher in a new age.[14] And, similar to the Nahua, a donation to Jerusalem continued to be a staple in Maya wills throughout the colonial period.[15]

Today the Apocalypse appears every day throughout the Americas, and the Nahua and Maya are often dragged into it all. In truth, contemporary society seems to have a thirst for the Apocalypse that the Nahua and Maya alone cannot slake, thus producing an overabundance of dystopian novels, zombie TV shows and movies, video games, and even influencing the choice of restaurant names (see figure 6.1).

Not even Christmas is immune from the Apocalypse. A recent film, *Anna and the Apocalypse*, appeared for the American holiday season of 2018. The movie combined the song and dance that made the *The Greatest Showman* and *La La Land* such successes with society's current insatiable desire for all things undead to produce (wait for it!) a zombie musical with a Christmas theme. Like so many of its zombie reincarnations, the Apocalypse, it seems, cannot die.

In reality, it is unable to. As the renowned theologian and historian Bernard McGinn stated, "Christianity was born apocalyptic and has remained so, not in the sense that apocalyptic hopes exhaust the meaning of Christian belief, but because they have never been absent from it."[16] Thus, Christianity and the Apocalypse are symbiotic dependents of one another in an inseparable relationship. Given that the large majority of the Americas' inhabitants are Christian, with Mexico alone boasting 95 percent of its population as believers, everyday encounters with the Apocalypse today and tomorrow seem assured.[17]

In the end, however, the Americas' encounter with the Apocalypse began centuries ago as ecclesiastics, Nahuas, and Mayas employed Old World theology to convey Christian concepts in a way conducive to New World worldviews and settings, thus producing new versions of the Apocalypse. Importantly, the religious texts examined and presented here provide insight into this encounter and the negotiations that took place during the colonial period and that continue for many Nahua and Maya today. In the 1960s, Nohoch Felix (Old Felix) became a member of a Yucatecan Pentecostal church that firmly upheld the gift of tongues and the Second Coming of Christ.[18] Indeed, Nohoch Felix and his wife frequently interpreted meteorological and spiritual events as evidence that Christ would soon return to administer his judgment. In 1987, Felix reported, "There was an earthquake in Xbek, so Christ is definitely going to come soon."[19]

Notes

Introduction

Epigraph 1: Shakespeare, *Hamlet*, act 2, scene 2.

1. McGinn, "John's Apocalypse," 10.
2. La Piana, "Roman Church." Here and throughout, I employ the capitalized "Apocalypse" to refer to the event prophesied in the Bible and associated with the Second Coming of Christ.
3. McGinn, "John's Apocalypse," 4–11; Underwood, *Millenarian World*, 14–15; and Fredriksen, "Christians," 603–5.
4. Of course, no Indigenous person ever referred to themselves as Aztec. "Aztec" became popular in the eighteenth century typically in reference to the pre-contact civilization that controlled central Mexico. They form part of a larger group of Nahuatl-speaking peoples, or the Nahua. For a useful explanation of terminology, see Restall, *Montezuma*, 359; Burkhart, *Aztecs on Stage*, 4; and Townsend, *Fifth Sun*, xi.
5. On the general topic of the Apocalypse, see, for example, the various works of Bernard McGinn and Richard K. Emmerson. See also Himmelfarb, *Apocalypse*; Whalen, *Dominion of God*; Meyer, *Medieval Allegory*; Emmerson, *Antichrist*; Palmer, *Apocalypse*; O'Hear and O'Hear, *Picturing the Apocalypse*; and Riedl, *Companion*, to name a few.
6. Baudot, *Utopia*, 83.
7. Fracas, "Almost Millenarian," provides a useful overview of the arguments of both Phelan and Baudot and their supporters and critics. For a few of many studies largely reinforcing Phelan and Baudot's works, see Weckmann, *Medieval Heritage* and "Las esperanzas milenaristas"; West, "Medieval Ideas"; León-Portilla, *Bernardino de Sahagún*; Timmer, "Providence and Perdition"; and Lara, *City, Temple, Stage*; and "Francis Alive." For works challenging Phelan

and Baudot see Sylvest, *Motifs*; Frost, "A New Millenarian"; and Fracas "Almost Millenarian."

8. Rovira, Salazar Anglada, and Sanchis Amat, *Homero Aridjis*, 11.

9. One need only search the web for "2012, Maya" to retrieve a list of examples. However, one work that received particular attention was Jenkins, *2012 Story*.

10. Restall and Solari have recently released an updated version of the work as *The Maya Apocalypse and its Western Roots* (2021).

11. Something Richard White discovered years ago. See his *Middle Ground*.

12. Notable exceptions exist including Sell and Burkhart's work on *Nahuatl Theater*; Burkhart's work consistently engages with Old World predecessors. For an illustrative example see her, "Voyage of Saint Amaro." An excellent example regarding the Maya is Bricker and Miram's examination of the Chilam Balam of Kaua (*Encounter of Two Worlds*); and Caso Barrera's *Chilam Balam of Ixil*.

13. For works engaging the Apocalypse and the colonial Nahua, see, for example, Burkhart's discussion of death and an overview of Nahuatl texts discussing the Final Judgment in her "Death and the Colonial Nahua"; and Schmidt, "End of the World." See also Magaloni-Kerpel, *Albores de la Conquista*. For the impact of the Apocalypse on Maya colonial texts see Knowlton, *Creation Myths*; Restall and Solari, *2012*.

14. Of course, sermons or discussions of the Apocalypse, the Final Judgment, and hell occur in various contexts. For three examples relating the pains of hell see Burkhart, *Holy Wednesday*, 263–78.

15. Burkhart observed this regarding the Nahua in her *Slippery Earth*, 79.

16. Bellitto, *General Councils*, 19, 104–7, 141–42.

17. Poggioli, "Pope Francis."

18. For an overview of the Church's history, see Hitchcock, *Catholic Church*.

19. Catholic Church, *Catechism*, para. 1042.

20. For more on the beliefs of the Catholic Church regarding the Final Judgment see, Catholic Church, *Catechism*, pt. 1, sec. 2, arts. 7 and 12.

21. Luther, "Christian Liberty," 326. The "stewards" is in reference to 1 Cor. 4:1.

22. Stuart, *Order of Days*, 209.

23. Stuart, *Order of Days*, 72–73. His chapter 7 provides a useful overview of Mesoamerican worldviews.

24. Numerous works detail the worldviews of the Nahua and Maya. For most relevant discussions see Restall and Solari, *2012*, 73–74; Léon-Portilla, *Native Mesoamerican Spirituality*, 27–30; López Austin, "El núcleo duro"; Díaz, "Reshaping the World"; Díaz, *Cielos e inframundos*; Carrasco, *Aztecs*, 61–77; Knowlton, *Maya Creation Myths*; Stuart, *Order of Days*; and Cecil and Pugh, *Maya Worldviews*. Of course, the surviving magnum opus of Maya worldviews is the Popol Vuh. See Christenson, *Popol Vuh*.

25. For studies on the stone and its significance in relation to period endings and beginnings and Western thought, see Restall and Solari, *2012*, 73–77; and Stuart, *Order of Days*, 203–9. For the stone in general, see Villela and Miller, *Aztec Calendar Stone*.

26. For more on the importance of prognostication among the Maya, see Gubler and Bolles, *Chilam Balam of Na*, 4–9.
27. The list of similarities is, actually, quite extensive. However, the primary difference between Catholic and Mesoamerican worldviews resides in the exclusive nature of the Christian deity versus the inclusive and dualistic nature of those from Mesoamerica and its cultures. That there could be only "one true God" surely must have been a strange concept to many Indigenous people and certainly proved difficult for ecclesiastics to convey. See Tavárez, "Naming the Trinity."
28. Peterson, "Images in Translation," 36n69.

Chapter 1. Old World Roots, New World Shoots

Epigraph 3: Motolinía, *Historia*, 161–66.

1. 2 Pet. 1–3.
2. For the persecutions of early Christians and their millenarian views, see Fredriksen, "Christians," 601–6. For the Black Death, see Aberth, *From the Brink*. For the presence of apocalypticism among Protestants, see Cunningham and Grell, *Four Horsemen*. For a general overview, see Himmelfarb, *Apocalypse*. For more on 2012, see Restall and Solari, *2012* and Stuart, *Order of Days*.
3. McGinn, *Visions*, 11; Latteri, "Jewish Apocalypticism," 67–102.
4. Underwood, *Millenarian World*, 14. His work provides an excellent overview, 14–23.
5. Both titles essentially carry the same meaning: "reveal." Taylor Halverson, personal communication, February 4, 2022.
6. McGinn, *Visions*, 11–27; McGinn, "Introduction: John's Apocalypse," 4–11. See also Ryan, *Companion*; and Whalen, *Dominion*.
7. Rev. 1:11.
8. McGinn, "Introduction: John's Apocalypse," 15–18; Poole, "Western Apocalypse Commentary," 103-104. Here and throughout, I employ the adjective "millenarian" as a way to connote an effort to bring about a paradisaical or millennial age here on earth that would usher in the Final Judgment. For an excellent overview of the term, see Graziano, *Millennial New World*, 7–8.
9. McGinn, *Visions*, 21; Restall, *2012*, 54–55. For example, fray Juan de Torquemada makes this connection in *Monarquía indiana*. See Kagan, *Urban Images*, 151–98; Graziano, *Millennial New World*, 138–41; and Phelan, *Millennial Kingdom*, 34–35.
10. McGinn, *Visions*, 26–27; Palmer, *Apocalypse*, 31–32. My thanks to Fr. Roger Corriveau A.A. for his insights. For more on apocalyptic interpretations of the New Jerusalem, see Meyer, *Medieval Allegory*.
11. Jerome, *Principal Works*, 269. Regarding the validity of Revelation in general among sixteenth-century theologians, see Backus, "Church Fathers," 651–66.
12. For an effective overview, see McGinn, *Visions*, 17–18; Restall and Solari, *2012*, 56.
13. Catholic Church, *Catechism*, paras. 668–77.
14. Underwood, *Millenarian World*, 15.

15. McGinn, "Introduction: John's Apocalypse," 16–19; Fredriksen, "Tyconius and Augustine," 20–37; Whalen, *Dominion*, 15–17. For more on amillennialism see Onyema, *Millennial Kingdom*, 33–34.

16. Jerome, *Commentarium in Danielem*, cited in Lerner, "Medieval Return," 51.

17. It should be noted that the scholarship on Joachim's interpretation of Revelation 20 and the millennial kingdom of Christ fails to agree on whether or not his views are amillennial or millennial. For a summary of the main points, see Onyema, *Millennial Kingdom*, 51–53; Lerner, "Medieval Return," 58.

18. Lerner, "Medieval Return," 57–71; Daniel, "Joachim of Fiore," 87.

19. McGinn, *Visions*, 25–26.

20. See Fredriksen, "Tyconius and Augustine," 35, for the invasion of Rome and 36n50 for the soldiers in the army of Otto I; for Islam, see Wainwright, "Mysterious Apocalypse," 60; and for the Muslim conquest, see Sahin, "Constantinople," 317–54.

21. Palmer, *Apocalypse*, 220.

22. For more on the Apocalypse and its role in shaping Western Christians' ideas of this world order see Whalen, *Dominion of God*, 12 and chap. 1 in general.

23. For an excellent discussion and examples, see O'Hear and O'Hear, *Picturing the Apocalypse*.

24. Emmerson, "Introduction," 294.

25. The role of the Apocalypse in medieval culture is well covered in Emmerson and McGinn, *Apocalypse*.

26. 2 Cor. 12:2.

27. Dante Alighieri, *Divine Comedy*, 3. For more on the work's influence on Dante, see Silverstein, "Dante," 397–99; and Herzman, "Dante," 398–413. See also Silverstein, *Visio Sancti Pauli*, 3–6; Gardiner, *Medieval Visions*, 179–94; and Bernstein, *Formation of Hell*, 292–305. For other spiritual journeys to heaven and hell, see Berlioz, "Infernal Visions," 101–19.For a translation of the Apocalypse of Paul, see Gardiner, *Visions*, 13–46.

28. Christensen, *Nahua and Maya Catholicisms*, 195–212; Christensen, *Translated Christianities*, 15–24.

29. Daniel "Joachim of Fiore," 78, 77. The chapter provides an excellent survey Joachim's interpretation of Revelation. See also McGinn, "Introduction: Joachim," 1–19. For Joachim's apocalyptic organization of historical events see Whalen, "Joachim the Theorist," 88–108.

30. For the carnal Church in Joachimist Theology, see Grosse, "Critiques," 159–60. Works on Joachim and his doctrine are ubiquitous, but see Baudot, *Utopia and History*, 76–80; Phelan, *Millennial Kingdom*, 14–15; and Daniel, "Joachim of Fiore," 72–88. It is important to note that much of what today is credited to Joachim actually derives from the pseudo-Joachimite commentaries of his predecessors. See Andrews, "Influence of Joachim."

31. Whalen, *Dominion of God*, 210.

32. Whalen, *Dominion of God*, 207–12; Lerner, *Feast*, 54–72, 61; McClure, *Franciscan Invention*, 164–67. Olivi argued for two Antichrists: a mystical Antichrist

serving as a corrupt pope and a great Antichrist. Whalen, *Dominion of God*, 210; Burr, *Spiritual Franciscans*, 77, 210–11, 249, 254.

33. For Olivi's influence, see West, "Medieval Ideas," 297. For a review of Joachim's impact on Franciscans, see Burr, *Spiritual Franciscans*, 285–90. Of course, Joachim's teachings influenced individuals from a variety of orders. See Samuel Edgerton, *Theaters of Conversion*, 13–34. For apocalyptic views of Jesuits in colonial Peru, see Pastore, "Mozas Criollas," 59–73.

34. Williams, "The Apocalypse Commentary," 222; and Covey, *Inca Apocalypse*, 78.

35. Fernández-Armesto, *Columbus on Himself*, 92. Arnold's works often ran afoul of religious authorities, who on several occasions burned his tract *Time of the Antichrist*. See Whalen, *Dominion*, 212–14.

36. Such is demonstrated throughout Covey, *Inca Apocalypse*, 71–108; and Magnier, *Pedro de Valencia*.

37. Magnier, *Pedro de Valencia*, 61.

38. Magnier, *Pedro de Valencia*, 1–31, 71–75, 126, 393; and Fernández-Armesto, *Columbus on Himself*, 92.

39. Phelan, *Millennial Kingdom*, 12–14; and Liss, *Isabel the Queen*, chap. 9. See also West, "Medieval Ideas," 300–301. For more on the general apocalyptic atmosphere in Spain, see Castro, *Aspectos del vivir hispanico*, 22–26.

40. McGinn, "Introduction: Joachim," 15.

41. Fernández-Armesto, *Columbus on Himself*, 91.

42. McGinn, "Introduction: Joachim," 15; and Fernández-Armesto, *Columbus on Himself*, 187.

43. Fernández-Armesto, *Columbus on Himself*, 188; Rev. 21:1; and Isa. 65:17.

44. It is not clear when, exactly, Columbus began to see himself and his achievements in such an apocalyptic light. As Felipe Fernández-Armesto notes, it is difficult to find Columbus's "authentic voice" among the highly edited documentation that exists today, *Columbus on Himself*, 9. For more on Columbus and his eschatological ideas, see Fernández-Armesto, *Columbus on Himself*. See also Phelan's *Millennial Kingdom*, 17–23.

45. Matt. 24:14.

46. See West, "Medieval Ideas," 304, 312–13.

47. Ricard, *Spiritual Conquest*, 20–23.

48. Some scholars question the impact of Joachim's teachings on the early Franciscans sent to the New World and their millenarian zeal and, by association, Phelan's *Millennial World* and Baudot's *Utopia and History*. See, for example, Saranyana and de Zabella Beascoechea, *Joaquín de Fiore*. Although direct connections with Joachim can be debated, his influence in the spread of apocalyptic thinking and view of history in general is more secure.

49. Ladero Quesada, "Spain circa 1492," 130.

50. Again, various works exist which expound upon the historical context of the evangelization program: Baudot, *Utopia and History*, 71–88; Phelan, *Millennial Kingdom*, 14–15; León-Portilla, *Bernardino de Sahagún*, 43–49; and West, "Medieval Ideas," 296.

51. West, "Medieval Ideas," 296.
52. Turley, *Franciscan Spirituality*, 15.
53. Keck, *Angels and Angelology*, 144; Burr, "Mendicant Readings," 102.
54. Morales, "Native Encounter," 148–49.
55. Turley, *Franciscan Spirituality*, 14–22. For more on Cisneros as a reformer, see Eire, *Reformations*, 118–20.
56. For a more detailed overview see Turley, *Franciscan Spirituality*, 18–24; García Oro, *Evangelización de América*; and León-Portilla, *Bernardino de Sahagún*, 45–60.
57. Turley, *Franciscan Spirituality*, 29–30, 43; and León-Portilla, *Bernardino de Sahagún*, 47–60.
58. Mendieta, *Historia eclesiástica*, 204. The *Instrucción* and the *Obediencia* can be found in Mendieta's *Historia eclesiástica indiana*. The parable is found in Matt. 20:1–16. West gives an excellent overview of the topic in his "Medieval Ideas." See also Phelan, *Millennial Kingdom*, 23–24; and Leeming, "Aztec Antichrist," chap. 1. For an English translation of the *Instrucción* and *Obediencia*, see Oroz, *Oroz Codex*, app. 1.
59. Ricard, *Spiritual Conquest*, 21; and Turley, *Franciscan Spirituality*, 31.
60. Valadés, *Retórica cristiana*, part 4:223, 204; León-Portilla, *Bernardino de Sahagún*, 60.
61. This would be Ps. 58:14 in the Vulgate.
62. Motolinía, *Historia*, 161–63; and West, "Medieval Ideas," 309. Many works have noted Valencia's plea. For example, see Baudot, *Utopia*, 84–85; and Segundo Guzmán, "El horizonte," 50–53. Also, Valencia became increasingly pessimistic toward the Indigenous people of central Mexico and eventually viewed those of Asia as preferable candidates for Christianity. For a discussion, see Tavárez, *Invisible War*, 30–31. Sahagún shared this sentiment. See Boruchoff, "New Spain," 17; and León-Portilla, *Bernardino de Sahagún*, 253.
63. Phelan, *Millennial Kingdom*, 45. For more on the Spiritual Franciscans and the pseudo-Joachimite traditions, see Burr, *Spiritual Franciscans*.
64. Turley, *Franciscan Spirituality*, 28.
65. Turley, *Franciscan Spirituality*, 3, 13, and demonstrated throughout the work. For an insightful discussion highlighting the differences within the Franciscan order, see Poiré, "Discalced Franciscans." For a useful overview of the early friars and millenarian beliefs, see Weckmann, *Medieval Heritage*, 208–16; McClure, *Franciscan Invention*.
66. Martin Nesvig's *Forgotten Franciscans*, 4, 4n2.
67. For a poignant example concerning Guatemala, see Sparks, *Rewriting Maya Religion*.
68. See Whalen, *Dominion of God*, 160–61, 173, 196.
69. Burr, "Mendicant Readings," 101–2.
70. Mendieta, *Historia eclesiástica*, 513. For the Nahua's role in employing the omens to create a Nahua-Christian, eschatological narrative of the conquest, see Magaloni-Kerpel, "Painting a New Era." A full study on the role of disease in evangelization lies beyond the scope of this work, yet merits further attention. Peterson and Terraciano's recent edited volume, *Florentine Codex*, con-

tains various chapters that expose the effects of sixteenth-century epidemics on Sahagún and his work.

71. For an excellent assessment of how the eschatological thinking of various friars influenced the Franciscans' view of the New World, see McClure, *Franciscan Invention*, 131–38, 159–88; and Segundo Guzmán, "El horizonte escatológico," 30–57. See also Roest, "Early Mendicant Mission," 197–217.

72. *Colección de documentos*, 13:424; and Phelan, *Millennial Kingdom*, 47.

73. Phelan's *Millennial Kingdom* continues to be the definitive work on Mendieta's eschatological views, although, as mentioned, some scholars question his conclusions. Bernardino de Sahagún likewise participated in the glorification of Cortés in his account of the conquest. See Cline, "Revisionist Conquest History," 93–106. For the apocalyptic views of the lesser-known Franciscan, Cristóbal Cabrera, see Laird, "Classical Letters," 78–108.

74. García Icazbalceta, *Bibliografía mexicana*, 1:316. The quotation is from Jer. 1: 9–10. See Boruchoff, "New Spain," 12.

75. García Icazbalceta, *Bibliografía mexicana*, 1:316–17. For additional references to the New Church, see *Códice franciscano*, xviii, xxvii, xxix, 115, 194, 217; also Sahagún, *Florentine Codex*, bk.10, prologue. For a good survey of Sahagún's work and attitude, see SilverMoon, *Imperial College*, 244–318; León-Portilla, *Bernardino de Sahagún*, 231–33.

76. Mendieta, *Historia eclesiástica*, 443–45. See also León-Portilla, *Los franciscanos vistos*, 75–79.

77. For more on Franciscan poverty, see McClure, *Franciscan Invention*, 142–47, 177.

78. Although much has been made of the formation of an Indigenous clergy as a foundational role of the college, there is little evidence of supporting the claim. See SilverMoon, *Imperial College*, 56–57, 174–75; and Laird, "Teaching of Latin."

79. Molina, *Confesionario mayor*, 2v; and Bautista, *Libro de la miseria*, prologue. An excellent overview of the college remains Burkhart's *Holy Wednesday*, 55–65. See also Tavárez, "Nahua Intellectuals," 203–35; and Nesvig, *Forgotten Franciscans*, 4–5.

80. Oroz, *Oroz Codex*, 201.

81. For more on the education of Indigenous people and their roles as surrogate priests see Christensen, "Missionizing Mexico," 27–36; Christensen, *Teabo Manuscript*, 3–5; Collins, "Maestros Cantores." In general see Morales, "Native Encounter"; and Hanks, *Converting Words*, 59–84. For an intriguing study of Indigenous assistants in Bolivia, see Falkner, "Sermones chiquitanos," 289–307; and for Oaxaca, see Farriss, *Tongues of Fire*, 38–42.

82. Magaloni-Kerpel, "Painting a New Era," 126.

83. See Magaloni-Kerpel, *Albores de la Conquista*; and Peterson, *Paradise Garden Murals*, 138–51. For the inclusion of Christian eschatology within the Maya worldview in the Books of Chilam Balam, see Restall and Solari, *Maya Apocalypse*, chap. 5; and Knowlton, *Maya Creation Myths*.

84. For an excellent examination of this among the Maya, see Hanks, *Converting Words*.

85. For Africa, see Strathern, "Catholic Missions," 158–59; for Japan see Ucerler, "Christian Missions," 314–17.

86. Nesvig, *Forgotten Franciscans*, 4–5; and Pollnitz, "Old Word," 123–52. For more on the Indigenous clergy, see SilverMoon, "Imperial College," 56–57; and Poole, "Church Law."
87. For this and more on the works produced by early Franciscan and Nahua collaboration, see Tavárez, "Aristotelian Politics."
88. Phelan, *Millennial Kingdom*, 46. For more on the Franciscans and motivations for education, see Carreño, *Don fray Juan*, 83–84; and Flint and Flint, *Most Splendid Company*, 27.
89. See SilverMoon, "Imperial College," 155–56. Baudot argues millenarian roots to the college in his *Utopia*, 72, 104–20; see also Morales, "Native Encounter." For possible millenarian influences on the *Florentine Codex*'s account of the conquest, see Magaloni-Kerpel, "Painting a New Era." Such a connection has been attempted in examining early religious architecture with varying degrees of success. See McAndrew, *Open Air Churches*; Edgerton, *Theaters of Conversion*; and Jaime Lara, *City Temple, Stage*. Lara, in particular, at times overreaches with his conclusions.
90. For an excellent discussion of the Franciscan's contribution to the rebuilding of Tenochtitlan, see Mundy, *Death of Aztec Tenochtitlan*, generally and regarding Gante, see 116–19.
91. Baudot, *Utopia*, 88–89. See also Curcio-Nagy, "Faith and Morals," 145.
92. For more on the use of Nahuatl, see Robert Schwaller, "Language of Empire."
93. Or as Francisco Morales would have it, that the school was formed under the "persuasion that higher education for the natives constituted an indispensable lay support for the Franciscan missionary effort." Morales, "Native Encounter," 147. Baudot, *Utopia*, 105–20.
94. Molina, *Confesionario mayor*, 2v; Bautista, *Libro de la miseria*, prologue.
95. Data taken from Sell, "Friars, Nahuas, and Books," app. 1.
96. For examples in Peru, see Lara, "Francis Alive," 139–63. For examples in Paraguay and Brazil see Graziano, *Millennial New World*, 169–71.
97. For older interpretations, see Clendinnen, *Ambivalent Conquests*. For studies examining a millenarian context see Roest, "Reconquista to Mission," 352; Timmer, "Providence and Perdition," 477–88; and Davis, "Evangelical Prophecies," 86–103. See also Chuchiak, "*In Servitio Dei*," 627n52.
98. Restall and Solari, 2012, 93–97.
99. Landa, *Relación*, 166–67. For more on the disposition and frustrations of Landa, see Chuchiak, "*In Servitio Dei*," 611–46.
100. Sparks, *Rewriting Maya Religion*, 155.
101. Scholes et al., *La iglesia*, 2:22–23.
102. Beltrán, *Novena de christo*, 2.
103. This waning of zeal is attributed not only to the persistence of Indigenous beliefs and practices but also to the incompatibility of a Christian utopia and the desire to make profits in the New World. See Graziano, *Millennial New World*, 166–71.
104. This belongs to a larger conversation regarding confessionalization. For an overview see Shore, "European Confessional State"; Schilling, *European Civilization*; Moreno and García Cárcel, "Introduction."

105. The metaphor, of course, derives from Richard White's *The Middle Ground*.
106. Solórzano Pereira, *Política indiana*, 29; and West, "Medieval Ideas," 313.
107. León, *Camino del cielo*, prolog.
108. Phelan, *Millennial Kingdom*, 106.
109. Prien, *Christianity*, 81; and Cline, "Revisionist Conquest History," 93–106. For a study that includes how such views affected land ownership in the seventeenth and eighteenth centuries, see Medrano, *Mexico's Indigenous Communities*, 79–150.
110. Zeller, *Prophets and Protons*, 123, 127.
111. For a summary, see Balch and Taylor, "Making Sense"; and Zeller, *Prophets and Protons*, pt. 3. The term "technological rapture" comes from Zeller, *Prophets and Protons*, 133.
112. McKinnie, "Mansion of Death."
113. For more on the evolving Antichrist, see Whalen, *Dominion of God*, chap. 1
114. See, for example, Grosse, "Thomas Aquinas," 144–89.
115. Nor were they limited to New Spain. For other millenarian missions see Graziano, *Millennial New World*, 164–71.
116. García Icazbalceta, *Bibliografía mexicana*, 319–21.

Chapter 2. The Personal Apocalypse

Epigraph: Aridjis, *El señor*, 33.

1. Woolf and Schoomaker, "Life Expectancy," 1998.
2. Catholic Church, *Catechism*, paras. 1021–41. For a general overview, see White, *Light of Christ*, chap. 7.
3. From *Seno de Abrahan*. Catholic Church, *Catechism*, para. 633.
4. Luke 16:19–31. For more on the parable and its development of hell, see Bernstein, *Formation of Hell*, 239–41.
5. Luke 23:43.
6. Catholic Church, *Catechism*, para. 1021.
7. Le Goff, *Birth of Purgatory*, 3; and Foster, *Three Purgatory Poems*, 4–5. See also Augustine, *City of God*, 238.
8. Le Goff, *Birth of Purgatory*, 3 (emphasis in original), for the ancient influences of purgatory, see 17–51.
9. McGuire, "Purgatory, the Communion," 81. For an overview of the counterarguments against Le Goff, see McGuire, "Purgatory, the Communion," 61–84; and Edwards, "Purgatory," 634–46.
10. Logan, *History*, 269–75.
11. Le Goff, *Birth of Purgatory*, 84, 357; and Van Deusen, *Souls of Purgatory*, 35.
12. Le Goff, *Birth of Purgatory*, 327–28; and Logan, *History*, 274–75. For examples in England, see Brown, *Church and Society*, 122–29.
13. For dates on its Spanish translations see Delbrugge, *Scholarly Edition*, 46. For an overview of the *devotio*, the *Imitatio*, and its translation into Nahuatl, see David Tavárez, "Nahua Intellectuals." For more on the *devotio moderna*, see Post, *Modern Devotion*.

14. Kempis, *Imitation of Christ*, 43–44.
15. See Eire, *From Madrid*. For the role of women and the "feminization of purgatorial piety," see Van Deusen, *Souls of Purgatory*.
16. Kelly, "Hell with Purgatory," 128–35. Augustine, "Treatise," chaps. 21–22.
17. Burkhart, *Slippery Earth*, 52–53.
18. Burkhart, "Introduction," 5–6. Burkhart's work, along with others, on the topic is pioneering and can be seen the various volumes of *Nahuatl Theater* (Sell and Burkhart).
19. Sell and Burkhart, *Nahuatl Theater*, 1:241.
20. Sell and Burkhart, *Nahuatl Theater*, 1:165–89. See also Burkhart's comments on limbo and hell in her *Holy Wednesday*, 211–14.
21. Anunciación, *Sermonario*, 236v–37r. For more on limbo, see Burkhart, *Slippery Earth*, 52–54. Anunciación likewise relates a biography of sorts on Saint Nicholas de Tolentino, patron of the souls of purgatory, in *Sermonario*, 190r–94v. Italics denote the Spanish term, *seno de Abraham*, in the Nahuatl passage.
22. Anunciación, *Doctrina*, 25r. The descriptive phrase of *tlayohuan, mixtecomac* appears in other texts as well including various plays. See Sell and Burkhart's *Nahuatl Theater*, 1:138, 2:214.
23. León, *Camino*, 37r.
24. Kelly, "Hell with Purgatory," 134–35; International Theological Commission, "Hope of Salvation."
25. For examples in colonial Oaxaca, see Farriss, *Tongues of Fire*, 178–84.
26. Although various hagiographies mention the saint and contain descriptions of his work, the most valuable work regarding his legend and spread to the New World, and the one employed here, is Smoller, *Saint*, in particular 1–15.
27. Smoller, *Saint*, 274–98. Ben Leeming does excellent work on Vincent and his colonial influence in his "Aztec Antichrist," 54–55, 70–72. Moreover, see the various articles found in *Anuario de estudios medievales* 49, no. 1.
28. Smoller, *Saint*, 291–93.
29. Leeming, "Aztec Antichrist," chap. 2.
30. Another example is Quintana's *Confessonario*. See also Smoller, *Saint*, 280.
31. Zulaica y Gárate, *Los franciscanos*, 218–21; Burkhart, *Holy Wednesday*, 51, 68; and Sell, "Friars, Nahuas, and Books," 146–47; Tavárez, "Naming the Trinity," 29.
32. See Eire, *Madrid to Purgatory*, 175–76. See also Adams, *Visions*, 17–54.
33. There are various versions of this story which differ in details and number of masses offered for Francisca's soul. The one used here derived from the eighteenth-century Vidal y Micó, *Historia*, 129–31. For mention of the tale in other works, see Martínez Gil, *Muerte y sociedad*, 225–27.
34. Biblioteca Nacional de Antropología e Historia, *Manuscritos mexicanos*, MS. 1493, fols. 349–52. Danièle Dehouve provides a summary of the MS 1493 sermon in her *Relatos de pecados*, 335–37. The CD-ROM accompanying the work contains the transcription and French and Spanish translation of the sermon. The use of exempla among the Jesuits in Mexico was not uncommon. See Dehouve, *Rudingero el borracho*.

35. MS 1493, fols. 349–52 as transcribed in Dehouve, *Relatos de pecados*, 283–85.
36. Sahagún, *Florentine Codex*, bk. 4, 69; Kerkhove, "Dark Religion?," 141–42.
37. Sahagún, *Exercicio* in Chimalpahin, *Codex Chimalpahin*, 2:154–55.
38. See Inga Clendinnen's excellent description in her *Aztecs: An Interpretation*, 356–58. See also Sigal, *Flower*, 151; and Bassett, *Fate of Earthly Things*, 53–56.
39. Larkin, "Liturgy," 515n72. For more on the role of trentals in medieval Europe, see Martínez Gil, *Muerte y sociedad*, 209–40.
40. Carrillo Cázares, *Manuscritos*, 3:180.
41. Larkin "Liturgy," 514–15. See also Smoller, *Saint*, 285–87.
42. Words or phrases in italics denote Spanish words in the Nahuatl text.
43. *bulto*, "image, shape."
44. Paredes, *Promptuario*, "Razon de la obra." Sell, "Friars, Nahuas, and Books," 235–45; Christensen, *Catholicisms*, and *Translated Christianities*.
45. Pasulka, *Heaven Can Wait*, 30–58.
46. Aquino, "Sermones y miscelánea," Hispanic Society of America, NS 3–1, 41r–41v. My thanks to Ben Leeming for sharing this manuscript with me.
47. Granada, *Libro de la oración*, 50–51.
48. This task was hastily performed on Good Friday as the Sabbath was quickly approaching. It was upon their return to the tomb to finish the job that they discovered it empty and Christ appeared to Mary Magdalene. Warner, *Alone of All Her Sex*, 230–32.
49. Burkhart, *Slippery Earth*, 51–56; Cervantes, "Changing Visions," 109–15.
50. The ninth sermon includes details on the end of the world, the resurrection, and final destination of saved and condemned souls, omitted in the translation here for sake of brevity. Words or phrases in italics denote Spanish and Latin words in the Nahuatl text.
51. Paredes made a Nahuatl redaction of Jerónimo de Ripalda's Spanish catechism in 1758, which was titled *Catecismo mexicano*. He is likely referencing this work as he had hoped that it would be the sole Nahuatl catechism used "to remove the variety that exists" in the doctrine. Moreover, the work contains instructions on how to baptize children in the case of an emergency. Ripalda, *Catecismo mexicano*, preliminary leaf, 164–69. For more on the influence of Ripalda's work on baptisms, see Christensen, *Catholicisms*, 148–57; Christensen, *Translated Christianities*, 68–70, contains a translation of Paredes's instructions on how to baptize in the case of an emergency; and Burkhart, "'Little Doctrine,'" 167–206.
52. Here, Paredes employs the term *quimopieliaya*. Although he attempts to be a purist in his use of Nahuatl, he ascribes to *pia* the common, mid-eighteenth century definition of the Spanish *tener*, "to have" instead of its original "to guard."
53. The meaning here and leading up to the event is that Christ resurrected through his own power, by his own will. No one helped him.
54. *Multa corpora sanctorum, qui dormierant surreserunt.* Paredes gives Matt. 22:57 as the citation, but it is actually Matt. 27:52.
55. *Quod si nosmet ipsos dijudicaremus, non utique judicaremur.* 1 Cor. 11:31.

56. Cogolludo gives a lengthy account of Coronel in his *Historia*, bk. 12, chap. 18. See also Roys, "The Franciscan Contribution," 422–23; Adams, "A Bio-Bibliography," 459–60; and Bandelier, "Juan Coronel," 386.

57. Coronel, "Discursos," viii. Here and throughout the book, I employ David Bolles's transcription of the *Discursos* that appears on the FAMSI website. For more on Coronel and his works, see Hanks, *Converting Words*.

58. For more on the Genesis Commentary and its circulation see Bricker and Miram, *Encounter*; Knowlton, "Dynamics"; and Christensen, *Teabo Manuscript*, 25–102. For examples of intertextuality in Highland Guatemala, see Sparks, *Rewriting*.

59. For more details, see Christensen, *Teabo Manuscript*, 216; and Whalen, "Annotated Translation." For more on the Books of Chilam Balam in general, see Love, "Los *Libros*"; and Scandar, "Juan Pío Pérez."

60. Acuña, "Escritos Mayas," 168–69. Acuña examines Landa's letter reporting the state of Maya text production (Archivo General de la Nación, Inq., vol. 90, exp. 42). See also Whalen, "Annotated Translation."

61. Coronel, "Discursos," vii.

62. William Hanks thoroughly discusses the eclectic and ongoing nature of such colonial dictionaries in his *Converting Words*, 120–27. In Coronel's discussion of the seventh Articles of Faith, he employs the sentence, "Teex cex tanolmail, yetel, nenmaic a uolex v dzoclukçabal, yetel v beeltabal dzayatzil cuchie" ("Discursos," 31v.), which likewise appears in the Motul. Ciudad Real, *Diccionario de motul*, John Carter Brown Library, Codex Ind 8, vol. 1, 326r.

63. See Christensen, *Catholicisms*, 122. For more on Beltrán's corrections of Coronel, see Hanks, *Converting Words*, 247–49.

64. Matt. 20:16.

65. For other examples of sarcasm, see Restall, *Maya World*, 141–43; Chuchiak, "Sin, Shame, and Sexuality," 195–219; and "Secrets behind the Screen," 106n53.

66. Perhaps referring to the second or final resurrection, which takes place immediately before the Last Judgment.

67. For the dating of the Morley Manuscript, see Whalen, "An Annotated Translation"; and Knowlton, "Dynamics," 90–112. Like all Maya Christian copybooks that serve as copies of originals compiled over the centuries, a specific date for text within the manuscript remains uncertain and warrants further study.

68. For more on the exempla and their translations, see Christensen, *Translated Christianities*, 27–44.

69. The quotation derives from John M. Weeks's study of Berendt's collection in "Karl Hermann Berendt," 677. Berendt's collection of manuscripts was later purchased by Daniel Brinton, who left it to the University of Pennsylvania. See Weeks, *Library*. Here, the manuscript appears as item 1081. Today, the manuscript can be found at the University of Pennsylvania, Berendt-Brinton Linguistic Collection as "Coleccion de platicas doctrinales y sermones en lengua maya por diferentes autores," MS collection 700, items 46 and 47.

70. Berendt, "Colección de platicas," "Sermones en lengua maya," 120.

71. This is not to say, of course, that the Maya were somehow incapable of mastering Latin. Only that the religious texts they produced often reflect an indifference toward accuracy in their Latin translations, which were often spelled phonetically. Most likely, Latin for the colonial Maya was similar to how Latin is for the majority of Christians today: a language not understood yet given reverence and importance for its use in religious contexts and foreign nature.

72. Molina, *Confesionario mayor*, 31r–v.

73. For Augustine and Aquinas, see Seymour, *A Theodicy*, 164–65; Augustine, *City of God*, bk. 13, 250–52, 259; Aquinas, *Summa theologiae*, supp., question 98, art. 9. See also Granada, *Libro de la oración*, 94.

74. Coronel, "Discursos," 201v–2r; and Whalen, "Annotated Translation," 346. For a translation and analysis, see Christensen, *Translated Christianities*, 41–42.

75. I thank Amara Solari for her insights, personal communication, May 18, 2020. For studies examining similar processions in Huejotzingo, see Webster, "Art, Ritual, and Confraternities," 35–39; see also Kirkland-Ives, "Alternate Routes," 266.

76. Matovina, *Latino Catholicism*, 166–70.

77. Aguiló y Fuster, *Recull de eximplis*, 2:260. For more examples, see Tubach, *Index Exemplorum*, 345, no. 4541. In another exemplum, a wrongfully denounced priest is redeemed by all the souls he had saved through requiem masses. Sánchez de Vercial, *Book of Tales*, 199–200, and also 36.

78. Landa described metnal in a Christian-like manner thus making it difficult to arrive at a clear, precontact understanding of the afterlife. Landa, *Relación*, 60. For more discussion on metnal, see Christensen, *Catholicisms*, 42.

79. Redfield and Villa Rojas claim that the maestro cantores "can repeat, in a low, rapid gabble for as much as an hour, Latin and Spanish prayers with little or no repetition." Redfield and Villa Rojas, *Chan Kom*, 73.

80. Christensen, *Teabo Manuscript*, 186–87; Ciudad Real, *Diccionario de motul*, Codex Ind 8, 221r.

81. Redfield and Villa Rojas, *Chan Kom*, 116–17.

82. For more on cold and winds in general, see Redfield and Villa Rojas, *Chan Kom*, 161–68.

83. Christensen, *Teabo Manuscript*, 94–95.

84. *Spes que difert afligit animum.* Prov. 13:12.

85. *O vos omnes qui transitis per viam, atendite et videte si est dolor sicut dolor meus.* This is a responsory, or sung chant, offered during Holy Week from Lam. 1:12; Long and Sawyer, *Bible in Music*, 177. But the full verse assigns responsibility of the torments to God, which is more reflected in the Maya text. The biblical text states that "the Lord afflicted me on the day of his blazing wrath."

86. *Miseremini mei.*

87. The final words of this page are missing.

88. *Beati misericordes, quoniam ipsi misericoriam consequentar.* Matt. 5:7.

89. *Beatus vir, qui intelligit super agenum et pauperem.* Ps. 41:1

90. García Icazbalceta, *Bibliografía mexicana*, 320.

91. García Icazbalceta, *Bibliografía mexicana*, 320. For more, see Dibble, "Sahagun's Appendices," 117–18.

92. For more on the topic, see Burkhart, *Slippery Earth*, 51–56; Cervantes, *Devil*, 47–53.

93. Many works examine the demographic collapse. For a good synthesis, see Alchon, *A Pest*; and Cook, *Born to Die*.

94. Oviedo y Valdés, *Historia general*, 1:105; Cook, *Born to Die*, 63.

95. Lane, *Defending the Conquest*, 147.

96. Gruzinski, *Man-Gods*, chap. 3.

97. For more on Maya medicine and its role in colonial Yucatan, see Gubler and Bolles, *Chilam Balam of Na*; Knowlton, "Filth and Healing,"; and Kashanipour, "World of Cures." For additional information on the Na and its authors, see Suárez Castro, "*Chilam Balam de Na*."

98. Cogolludo, *Historia*, bk. 11, 628.

99. Redfield and Villa Rojas, *Chan Kom*, 198–204.

100. Rosica, "Why."

101. Pew Research Group, "Belief in Hell."

102. Knapp, "No."

Chapter 3. Signs of the Times

Epigraph 1: Bautista, *Sermonario*, 160. Although the work bears the name of Bautista, one of his Nahua aides, Valeriano, commonly is credited with the glosses found throughout.

Epigraph 2: Saint Augustine, *Letters*, 362; Regan, *Advent to Pentecost*, 7.

Epigraph 3: Morris, *Cursor Mundi*, 21, lines 213–16; modified slightly from the Middle English.

1. From Hatfield, "Botticelli's," 98.

2. Hatfield, "Botticelli's," 89–114; Patrick, *Renaissance and Reformation*, 137–38.

3. Cyril of Jerusalem, *Works*, 53; Regan, *Advent to Pentecost*, 6.

4. An excellent overview of the development of Advent is Regan's, *Advent to Pentecost*, chap. 1.

5. Sell, "Friars, Nahuas, and Books," 142. For the production of collections of sermons in the early colonial period, see Sell, "Friars, Nahuas, and Books," Appendix I; and Burkhart, *Holy Wednesday*, 165.

6. The Maya Sermons text resides in Princeton University Library, Department of Rare Books and Special Collections, Garrett-Gates Mesoamerican Manuscripts (C0744), no. 65, Maya Sermons, 17–18; the Teabo Manuscript is located in Brigham Young University, L. Tom Perry Special Collections, MSS 279, box 74, folder 3, Christian doctrine, 33–35. The Chilam Balam of Tusik likewise contains *The Fifteen Signs* and concluding sermons that parallel those in the Teabo Manuscript and Maya Sermons text. It is possible, if not likely, that the Tusik text likewise derived from an Advent sermon.

7. For some examples of Nahuatl texts, see Christensen, "Predictions and Portents," 247–53. The popularity of *The Fifteen Signs* was well entrenched in

Europe. See, for example, the fifteenth-century advent sermons in Powell, *Advent and Nativity*, 72-73.

8. Matt. 24:36.

9. For the *Cursor Mundi*, see Morris's 1984 version. For more on the appearance of the signs in the Americas and their scholarly treatment, see Christensen, *Teabo Manuscript*, 137–72, and "Predictions and Portents," 242–60. The seminal work on the signs themselves remains to be Heist, *Fifteen Signs*.

10. For more on the works that inspired medieval scholars in Spain, see Nepaul-singh, *Towards a History*, 64. For details on the origins of Berceo's poem, see Dutton, "Source," 247–55.

11. According to Erik Alder, *trovar* is related to "troubadour," a lyric poet of the time, who typically composed songs of courtly love. Berceo famously spiritualized this type of poetry and is playing a bit with trovar in the poem. Personal correspondence, April 19, 2021.

12. The poem's signs are listed and analyzed by James W. Marchand in his "Gonzalo," 283–95, from which I derive the Spanish. The English translation was a cooperative endeavor by Travis Meyer, Erik Alder, Valerie Hegstrom, Lin Sherman, and myself.

13. Granada, *Libro de la oración*, 82.

14. For more on the signs and their origins see Heist, *Fifteen Signs*. Recent studies continue to add to the corpora of texts containing *The Fifteen Signs* and thus the origin of the signs themselves remain a topic of study and debate. See Hawk, "Fifteen Signs," 443–57.

15. Musper, *Der Antichrist*. The Apocalypse, in general, was a popular theme of such books. See Bing, "Apocalypse Block-Books," 143–58. For more on woodcuts and block books, see Parshall and Schoch, *European Printmaking*.

16. Heist, *Fifteen Signs*, 203.

17. See Christenson, *Burden*.

18. For examples, see Knowlton, *Creation Myths*; and Christensen, *Teabo Manuscript*, 25–102, 137–72.

19. Roys, *Book*, 106–7, 163–69. For further insights into the impact of European sources on the Books of Chilam Balam, see Bricker and Miram, *Kaua*; Knowlton, *Creation Myths*, chap. 4; and George, "Fuentes europeas."

20. Sullivan, *Unfinished Conversations*, 205–10.

21. See Christensen, *Teabo Manuscript*, 137–72 for more on these textual similarities and differences.

22. *-ob* is the Yucatec plural marker, equivalent to *-s* in English.

23. For more on the ah kinob see Chuchiak, "Pre-Conquest," 135–160; and Caso Barrera, *Caminos*, 109–22.

24. Lizana, *Historia de Yucatán*, 5r.

25. For more on tumen mactzil, see Christensen, *Teabo Manuscript*, 150–53.

26. From *dominica adventus cum veneris filius hominis*. This preface, though not the signs, likewise appears translated in Christensen, *The Teabo Manuscript*, and is reproduced here with permission.

27. The marginal numbering ends with this sign, but I have included them for convenience.
28. Here the line continues on the next page, but I think the author accidentally omits a line indicating the trees from which the blood descends.
29. Sell, "Friars, Nahuas, and Books," 142–86; Burkhart, *Before Guadalupe*, 14–15. Tavárez also includes insightful discussions of Bautista and his *Sermonario* in his "Naming the Trinity," and "Nahua Intellectuals."
30. Bautista, *Sermonario*, prologue.
31. See Sell, "Friars, Nahuas, and Books," 162–63; Burkhart, *Holy Wednesday*, 52–54.
32. See Christensen, *Translated Christianities*, 46–48.
33. Schwaller, "Pre-Hispanic Poetics," 315–32.
34. For more, see Tavárez, "Naming the Trinity," 28–29, and "Nahua Intellectuals," 206–9.
35. Bautista, *Sermonario*, prologue.
36. Bautista, *Sermonario*, aprobación.
37. Bautista included some of the signs, though unlisted, in his earlier 1604 work *Libro de la miseria y breuedad de la vida del hombre* that Tavárez has illustrated to have been drawn from fray Luis de Granada's 1554 *Libro de la oración y meditación*. See Christensen, "Predictions and Portents," 253; and Tavárez, "Dominican Invention," 41. Stephanie Schmidt provides another examination of Bautista's apocalyptic discourse in her "End of the World."
38. Personal communication, May 16, 2016.
39. Variations, of course, exist among the many versions. For details, see Heist, *Fifteen Signs*.
40. Literally, "fifteen lengths from the elbow to the tip of the middle finger," which, after all, is the measurement of a cubit.
41. The *Livre de la vigne nostre seigneur* is located in the Bodleian Library at the University of Oxford, MS Douce 134, ff. 41v–50v
42. Christensen, *Teabo Manuscript*, 144–46, and "Predictions and Portents," 248–50.
43. Fredriksen, "Apocalypse and Redemption," 151. See, for example, Tyconius's commentary on Rev. 6:7–8 in his *Exposition*, 74–77. For more on medieval exegeses on Revelation, see Poole, "Western Apocalypse."
44. Fredriksen, "Tyconius," 27. For an excellent study of Tyconius, see Hoover, *Donatist Church*, chap. 5.
45. Rev. 18:7.
46. Wis. 11:16.
47. Dante Alighieri, *Divine Comedy*, 8, 13.
48. Kempis, *Imitation of Christ*, 44.
49. Granada, *Libro de la oración*, 98. For more on such works and the *devotio*, see Tavárez, "Nahua Intellectuals."
50. Thayer, *Penitence*, 21–23, 40–41.
51. Mathes, *America's First*, 53.

52. That said, the order of the signs varies somewhat between the texts.
53. Herolt, *Sermones discipuli*, 19.
54. Compare, for example, Bautista's citations with those found in Magnus, *Enarrationes*, 23:645–47.
55. Burkhart, *Slippery Earth*, 64. See also Dehouve, *Relatos de pecados*, 191–92, 263–62.
56. Sahagún, *Florentine Codex*, bk. 5, 151–56.
57. Molina, *Confesionario mayor*, 21r.
58. Bautista, *Confessionario*, 21v–28v. See Alcántara Rojas, "El dragon y la mazacóatl."
59. Cárdenas y León, *Breve práctica*.
60. Lockhart, "Language," 65.
61. Sahagún, *Florentine Codex*, bk. 1, 1; bk 3, 5; and Schwaller, *Fifteenth Month*, 17, 70.
62. For more on the visual representation of the eight signs see Magaloni-Kerpel, "Visualizing," 193–221.
63. Sahagún, *Florentine Codex*, bk. 12, 1–3; Magaloni-Kerpel, "Visualizing."
64. For the use of tetzahuitl with the medieval genre of exempla, see Dehouve, *Rudingero el borracho*, 116, 120.
65. Burkhart's *Slippery Earth* remains essential reading in this regard.
66. For more on gluttony in Nahua culture and in religious texts, see Burkhart, *Slippery Earth*, 159–63. For additional insights on this sign, see Schmidt, "End of the World," 130–33.
67. *Xayocomitl*. Such vessels could be used with pulque. Sahagún, *Florentine Codex*, bk. 8, 69; bk. 1, 2nd ed., 49.
68. Leeming, "'Jade Water.'"
69. Truitt, *Sustaining the Divine*, 90–107.
70. For more on this and other metaphorical couplets see Sell, "Classical Age," 22; Edmonson, *Sixteenth-Century Mexico*, 99; and Montes de Oca Vega, *Los difrasismos*.
71. Sahagún, *Florentine Codex*, bk. 3, 2nd ed., 3; Carrasco, *Aztecs*, 73; and Hosler, *Sounds and Colors*, 241.
72. The definitive work on the subject of tlazolli remains Burkhart, *Slippery Earth*. Relevant here is 93–95, 102, and all of chap. 4.
73. Burton, "Repentance."
74. *Sermon II. Sobre el evangelio. De otras muchas y no menos espantosas, y terribles señales, que precederan al espantoso y terrible dia del Iuyzio.*
75. *Et erunt signa in Sole, & Luna, & Stellis: & in terries praessura gentium prae confusion sonitus maris & fluctuum, areseétibus [sic] hominibus prae timore & expectatione, quae superuenient uniuerso orbi.* The passage derives from Luke 21:25–26.
76. From *ilhuica atl* giving the meaning "the water that meets the heavens," or "the ocean." This reflects an early style of Nahuatl. Broda, "Provenience of the Offerings," 223–24.

77. This is in reference to the flood as recorded in Gen. 7:20 which reads, "the crest rising fifteen cubits higher than the submerged mountains."

78. *Mirabiles elationes maris, mirabilis in altis Dominus.* Following the Septuagint numbering, this is from Ps. 92:4. Bonaventure quoted this passage in his *Sermones de diuresis*, vol. 2, sermon 42 (as loosely cited in the gloss).

79. *Ego sum Dominus tuus, qui conturbo mare, intumescunt fluctus eius.* The Latin text differs slightly from that of the Vulgate (Isa. 51:15). It is possible that the author(s) were referencing works other than the Vulgate for their biblical passages.

80. *Cor impij quasi mare feruens, quod quiescere nó potest.* Isa. 57:20. Note that the Nahuatl translation differs from the Latin.

81. *Inter superbos semper sunt iurgia.* Prov. 13:10.

82. *Seruus Dei non quaerit, quomodo alijs appareat maior: sed quomodo inferior omnibus videatur.*

83. *Dedit abissus vocem suam.* Hab. 3:10.

84. *Increpans mare, & exiccans illud, & omnia flumina ad desertum deducens.* Nah. 1:4.

85. *Omnis qui se exaltat humiliabitur.* From Luke 14:11, not Luke 18 as cited in the marginalia.

86. *Superbum sequitur humilitas.* Prov. 29:23.

87. *Vae vobis qui nunc ridetis quia lugebitis.* Luke 6:25.

88. *Beati qui nunc fletis, quia ridebitis.* Luke 6:21.

89. *Presentia gaudia sequuntur paerpetua lamenta.*

90. *Pars illorum erit in stagno ardenti igne, & sulphure.* Rev. 21:8.

91. *Quantum glorificauit se, & in delitijs fuit: tantum date illi tormentum, & luctum.* Rev. 18:7.

92. *Et dabo prodigia in Caelo, & in terra, sanguinem, & ignem, & vaporem fumi. Sol conuertetur in tenebras, & Luna in sanguinem antequám veniat dies Domini magnus & horribilis.* Joel 2:30–31.

93. *Inebriabitur terra sanguine, quia dies vltionis Domini, annus retributionis iudicij Syon.* Isa. 34:7–8.

94. *Vox sanguine fratris tui Abel, clamat ad me de terra.* Gen. 4:10.

95. This is in reference to Cain's murder of Abel as recorded in Gen. 4:10.

96. *In domo patris mei mansiones multae sunt.* John 14:2.

97. *Vae qui conjungitis domum ad domum, & agrum agro copulatis, usq; ad terminum loci.* Isa. 5:8.

98. Two-story homes were commonly associated with the Nahua nobility and rulers: the wealthy. Sousa, *Woman*, 227.

99. *Et terremotus factus est magnus, quails non fuit, ex quo homines fuerunt super terram, talis terremotus, sic magnus.* Rev. 16:18.

100. *Montes sicut cera fluxerunt a facie Domini: a facie Domini omnis terra.* Ps. 96:5.

101. *Omnis vallis implebitur, & omnis mons humiliabitur, & erunt praua in directa & aspera in vias planas. Et videbit omnis caro salutare Dei.* Isa. 40:4.

102. *Filius hominis reddet unicuiq; secundum opera eius.* Matt. 16:27.

103. *Conterriti sunt in Syon peccatores, possedit tremor hypocritas.* Isa. 33:14.

104. *Ecce ego aperiam tumulos vestros, æduca vos de sepulebris vestris.* Ezek. 37:12.
105. *Nihil enim est opertum, quod non reuelabitur: & occultum, quod non scietur.* Matt. 10:26.
106. *Stellae cadent de Caelo, & virtutues Caelorum commevebuntur.* Matt. 24:29.
107. The Spanish gloss says, "it is composed from *tletl* and *tzontli*, hair, because when they burn, they fall like hairs of fire." Bautista, *Sermonario*, 175.
108. From *chicotlaneltocani*, which appears in Quauhtlehuanitzin's *Annals of his Time* for the English "heretic," 305.
109. *Super eum rugierunt leones, & dederunt vocem suam.* Jer. 2:15.
110. Dickerson, "Brexit."

Chapter 4. The Apocalypse of the Body

1. Billboard Staff, "Mayan Apocalypse Playlist"; and Bick, "It's the End."
2. For gas prices, see United States Department of Energy, "Historical Gas Prices."
3. Rev. 21:1; see also 2 Pet. 3:13.
4. Tillard, *Church of Churches*, 87. My thanks to Taylor Halverson for his insight on the Greek (personal communication May 31, 2019).
5. Wooden, "World."
6. Paul IV, *Lumen Gentium*, chap. 7.
7. Catholic Church, *Catechism*, paras. 1043 and 1047.
8. Lynch and Adamo, *Medieval Church*, 16–18; Catholic Church, *Catechism*, paras. 13 and 14.
9. Ashwin-Siejkowski, *Apostles' Creed*, 4.
10. Marthaler, *Creed*, 11–13.
11. Burkhart, "Little Doctrine," 169, 170.
12. Aquinas, *Summa theologiae*, pt. 2 of second pt., question 1, art. 8.
13. Sell, "Friars, Nahuas, and Books," 210–11. The Dominican order's publications in Mixtec and Zapotec received much more prominence than those in Nahuatl. For their work in Oaxaca and Zapotec, see Tavárez, "Reframing Idolatry," 164–81. For a general discussion, see Farriss, *Tongues of Fire*.
14. Díaz Balsera, "Instructing the Nahuas," 106.
15. For a more detailed study of the case see Nesvig, *Ideology and Inquisition*, 156–60. Ideological differences between, and even within, the orders regarding translation affected and diversified evangelization efforts in varied degrees. For a variety of essays examining the topic, see the recent Dedenbach-Salazar Sáenz, *La transmission*; Sparks, *Rewriting*; and Yáñez Rosales, "De 'Dios.'"
16. León, *Camino*, unnumbered introduction. See also Sell, "Nahuatl Theater, Nahua Theater," 68n5.
17. León, *Sermonario*, "dedicatoria."
18. León, *Camino*, prólogo.
19. Sell, "Friars, Nahuas, and Books," 209, 206–11.
20. One example that stands out is his preferential use of the construction *cemanahuac tlalticpac*, "the world, the earth." Although parallel constructions regarding "the world" are not uncommon, this particular one appears sparingly at

best in other works and León's liking for it here and in his sermonary, perhaps, demonstrates a personal preference.

21. Keck, *Angels*, 26–27.
22. Stephanie Schmidt, "Conceiving the End," expounds on the matter; and Bautista, *Sermonario*, 197.
23. For example, see Granada, *Libro de la oración*, 88–89. The topic also appears in various Nahuatl texts including one frequently attributed to the Jesuit Horacio Carochi, titled *De judicio finali* (Bancroft Library M-M 464, "Santoral en Mexicano," *De judicio finali*, 277v).
24. Dimant, "Resurrection," 527.
25. Bynum's *Resurrection* discusses in detail Paul's writings. See, for example, Acts 17:32; 1 Cor. 15:12–58; and 2 Tim. 2:18 (and many others). For the dispute between the Pharisees and Sadducees, see Acts 23:6–10.
26. Augustine, *Expositions*, 514; as revealed by O'Collins, *Saint Augustine*, 2. For more on Augustine and the resurrection, see Van Dyke, "Aquinas's," 269–92.
27. Alkier, "Ways of Presence," 54. See John 20:19, 26; and Luke 24:13–36. Bynum, Resurrection, 4–5, 336, 338–39.
28. See, for example, Matt. 13:43.
29. Prusak, "Bodily Resurrection," 64.
30. Bynum, *Resurrection*, 235, quotation from 367n67; Aquinas, *Summa*, supplement to the third part, questions 82–85. Interestingly, fray Domingo de Vico's sixteenth-century *Theologia Indorum*, composed in K'iche' Maya for Highland Guatemala, contains a section titled, "About the four endowments or gifts in the loosing of our body after the judgment." See Vico in Sparks, *Americas' First Theologies*, 46.
31. For example, the Colegio de Santa Cruz held multiple copies of the *Summa*. Mathes, *America's First*, 51–73.
32. Burkhart, *Slippery Earth*, chap. 4.
33. Sahagún, *Florentine Codex*, bk. 10, 37–38, 55. See also Burkhart, *Slippery Earth*; and Christensen, "Predictions and Portents," 252. For more on the negative descriptors of book 10 regarding sexual deviancy, see Sigal, *Flower*, 177–206.
34. Sahagún, *Florentine Codex*, bk. 6, 105–23.
35. For an excellent example of a study that balances the Christian and Indigenous influences on the *Florentine Codex*, see Sousa, "Flowers and Speech."
36. Bonaventure, *Sunday Sermons*, 222.
37. Granada, *Libro de la oración*, 120.
38. Von Cochem, *Four Last Things*, 130. The Dominican Luis de Granada discusses the stench of the normal human body in his *Libro de la oración*, 78–79. See Tavárez, "Performing," 39–40.
39. Mendieta, *Historia eclesiástica*, 650–51; Oroz, *Oroz Codex*, 271.
40. Thomas Aquinas, *Summa contra gentiles*, bk. 4, chap. 89; Van Dyke, "Aquinas's," 276n19. In Aquinas's day, much like today, debate among theologians existed regarding the resurrected body of the damned. See Aquinas, *Summa theologiae*, question 86, art. 1.

41. Numerous scholars have exposed this in their research, but for a recent example concerning the *Florentine Codex*, see Peterson, "Rhetoric as Acculturation," 176–77.
42. This "insult by omission" is covered well by Sell, "Nahuatl Theater," 56, 69n8.
43. From the Spanish, *articulo*. As noted, italics denote Spanish or Latin terms in the text.
44. Likely from Isa. 2:14.
45. *Surgite morui & venite ad iuditium.* Derived from 1 Thess. 4:16 but attributed to Saint Jerome.
46. From *cemanahuac tlalticpac*.
47. *Venite benedicte Patris mei percipite regnum quod paratum est vobis, &.* From Matt. 25:34.
48. *Ite maledicte Patris mei in ignem eternum, &.* Matt. 25:41.
49. Ciudad Real, *Diccionario de motul*, fol. 410v. The progressive and collaborative compilation of the Motul and the other four colonial dictionaries is expertly discussed in Hanks, *Converting Words*, 118–56.
50. Catholic Church, *Catechism*, para. 234.
51. The phrase appears verbatim as part of a sentence included in the Vienna dictionary under a few entries such as *numzabenil ti ya*, yet Coronel's text is missing the word for agility, *çaçalil*. Bolles, "Vocabularies," 1516.
52. Anunciación, *Sermonario*, 239r.
53. Paredes, *Promptuario*, 68.
54. Burr, *Spiritual Franciscans*, 210–12.
55. Motolinía, *Epistolario*, 187. Turley's, *Franciscan Spirituality*, 99–100, first made me aware of this letter. For more on tensions with the secular clergy, see the same 90–106.
56. For the differences between Franciscans and Dominicans on the matter in Guatemala, see Sparks, *Rewriting Maya Religion*.
57. See Farriss, *Maya Society*, 233–35; Hanks, *Converting Words*, 31–32; and Chuchiak, "Ah Dzib Cahob."
58. Cogolludo, *Historia de Yucatán*, bk. 5, chap. 6.
59. Scholes and Roys, "Fray Diego de Landa"; and Chuchiak, "Pre-Conquest," 135–60.
60. Hanks, *Converting Words*, 78–79, 368–69; Farriss, *Maya Society*, 233–35; and Collins, "Maestros."
61. Aguilar, *Informe*, 153–54; Caso Barrera, *Caminos*, 121; and Chuchiak, "Papal Bulls," 78.
62. Sergio Quezada, *Maya Lords*, 12–14.
63. Hanks discusses the matter in more detail in his *Converting Words*, 163, 294, 326.
64. Bolles and Bolles, *Grammar*, 26.
65. For an example in Nahuatl, see Christensen, *Translated Christianities*, 15–26.
66. Ciudad Real, *Diccionario de motul*, fol. 55r.

67. More and more scholars question the layered structure of the Maya (and Nahua) universe suggesting it to be a European influence. See Nielsen and Reunert, "Dante's Heritage."

68. For more see Knowlton, *Maya Creation Myths*, 57–58.

69. For more on the number thirteen and the Maya calendar, see David Stuart, *Order of Days*, 91–92, 241–45. For the translation of "oxlahun," see Brinton, *Maya Chronicles*, 129–30.

70. *Tha. In carne mea videbo Deum Saluatorem meum.* Job 19:26. The phrase inserted here differs slightly from that of the Vulgate but matches the Roman Breviary. *Breuiarium Romanum*, 63v.

71. From *gloriae*.

72. Here, Coronel employs two terms for baptism, *oc ha ti pol* and *caput çihil*, with literal meanings of "water enters on the head" and "twice born," respectively. Both commonly appear in colonial documents. For more on the philology of the words and their original composition, see Hanks, *Converting Words*, 129–31, 188–89.

73. From *Sanctos. y. Sa[n]ctasobe.*

74. This subheading derives from the Spanish and Latin, *Como à de venir a juzgar a los viuos, y muertos. Tha. Iudicauit populos in equitate.* The latter derives from Ps. 95:10.

75. Thus, because our works are always with us, they speak against us.

76. *Articulos de la Fe.*

77. *Eva[n]gelio.*

78. *Qui crediderit & baptizitus fuerit. &c.* Mark 16:16.

79. Townshend, "Cemetery."

80. Farrow, "Why Christians Believe."

81. "Resurrection."

82. Farrow, "Why Christians Believe."

Chapter 5. Heaven, but Mostly Hell

Epigraph 1: Virgil, *Aeneid*, 169.
Epigraph 2: Reese, "Commentary."
Epigraph 3: Twain, *Mark Twain's Notebooks*, 538.

1. Carroll, *Alice's Adventures*, 75–76.

2. Ellens, "Afterlife and Underworld," 1.

3. Rituals performed by the living and the life led on earth could influence somewhat one's condition in Sheol. See McDannell and Lang, *Heaven*, 3–6. For Hades as a neutral location, see Bernstein, *Formation of Hell*, chap. 1.

4. Ellens, "Heaven," 83–102, quotation from 85; and Helsel, "Hades, Hell, and Sheol," 104–9; Ellens, "Afterlife and Underworld"; and Bernstein *Formation of Hell*. All offer use useful overviews and opinions on the development of hell. The biblical passage comes from Luke 16:23.

5. Helsel, "Hades, Hell, and Sheol," 103–20; and Bernstein, *Formation of Hell*, 292–333. For texts representing stages in the development of hell, see Bruce, *Penguin Book*.

6. See Augustine, *City of God*, bk. 21; and Bernstein, *Formation of Hell*, 1.
7. McDannell and Lang, *Heaven*, 22.
8. Von Ehrenkrook, "Afterlife in Philo," 99.
9. McDannell and Lang, *Heaven*, 23–46.
10. Farriss, *Tongues of Fire*, 16.
11. Sahagún, *Coloquios*, 168–75; and Bremer, "Sahagún Dialogues," 21. For more on Sahagún and his writings see Schwaller, *Sahagún at 500*. For Guatemala, fray Domingo de Vico produced his sixteenth-century *Theologia Indorum* in K'iche' Maya. The second part of this work discusses the Final Judgment. Vico in Sparks, *Americas' First Theologies*, 46.
12. For the use of images and signs among early friars, see Farriss, *Tongues of Fire*, 12–26.
13. Pérez de Ribas, *History*, 371.
14. Burkhart, *Aztecs on Stage*, 62–63, 67–78. For more details on the play itself, see Mosquera, "Nahuatl Catechistic Drama," 71–78.
15. Schuessler, *Foundational Arts*, 131–33.
16. Burkhart, *Aztecs on Stage*, 64, 76.
17. Schuessler, *Foundational Arts*, 124–58. Ecclesiastics in the Andes likewise used such visual mediums to convey the horrors that await the wicked. See Cohen-Suarez, *Heaven*.
18. For some examples, see Edgerton, *Theaters of Conversion*, 53, 196–205; and Jackson, *Conflict and Conversion*, 85–144.
19. Many examples exist, but for examples of violence against women, see Sousa, *Woman*.
20. For an excellent article discussing the development of *ilhuicatl*, the chosen Nahuatl word for "heaven," see Schwaller, "Ilhuica," 391–412.
21. Seymour, *Theodicy*, 164–72. Alonso Rodriguez was a Jesuit whose extremely popular, early seventeenth-century *Exercicio de perfección y virtudes cristianas* mentions the importance of imagining the torments of hell so as to withstand temptation (O'Malley, *Saints or Devils*, 131–35). Rodriguez, *Exercicio*, 243. For an examination of ecclesiastics, including Paredes, employing fear in their sermons, see Chinchilla Pawling, "Predicación y miedo," which also includes a Spanish translation of an excerpt from Paredes's sermon.
22. Pinamonti and his companion, Paolo Segneri, were famed missionaries in the Italian countryside. For more on Pinamonti and Segneri, see Bireley, *Refashioning of Catholicism*, 98–100; Cheng, "James Joyce," 172–73; and Doherty, "Hell Opened to Christians."
23. Granada, *Libro de la oración*, 97; Segneri, *Infierno abierto*, 70.
24. Kempis, *Imitation of Christ*, 44.
25. The pioneering work on this manuscript and its connections to the *devotio moderna* and other texts remains Tavárez, "Nahua Intellectuals."
26. Granada, *Libro de le oración*, 95.
27. Segneri, *Infierno abierto*, 46.
28. Granada, *Libro de le oración*, 93.
29. Segneri, *Infierno abierto*, 32.

30. Vitry, *Exempla*, 236–37.
31. For yet another example of the impact of Old World discourses on that of the New, see David Tavárez, "Aristotelian Politics."
32. For an excellent study on caves in Mesoamerican worldviews and rituals, see Brady and Prufer, *Maw.*
33. Sahagún, *Florentine Codex*, bk. 3, 2nd ed., 37n5. It also appears in religious play discussed in Sell and Burkhart, *Nahua Christianity*, 380.
34. Granada, *Libro de la oración*, 99.
35. *Propterea vos non auditis: quia ex Deo non estis.* John 8:47.
36. *Quis poterit habitare de vobis cum igne devorante? Quis habitabit ex vobis cum ardoribus sempiternis?* Isa. 33:14.
37. *Descendant in Infernum viventes; ne descendant morientes.*
38. From *Quauhtla tlamacehuani*: literally, "one who merits things in the wild or woods."
39. *Quisquis mortem, que porta est ad vitae, aut mortis aeternitatem, serio cogitaverit, in aeternum non peccabit, nec peribit.*
40. *Descendant in Infernum viventes.* Ps. 54:16.
41. *Ne descendant morientes.*
42. *Qui paratus est Diabolo, & Angelis ejus.* Matt. 25:41.
43. *Projectus sum a facie oculorum tuorum.* Ps. 30:23.
44. *Per quae peccat quis, per haec et torquetur.* Wisd. of Sol. 11:17.
45. *Venient super eum horribiles.* Job 20:25.
46. From *ahuilnenque*, literally "those who live in pleasure."
47. Following this is the Spanish sentence, *Aqui se hace, y se repite el Acto de Contricion* (here is made and repeated the Act of Contrition).
48. Christensen, "The Tales"; and Christensen, *Catholicisms*, 195–212.
49. For more on Aquino, see Leeming's dissertation, "Aztec Antichrist."
50. Milton, *Paradise Lost*, bk. 1, lines 61–65.
51. See Boone, "Incarnations," i–iv, 1–107; and Cervantes, *Devil.*
52. Leeming likewise makes this observation in his "Aztec Antichrist," 272.
53. Dante Alighieri, *Divine Comedy*, 8–9.
54. Townsend, *Here in This Year*, 125, see also 95, 145, 149, 165, 173, 175.
55. For a lengthier discussion see the various works in Brady and Prufer, *Maw.*
56. Aquino, *Sermones*, 49r–51r. Ben Leeming shared his images, thoughts, and his tentative transcription and translation of the text up to a part of fol. 49v, and I thank him for his generosity. That said, the translation here reflects my own work with the text.
57. See Job 8:9; Ps. 144:4; 1 Chron. 29:15; Eccles. 6:12; Kempis, *Imitation of Christ*, 42; and Granada, *Libro de la oración*, 96.
58. For more on disease among the Maya, see Bricker and Hill, "Climatic Signatures"; and Kashanipour, "World of Cures."
59. For more on the dictionaries, see Hanks, *Converting Words*, 118–56. The reference for the San Francisco dictionary came from Bolles, "Vocabularies," 2432; for the Motul, see Ciudad Real, *Diccionario de motul*, codex ind. 8, vol.1, fol. 54v; for the Morley Manuscript, see Whalen, "Annotated Translation."

60. Bolles, "Vocabularies," 1510; Nielsen and Reunert, "Dante's Heritage," 399–413; and, more recently, Nielsen and Reunert, "Colliding Universes," 31–69.

61. Gen. 41.

62. The story of Joseph appears in a few Maya texts: the Morley Manuscript provides the most detailed account, which relates the story of Joseph and Potiphar's wife, but it likewise appears in Coronel's *Discursos*. See Gen. 39; and Whalen, "Annotated Translation." For more on plagues of locusts and famines among the prognostications of the Maya, see García Quintanilla, "*Saak'*."

63. From the Spanish, *Quan grandes son las penas del infierno.*

64. *Tha. Dolores inferni circumdederunt me.* Ps. 17:6.

65. Also could be translated as "he who endures suffering."

66. *Como seran premiados los Buenos y castigados los malos.*

67. *Tha. Qui bene exerunt ibunt in vitam eternum &c.* John 5.

68. From the Latin *Erranimus & lixati sumus.* Likely Prov. 14:22.

69. From the Latin *Erranimus &c.*

70. Vitry, *Exempla,* 236–37. Saak notes a similar exemplum located in Jordan of Saxony's fourteenth-century *Liber vitasfratrum.* Saak, *Creating Augustine,* 207.

71. From the Latin *Recordare.*

72. From the Spanish, *La deferencia que ay de tormentos, en el infierno.*

73. From the Latin, *Dissipat sunt ossa nostra secus infernum.*

74. From *ah pochilob u than Dios,* which also refers to blasphemers.

75. From the Spanish, *Como son sin fin las penas del infierno.*

76. From the Latin, *Quia in inferno, nulla est redemptio.*

77. One *tostón* equals four reales or half a peso.

78. The following translation and some of the commentary can also be found in my full examination in Christensen, *Teabo Manuscript.*

79. Edmonson, *Heaven Born Merida,* 249–52; and Grupo Dzíbil, *Chilam Balam,* 31–34. The Tusik, however, only contains the part of the sermon where the righteous go to heaven and the wicked to hell.

80. Acts 1:18.

81. Dante Alighieri, *Divine Comedy,* 32–33, 60–61; and Lansing, *Dante Encyclopedia,* 573–75, 781–82.

82. Granada, *Libro de la oración,* 96–97.

83. For a more detailed discussion on some of these Maya contributions, see Christensen, *Teabo Manuscript,* 108–13.

84. Kelly, "Hell with Purgatory," 126.

85. Sousa, *Woman,* 23; Díaz Balsera, *Guardians of Idolatry,* 36–52.

86. Knowlton and Vail, "Hybrid Cosmologies," 711; Stuart, *Order of Days,* 78–87; and Restall, *Maya World,* 189–99.

87. From *aa qua perducat aD uitame ternam* which should read *ad quam nos perducat ad uitam aeternam.*

88. Pew Research Group, "Belief in Heaven"; and Pew Research Group, "Belief in Hell."

89. Hudson, *Heaven and Hell,* 173.

90. Clark, "Saw."

Conclusion

Epigraph 1: David Mitchell, *Cloud Atlas*, 453.
Epigraph 2: Chomsky, *Failed States*, 14.

1. For a few examples, see Morris, "Claire's"; and Morris, "Country's Biggest Mall."
2. Motolinía, *Historia*, 18.
3. Motolinía, *Historia*, 300n1.3; and Lomnitz, *Death and the Idea of Mexico*, 70–71.
4. Motolinía, *Historia*, 29.
5. Burkhart, *Aztecs on Stage*, 16.
6. Bagge, "Christianizing Kingdoms," 117, 127.
7. Restall and Solari, *Maya*, 88.
8. Don, *Bonfires of Culture*, 107; Poole, *Lady of Guadalupe*, 24, 106–33; and Jeanette Favrot Peterson, "Creating the Virgin," 592.
9. Townsend, *Here in This Year*, 123, 139, 145.
10. Mendieta, *Historia eclesiástica*, 456.
11. Melton-Villanueva, *Aztecs at Independence*, 178–82.
12. Robert Patch, *Maya Revolt*, 146.
13. Edmonson, *Chumayel*, 265; Bricker, *Indian Christ*, 28. See also Knowlton, *Creation Myths*, 55–81; Restall and Solari, 2012, 101–7.
14. See Bricker, *Indian Christ*, 156–59, and chap. 8.
15. For examples from the town of Ixil, see Christensen and Restall, *Return to Ixil*.
16. McGinn, *Visions*, 11. For an interesting read on the lasting effects of the Apocalypse, see Aridjis, *Apocalipsis con figuras*.
17. Pew Research, "Global Christianity."
18. Offering a personal and intimate experience with the divine, Pentecostal denominations have won the hearts of many Latin Americans over the decades comprising 73 percent of Protestants as of 2006. Pew Research Group, "Overview: Pentecostalism."
19. Goodman, *Maya Apocalypse*, xv, 2, 515, 522. Goodman's work is an insightful narrative of the impact of Pentecostalism in the lives of the Yucatec Maya, particularly women.

Bibliography

Aberth, John. *From the Brink of the Apocalypse: Confronting Famine, War, Plague, and Death in the Later Middle Ages*. New York: Routledge, 2001.

Acuña, René. "Escritos Mayas inéditos y publicados hasta 1578: Testimonio del obispo Diego de Landa." *Estudios de cultura maya* 21 (2001): 165–79.

Adams, Eleanor B. "A Bio-Bibliography of Franciscan Authors in Colonial Central America." *Americas* 8, no. 4 (1952): 431–73.

Adams, Gwenfair Walters. *Visions in Late Medieval England: Lay Spirituality and Sacred Glimpses of the Hidden Worlds of Faith*. Leiden, Netherlands: Brill, 2007.

Aguiló y Fuster, Marian. *Recull de eximplis e miracles gestes e faules e altres ligendes ordenades per A.B.C.* 2 vols. Barcelona: Llibreria d'alvar verdaguer, 1881.

Andrews, Frances. "The Influence of Joachim in the 13th Century." In *A Companion to Joachim of Fiore*, edited by Matthias Riedl, 190–266. Leiden, Netherlands: Brill, 2018.

Alcántara Rojas, Berenice. "El dragón y la *mazacóatl*: Criaturas del infierno en un *exemplum* en Náhuatl de fray Ioan Baptista." *Estudios de cultura Náhuatl* 36 (2005): 383–422.

Alchon, Suzanne. *A Pest in the Land: New World Epidemics in Global Perspective*. Albuquerque: University of New Mexico Press, 2003.

Alkier, Stefan. "Ways of Presence and Modes of Absence in the Gospel of Luke— Or: How Scripture Works." In *The Presence and Absence of God*, edited by Ingolf U. Dalferth, 41–55. Tübingen, Germany: Mohr Siebeck, 2009.

Anunciación, Juan de la. *Sermonario en lengua mexicana*. Mexico City: Antonio Ricardo, 1577.

Anunciación, Domingo de la. *Doctrina Xpiana breue y co[m]pendiosa*. Mexico City: Pedro Ocharte, 1565.

Aquinas, Thomas. *Of God and His Creatures: An Annotated Translation (with some Abridgement) of the* Summa Contra Gentiles *of Saint Thomas Aquinas.* Translated by Joseph Rickaby, S.J. London: Burns and Oates, 1905.

———. *Summa theologiae.* Translated by Father Laurence Shapcote. 2nd ed. 2 vols. Chicago: Encyclopedia Britannica, 1990.

Aquino, Fabián de. Sermones y miscelánea de devoción. n.s. 3/1, Hispanic Society of America, New York.

Aridjis, Homero. *Apocalipsis con figuras: El hombre milenario.* Mexico City: Taurus, 1997.

———. *Arte y mística del barroco. Catálogo de exposición, marzo-junio 1994.* Mexico City: Universidad Autonoma de Mexico, and Consejo Nacional para la Cultura y las Artes, 1994.

———. *El senor de los últimos días: Visiones del ano mil.* Barcelona: Edhasa, 1994.

Ashwin-Siejkowski, Piotr. *The Apostles' Creed: The Apostles' Creed and its Early Christian Context.* London: T and T Clark, 2009.

Augustine of Hippo, Saint. *The City of God.* Edited with an introduction by Vernon J. Bourke. New York: Image Books, 2014.

———. *Expositions of the Psalms 99–120,* pt. 3, vol. 19. Edited by Boniface Ramsey. Translated by Maria Boulding. Hyde Park, New York: New City, 2003.

———. *Letters: Volume IV (165–203).* Translated by Sister Wilfrid Parsons. The Fathers of the Church: A New Translation 30. Washington, DC: Catholic University of America Press, 1981.

———. "A Treatise on the Merits and Remission of Sins, and on the Baptism of Infants." In *Augustine: Anti-Pelagian Writings,* vol. 5 of *A Select Library of the Christian Church: Nicene and Post-Nicene Fathers,* edited by Philip Schaff, 15-78. Translated by Peter Holmes, Robert Ernest Wallis, and Benjamin B. Warfield. 1887. Reprint. Peabody, MA: Hendrickson, 1995.

Backus, Irene. "The Church Fathers and the Canonicity of the Apocalypse in the Sixteenth Century: Erasmus, Frans Titelmans, and Theodore Beza." *Sixteenth Century Journal* 29, no. 3 (1998): 651–66.

Bagge, Sverre. "Christianizing Kingdoms." In *The Oxford Handbook of Medieval Christianity,* edited by John H. Arnold, 114–31. Oxford: Oxford University Press, 2014.

Balch, Robert, and David Taylor. "Making Sense of Heaven's Gate Suicides." In *Cults, Religion, and Violence,* edited by David G. Bromley and J. Gordon Melton, 209–28. Cambridge: Cambridge University Press, 2002.

Bandelier, A. F. "Juan Coronel." In *Catholic Encyclopedia,* edited by Charles G. Herbermann, Edward A. Pace, Conde B. Pallen, Thomas J. Shahan, and John J. Wynne, vol. 4, 386. New York: Robert Appleton, 1908.

Bassett, Molly H. *The Fate of Earthly Things: Aztec Gods and God-Bodies.* Austin: University of Texas Press, 2015.

Baudot, Georges. *Utopia and History in Mexico: The First Chroniclers of Mexican Civilization (1520–1569).* Translated by Bernard R. Ortiz de Montellano and Thelma Ortiz de Montellano. Niwot, CO: University Press of Colorado, 1995.

Bautista Viseo, Juan. *Confessionario en lengua mexicana y castellana*. Mexico City: Casa de Melchior Ocharte, 1599.

———. *Libro de la miseria, y breuedad de la vida del hombre: y de sus quatro postrimerias, en lengua mexicana*. Mexico City: Diego López Dávalos, 1604.

———. *Sermonario en lengua mexicano*. Mexico City: Diego López Dávalos, 1606.

Bellitto, Christopher M. *The General Councils: A History of the Twenty-One Church Councils from Nicaea to Vatican II*. New York: Paulist, 2002.

Beltrán de Santa Rosa María, Pedro. *Novena de christo crucificado con otro oraciones en lengua maya*. Mexico City: don Francisco de Xavier Sánchez, 1740.

Berendt, Carl Hermann. Coleccion de platicas, doctrinales y sermones en lengua maya por diferentes autores. Berendt-Brinton Linguistic Collection, MS Collection 700, items 46 and 47. University of Pennsylvania.

Berlioz, Jacques. "Infernal Visions and Border Conflicts: Two Tales from the Fifteenth-Century *Recull de eximplis e miracles*." Translated by Diana Conchado. In *Telling Tales: Medieval Narratives and the Folk Tradition*, edited by Francesca Canadé Sautman, Diana Conchado, and Giuseppe Carlo Di Scipio, 101–19. New York: St. Martin's, 1998.

Bireley, Robert. *The Refashioning of Catholicism, 1450–1700: A Reassessment of the Counter Reformation*. New York: St. Martin's, 1999.

Bernstein, Alan E. *The Formation of Hell: Death and Retribution in the Ancient and Early Christian Worlds*. Ithaca, NY: Cornell University Press, 1993.

Bick, Emily. "It's the End of the World as We Know It (And I Feel Fine)—R.E.M.'s 1987 song is suddenly popular again." *Financial Times*, March 29, 2020. https://ig.ft.com/life-of-a-song/end-of-the-world.html.

Billboard Staff. "Mayan Apocalypse Playlist: 15 Doomsday Songs for 12/21." *Billboard*, December 20, 2012. https://www.billboard.com/articles/list/1481281/mayan-apocalypse-playlist-15-doomsday-songs-for-1221.

Bing, Gertrud. "The Apocalypse Block-Books and their Manuscript Models." *Journal of the Warburg and Courtauld Institutes* 5 (1942): 143–58.

Bolles, David. "Combined Mayan-Spanish and Spanish-Mayan Vocabularies." 2012. http://www.famsi.org/research/bolles/CombinedVocabularies.pdf

Bolles, David, and Alejandra Bolles. *A Grammar of the Yucatecan Mayan Language*. Lancaster: Labyrinthos, 2001.

Bonaventure. *The Sunday Sermons of St. Bonaventure*. Translated by Timothy Johnson. Bonaventure Texts in Translation Series 12. St. Bonaventure, NY: Franciscan Institute Publications, 2008.

Boone, Elizabeth. "Incarnations of the Aztec Supernatural: The Image of Huitzilopochtli in Mexico and Europe." *Transactions of the American Philosophical Society* 79, no. 2 (1989).

Boruchoff, David A. "New Spain, New England, and the New Jerusalem: The 'Translation' of Empire, Faith, and Learning (*translatio imperii, fidei ac scientiae*) in the Colonial Missionary Project." *Early American Literature* 43, no. 1 (2008): 5–34.

Brady, James E., and Keith M. Prufer, eds. *In the Maw of the Earth Monster: Mesoamerican Ritual Cave Use*. Austin: University of Texas Press, 2005.

Bremer, Thomas S. "Reading the Sahagún Dialogues." In *Sahagún at 500: Essays on the Quincentenary of the Birth of Fr. Bernardino de Sahagún*, edited by John F. Schwaller, 11–29. Berkeley: Academy of American Franciscan History, 2003.

Bricker, Victoria Reifler. *The Indian Christ, the Indian King: The Historical Substrate of Maya Myth and Ritual*. Austin: University of Texas Press, 1981.

Bricker, Victoria R., and Helga-Maria Miram, eds. and trans. *An Encounter of Two Worlds: The Book of Chilam Balam of Kaua*. New Orleans: Middle American Research Institute, Tulane University, 2002.

Bricker, Victoria R., and Rebecca E. Hill. "Climatic Signatures in Yucatecan Wills and Death Records." *Ethnohistory* 56, no. 2 (Spring 2009): 227–68.

Brinton, Daniel G. *The Maya Chronicles*. Philadelphia: D.G. Brinton, 1882.

Broda, Johanna. "The Provenience of the Offerings: Tribute and *Cosmovisión*." In *The Aztec Templo Mayor: A Symposium at Dumbarton Oaks 8th and 9th October 1983*, edited by Elizabeth Hill Boone, 211–56. Washington, DC: Dumbarton Oaks, 1987.

Brown, Andrew. *Church and Society in England, 1000–1500*. New York: Palgrave Macmillan, 2003.

Bruce, Scott G., ed. *The Penguin Book of Hell*. New York: Penguin, 2018.

Burkhart, Louise M. *Aztecs on Stage: Religious Theater in Colonial Mexico*. Norman: University of Oklahoma Press, 2011.

———. *Before Guadalupe: The Virgin Mary in Early Colonial Nahuatl Literature*. Austin: University of Texas Press, 2001.

———. "Death and the Colonial Nahua." In *Death and Life in Colonial Nahua Mexico*, edited by Barry D. Sell and Louise Burkhart, 29–54. Vol. 1 of *Nahuatl Theater*. Norman: University of Oklahoma Press, 2004.

———. *Holy Wednesday: A Nahua Drama from Early Colonial Mexico*. Philadelphia: University of Pennsylvania Press, 1996.

———. "The 'Little Doctrine' and Indigenous Catechesis in New Spain." *Hispanic American Historical Review* 94, no. 2 (2014): 167–206.

———. *The Slippery Earth: Nahua-Christian Moral Dialogue in Sixteenth-Century Mexico*. Tucson: University of Arizona Press, 1989.

———. "The Voyage of Saint Amaro: A Spanish Legend in Nahuatl Literature." *Colonial Latin American Review* 4, no. 1 (1995): 29–57.

Burr, David. "Mendicant Readings of the Apocalypse." In *The Apocalypse in the Middle Ages*, edited by Richard Kenneth Emmerson and Bernard McGinn, 89–102. Ithaca, NY: Cornell University Press, 1992.

———. *The Spiritual Franciscans: From Protest to Persecution in the Century After Saint Francis*. University Park: Pennsylvania State University Press, 2001.

Burton, Theodor M. "The Meaning of Repentance." Speech given at Brigham Young University, Provo, UT, March 26, 1985.

Bynum, Caroline Walker. *The Resurrection of the Body in Western Christianity, 200–1336*. New York: Columbia University Press, 2017.

Carrasco, Davíd. *The Aztecs: A Very Short Introduction*. New York: Oxford University Press, 2012.

Carreño, Alberto Maria. *Don fray Juan de Zumárraga, primer obispo y arçobispo de Mexico: Documentos ineditos*. Mexico City: José Porrúa e hijos, 1941.

Carrillo Cázares, Alberto, trans., ed. *Manuscritos del concilio tercero provincial mexicano (1585)*. 4 vols. Zamora, Michoacán: El Colegio de Michoacán, 2006–9.

Carroll, Lewis. *Alice's Adventures in Wonderland*. London: William-Heinemann; New York: Doubleday, 1907.

Caso Barrera, Laura. *Caminos en la selva: Migración, comercio y resistencia. Mayas yucatecos e itzaes, siglos XVII-XIX*. Mexico City: Colegio de México, Fondo de Cultura Económica, 2002.

———. *Chilam Balam de Ixil: Facsimilar y estudio de un libro Maya inédito*. Mexico City: Artes de México y del Mundo, 2011.

Castro, Américo. *Aspectos del vivir hispánico: Espiritualismo, mesianismo y actitud personal en los siglos xv al xvi*. Santiago, Chile: Cruz del Sur, 1949.

Catholic Church. *Catechism of the Catholic Church: Revised in Accordance with the Official Latin Text Promulgated by Pope John Paul II*. 2nd ed. Vatican City: Libreria Editrice Vaticana, 2019.

Cecil, Leslie G., and Timothy W. Pugh. *Maya Worldviews at Conquest*. Boulder: University Press of Colorado, 2009.

Cervantes, Fernando. *The Devil in the New World: The Impact of Diabolism in New Spain*. New Haven, CT: Yale University Press, 1994.

———. "Devils Conquering and Conquered: Changing Visions of Hell in Spanish America." In *Hell and its Afterlife: Historical and Contemporary Perspectives*, edited by Isabel Moriera and Margaret Toscano, 103–19. Surrey: Ashgate, 2010.

Cheng, Vincent J. "James Joyce and the (Modernist) Hellmouth." In *Hell and its Afterlife: Historical and Contemporary Perspectives*, edited by Isabel Moriera and Margaret Toscano, 165–74. Surrey: Ashgate, 2010.

Chimalpahin Quauhtlehuanitzin, Domingo de San Antón Muñón. *Annals of His Time: Don Domingo de San Antón Muñón Chimalpahin Quauhtlehuanitzin*. Edited and translated by James Lockhart, Susan Schroeder, and Doris Namala. Stanford: Stanford University Press, 2006.

———. *Codex Chimalpahin*. Edited and translated by Arthur J. O. Anderson and Susan Schroeder. 2 vols. Norman: University of Oklahoma Press, 1997.

Chinchilla Pawling, Perla. "Predicación y miedo." In *Una historia de los usos del miedo*, edited by Pilar Gonzalbo Aizpuru, Anne Staples, and Valentina Torres Septién, 203–21. Mexico City: El Colegio de México, 2009.

Chomsky, Noam. *Failed States: The Abuse of Power and the Assault on Democracy*. New York: Owl Books, 2006.

Christensen, Mark Z. "Missionizing Mexico: Ecclesiastics, Natives, and the Spread of Christianity." In *A Companion to Early Modern Catholic Global Missions*, edited by Ronnie Po-Chia Hsia, 17–40. Leiden, Netherlands: Brill, 2018.

———. *Nahua and Maya Catholicisms: Texts and Religion in Colonial Central Mexico and Yucatan*. Stanford: Stanford University Press and the Academy of American Franciscan History Press, 2013.

———. "Predictions and Portents of Doomsday in European, Nahuatl, and Maya Texts." In *Words and Worlds Turned Around: Indigenous Christianities in Colonial*

Latin America, edited by David Tavárez, 242–64. Boulder: University Press of Colorado, 2017.

———. "The Tales of Two Cultures: Ecclesiastical Texts and Nahua and Maya Catholicisms." *Americas* 66, no. 3 (2010): 353–77.

———. *The Teabo Manuscript: Maya Christian Copybooks, Chilam Balams, and Native Text Production in Yucatan*. Austin: University of Texas Press, 2016.

———. *Translated Christianities: Nahuatl and Maya Religious Texts*. University Park: Pennsylvania State University Press, 2014.

Christensen, Mark Z., and Matthew Restall. *Return to Ixil: Maya Society in an Eighteenth-Century Yucatec Town*. Louisville: University Press of Colorado, 2019.

Christenson, Allen J. *The Burden of the Ancients: Maya Ceremonies of World Renewal from the Pre-Columbian Period to the Present*. Austin: University of Texas Press, 2016.

———. *Popol Vuh: The Sacred Book of the Maya*. Norman: University of Oklahoma Press, 2007.

Chuchiak, John F., IV. "'*Ah Dzib Cahob yetel lay u katlilob lae*': Maya Scribes, Colonial Literacy, and Maya Petitionary Forms in Colonial Yucatán." In *Text and Context: Yucatec Maya Literature in a Diachronic Perspective*, edited by Antje Gunsenheimer, Tsubasa Okoshi Harada, and John F. Chuchiak, 159–84. Aachen: Bonner Amerikanistische Studien, 2009.

———. "*In Servitio Dei:* Fray Diego de Landa, the Franciscan Order, and the Return of Extirpation of Idolatry in the Colonial Diocese of Yucatán, 1573–1579." *Americas* 61, no. 4 (2005): 611–46.

———. "Papal Bulls, Extirpators, and the Madrid Codex: The Content and Probable Provenience of the M. 56 Patch." In *The Madrid Codex: New Approaches to Understanding an Ancient Maya Manuscript*, edited by Gabrielle Vail and Anthony Aveni, 57–88. Boulder: University Press of Colorado, 2009.

———. "Pre-Conquest *Ah Kinob* in a Colonial World: The Extirpation of Idolatry and the Survival of the Priesthood in Colonial Yucatán, 1563–1697." In *Maya Survivalism*, edited by Ueli Hostettler and Matthew Restall, 135–60. Markt Schwaben, Germany: Verlag Anton Saurwein, 2001.

———. "Secrets behind the Screen: Solicitantes in the Colonial Diocese of Yucatan and the Yucatec Maya, 1570–1785." In *Religion in New Spain*, edited by Susan Schroder and Stafford Poole, 83–109. Albuquerque: University of New Mexico Press, 2007.

———. "Sin, Shame, and Sexuality: Franciscan Obsessions and Maya Humor in the *Calepino de Motul* Dictionary, 1573–1615." In *Words and Worlds Turned Around: Indigenous Christianities in Colonial Latin America*, edited by David Tavárez, 195–219. Boulder: University Press of Colorado, 2017.

Ciudad Real, Antonio de. *Diccionario de motul, maya español*. John Carter Brown Library, Codex Ind. 8, vol. 1. Brown Digital Repository. Brown University Library.

Clark, Travis. "How 'Saw' Became a $1 Billion Horror Franchise After Nearly Going Straight-to-DVD, and What the Producers Have Planned for the Future. *Insider*. May 28, 2021. https://www.businessinsider.com/inside-saw-franchises-path-to-1-billion-at-box-office-2021-5.

Clendinnen, Inga. *Ambivalent Conquests: Maya and Spaniard in Yucatan, 1517–1570*. New York: Cambridge University Press, 1987.

———. *Aztecs: An Interpretation*. Cambridge: Cambridge University Press, 2014.

Cline, S. L. "Revisionist Conquest History: Sahagun's Revised Book XII." In *The Work of Bernardino de Sahagún: Pioneer Ethnographer of Sixteenth–Century Aztec Mexico*, edited by J. Jorge Klor de Alva, H. B. Nicholson, and Eloise Quiñones Keber, 93–106. Austin: University of Texas Press, 1988.

Cogolludo, Diego López de. *Historia de Yucatán*. Madrid: J. García Infanzón, 1688.

Cohen-Suarez, Ananda. *Heaven, Hell, and Everything in Between: Murals of the Colonial Andes*. Austin: University of Texas Press, 2016.

Colección de documentos inéditos relativos al descubrimiento, conquista, y organización de las antiguas posesiones españolas en América y Oceanía. Vol. 13. Madrid: José María Perez, 1870.

Collins, Anne C. "The Maestros Cantores in Yucatán." In *Anthropology and History in Yucatán*, edited by Grant D. Jones, 233–47. Austin: University of Texas Press, 1977.

Cook, Noble David. *Born to Die: Disease and New World Conquest, 1492–1650*. Cambridge: Cambridge University Press, 1998.

Coronel, Juan. *Discursos predicables, con otras diuersas materias espirituales, con la doctrina xpna, y los articulos de la fé*. Transcribed by David Bolles. Created July 8, 2009. http://www.famsi.org/reports/96072/corodoctorg.pdf.

Corvera Poiré, Marcela. "The Discalced Franciscans in Mexico: Similarities and Differences vis–à–vis the Observant Franciscans in Mexico and the Discalced in the Philippines." In *Francis in the Americas: Essays on the Franciscan Family in North and South America*, edited by John Frederick Schwaller, 27–44. Berkeley: Academy of American Franciscan History, 2005.

Covey, R. Alan. *Inca Apocalypse: The Spanish Conquest and the Transformation of the Andean World*. New York: Oxford University Press, 2020.

Cunningham, Andrew, and Ole Peter Grell. *The Four Horsemen of the Apocalypse: Religion, War, Famine and Death in Reformation Europe*. Cambridge: Cambridge University Press, 2000.

Curcio-Nagy, Linda A. "Faith and Morals in Colonial Mexico." In *The Oxford History of Mexico*, edited by William H. Beezley and Michael C. Meyer, 143–74. New York: Oxford University Press, 2010.

Cyril of Jerusalem. *The Works of Saint Cyril of Jerusalem*. Vol. 2. Translated by Leo P. McCauley, S. J., and Anthony A. Stephenson. The Fathers of the Church: A New Translation 64. Washington, DC: Catholic University of America Press, 1970.

Daniel, E. Randolph. "Joachim of Fiore: Patterns of History in the Apocalypse." In *The Apocalypse in the Middle Ages*, edited by Richard K. Emmerson and Bernard McGinn, 72–88. Ithaca, NY: Cornell University Press, 1992.

Dante Alighieri. *The Divine Comedy: The Inferno, Purgatorio, and Paradiso*. Translated by Lawrence Grant White. New York: Pantheon Books, 1948.

Davis, Mark Evan. "The Evangelical Prophecies over Jerusalem Have Been Fulfilled: Joachim of Fiore, the Jews, Fray Diego de Landa and the Maya." *Journal of Medieval Iberian Studies* 5, no. 1 (2013): 86–103.

De judicio finali. Santoral en Mexicano, Bancroft Library, M-M 464, University of California, Berkeley.

Dedenbach–Salazar Sáenz, Sabine, ed. *La transmisión de conceptos cristianos a las lenguas amerindias: Estudios sobre textos y contextos de la época colonial.* Sankt Augustin: Anthropos Institut, Academia Verlag, 2016.

Dehouve, Danièle. *Relatos de pecados en la evangelización de los indios de México (siglos XVI–XVIII).* Translated by Josefina Anaya. Mexico City: Centro de Investigaciones y Estudios Superiores en Antropología Social, 2010.

———. *Rudingero el borracho y otros exempla medievales en el México virreinal.* Mexico City: Centro de Investigaciones y Estudios Superiores en Antropología Social, 2000.

Delbrugge, Laura. *A Scholarly Edition of Andrés de Li's* Thesoro de la passion *(1494).* Leiden, Netherlands: Brill, 2011.

Díaz, Ana, ed. *Cielos e inframundos: Una revisión de las cosmologías mesoamericana.* Mexico City: Universidad Nacional Autónoma de México, 2015.

———. *Reshaping the World: Debates on Mesoamerican Cosmologies.* Louisville: University Press of Colorado, 2020.

Díaz Balsera, Viviana. "Instructing the Nahuas in Judeo-Christian Obedience: A *Neixcuitilli* and Four Sermon Pieces on the Akedah." In *Death and Life in Colonial Nahua Mexico,* edited by Barry D. Sell and Louise M. Burkhart, 85–111. Vol. 1 of *Nahuatl Theater.* Norman: University of Oklahoma Press, 2004.

———. *Guardians of Idolatry: Gods, Demons, and Priests in Hernando Ruiz de Alarcón's Treatise on the Heathen Superstitions.* Norman: University of Oklahoma Press, 2018.

Dibble, Charles E. "Sahagún's Appendices: 'There Is No Reason to Be Suspicious of the Ancient Practices.'" In *The Work of Bernardino de Sahagún: Pioneer Ethnographer of Sixteenth-Century Aztec Mexico,* edited by J. Jorge Klor de Alva, H. B. Nicholson, and Eloise Quiñones Keber, 107–18. Austin: University of Texas Press, 1988.

Dickerson, Ed. "Brexit: When Dreams Collide." *Signs of the Times,* October 2016.

Dimant, Devorah. "Resurrection, Restoration, and Time-Curtailing in Qumran, Early Judaism, and Christianity." *Revue de Qumrân* 19, no. 4 (2000): 527–48.

Doherty, James. "Joyce and 'Hell Opened to Christians:' The Edition He Used for His 'Hell Sermons.'" *Modern Philology* 61, no. 2 (1963): 110–19.

Don, Patricia Lopes. *Bonfires of Culture: Franciscans, Indigenous Leaders, and the Inquisition in Early Mexico, 1524–1540.* Norman: University of Oklahoma Press, 2010.

Dutton, Brian. "The Source of Berceo's *Signos del Juicio Final.*" *Kentucky Romance Quarterly* 20 (2010): 247–55.

Edgerton, Samuel. *Theaters of Conversion: Religious Architecture and Indian Artisans in Colonial Mexico.* Albuquerque: University of New Mexico Press, 2001.

Edmonson, Munro S., ed. *Sixteenth-Century Mexico: The Work of Sahagún.* Albuquerque: University of New Mexico Press, 1974.

———, trans., and ed. *Heaven Born Merida and Its Destiny: The Book of Chilam Balam of Chumayel*. Austin: University of Texas Press, 1986.

Edwards, Graham Robert. "Purgatory: 'Birth' or Evolution?" *Journal of Ecclesiastical History* 36 (1985): 634–46.

Eire, Carlos M. N. *From Madrid to Purgatory: The Art and Craft of Dying in Sixteenth-Century Spain*. Cambridge: Cambridge University Press, 1995.

———. *Reformations: The Early Modern World, 1450–1650*. New Haven, CT: Yale University Press, 2016.

Ellens, J. Harold. "Afterlife and Underworld in the Bible." In *End Time and Afterlife in Judaism*, edited by J. Harold Ellens, 1–5. Vol. 1 of *Heaven, Hell, and the Afterlife: Eternity in Judaism, Christianity, and Islam*. Santa Barbara, CA: Praeger, 2013.

———. "Heaven, Hell, and Afterlife in the Christian Creeds." In *End Time and Afterlife in Christianity*, edited by J. Harold Ellens, 83–102. Vol. 2 of *Heaven, Hell, and the Afterlife: Eternity in Judaism, Christianity, and Islam*. Santa Barbara, CA: Praeger, 2013.

Emmerson, Richard K. *Antichrist in the Middle Ages: A Study of Medieval Apocalypticism, Art, and Literature*. Seattle: University of Washington Press, 1981.

———. "Introduction: The Apocalypse in Medieval Culture." In *The Apocalypse in the Middle Ages*, edited by Richard Kenneth Emmerson and Bernard McGinn, 293–332. Ithaca, NY: Cornell University Press, 1992.

Emmerson, Richard K. and Bernard McGinn, eds. *The Apocalypse in the Middle Ages*. Ithaca, NY: Cornell University Press, 1992.

Falkner, Sieglinde. "Los sermones chiquitanos: Su origen y transformación." In *La transmisión de conceptos cristianos a las lenguas amerindias: Estudios sobre textos y contextos de la época colonial*, edited by Sabine Dedenbach–Salazar Sáenz, 289–307. Sankt Augustin: Anthropos Institut, Academia Verlag, 2016.

Farriss, Nancy. *Maya Society under Colonial Rule: The Collective Enterprise of Survival*. Princeton, NJ: Princeton University Press, 1984.

———. *Tongues of Fire: Language and Evangelization in Colonial Mexico*. New York: Oxford University Press, 2018.

Farrow, Mary. "Why Christians Believe in Resurrection, not Reincarnation." *Catholic News Agency*. October 24, 2018. https://www.catholicnewsagency.com/news/39710/why-christians-believe-in-resurrection-not-reincarnation.

Fernández-Armesto, Felipe. *Columbus on Himself*. Indianapolis: Hackett, 2010.

Flint, Richard, and Shirley Cushing Flint. *A Most Splendid Company: The Coronado Expedition in Global Perspective*. Albuquerque: University of New Mexico Press, 2019.

Foster, Edward E., ed. *Three Purgatory Poems: The Gast of Gy, Sir Owain, The Vision of Tundale*. Kalamazoo: Medieval Institute Publications, Western Michigan University, 2004.

Fracas, Simone. "Almost Millenarian: A Critical Reading of Gerónimo de Mendieta's Eschatological Thought and its Historiography." *International Journal of Latin American Religions* 1 (2017): 376–400.

Fredriksen, Paula. "Apocalypse and Redemption in Early Christianity. From John of Patmos to Augustine of Hippo." *Vigiliae Christianae* 45, no. 2 (June 1991): 151–83.

———. "Christians in the Roman Empire in the First Three Centuries C.E." In *A Companion to the Roman Empire*, edited by David S. Potter, 587–606. Malden, MA: Blackwell, 2006.

———. "Tyconius and Augustine on the Apocalypse." In *The Apocalypse in the Middle Ages*, edited by Richard Kenneth Emmerson and Bernard McGinn, 20–37. Ithaca, NY: Cornell University Press, 1992.

Frost, Elsa Cecilia. "A New Millenarian: Georges Baudot." *Americas* 36, no. 4 (April 1980): 515–26.

García Icazbalceta, Joaquín. *Bibliografía mexicana del siglo XVI*, vol. 1. Mexico City: Librería de Andrade y Morales, 1886.

———, ed. *Códice franciscano, siglo XVI*. Vol. 2 of *Nueva colección de documentos para la historia de México*. Mexico City: Imprenta de Francisco Díaz de León, 1889.

García Oro, José. *Prehistoria y primeros capítulos de la evangelización de América*. Caracas: Editiones Trípode, 1988.

García Quintanilla, Alejandra. *"Saak' y el retorno del fin del mundo: La plaga de langosta en las profecías del katun 13 Ahau."* *Ancient Mesoamerica* 16 (2005): 327–44.

Gardiner, Eileen. *Medieval Visions of Heaven and Hell: A Sourcebook*. New York: Garland, 1993.

———, ed. *Visions of Heaven and Hell Before Dante*. New York: Italica, 1989.

George, Amy. "Fuentes europeas en los *Libros del Chilam Balam*." *Arqueología mexicana* 28, no. 166 (2021): 52–56.

Goodman, Felicitas D. *Maya Apocalypse: Seventeen Years with the Women of a Yucatan Village*. Bloomington: Indiana University Press, 2001.

Graham, Elizabeth. *Maya Christians and Their Churches in Sixteenth-Century Belize*. Gainesville: University Press of Florida, 2011.

Granada, Luis de. *Libro de la oración y meditación*. Barcelona: Emprenta de Iayme Cendrat, 1594.

Graziano, Frank. *The Millennial New World*. New York: Oxford University Press, 1999.

Grosse, Sven. "Thomas Aquinas, Bonaventure, and the Critiques of Joachimist Topics from the Fourth Lateran Council to Dante." In *A Companion to Joachim of Fiore*, edited by Matthias Riedl, 144–89. Leiden, Netherlands: Brill, 2018.

Grupo Dzíbil. *Chilam Balam of Tuzik*. Mexico City: n.p., 1996.

Gruzinski, Serge. *Man-Gods in the Mexican Highlands: Indian Power and Colonial Society, 1520–1800*. Translated by Eileen Corrigan. Stanford: Stanford University Press, 1989.

Gubler, Ruth, and David Bolles, eds. *The Book of Chilam Balam of Na: Facsimile, Translation, and Edited Text*. Lancaster, CA: Labyrinthos, 2000.

Hanks, William F. *Converting Words: Maya in the Age of the Cross*. Berkeley: University of California Press, 2010.

Hatfield, Rab. "Botticelli's *Mystic Nativity*, Savonarola, and the Millennium." *Journal of the Warburg and Courtauld Institutes* 58 (1995): 89–114.

Hawk, Brandon W. "The *Fifteen Signs before Judgment* in Anglo-Saxon England: A Reassessment." *Journal of English and Germanic Philology* 177, no. 4 (2018): 443–57.

Heist, William W. *The Fifteen Signs before Doomsday*. East Lansing: Michigan State College Press, 1952.

Helsel, Philip Samuel Browning. "Hades, Hell, and Sheol: The Reception History of the King James Version in American Fundamentalism." In *End Time and Afterlife in Christianity*, edited by J. Harold Ellens, 103–19. Vol. 2 of *Heaven, Hell, and the Afterlife: Eternity in Judaism, Christianity, and Islam*. Santa Barbara, CA: Praeger, 2013.

Herolt, Fray Johannes. *Sermones discipuli de tempore. & de sanctis*. Venice: Antonium Bertanum, 1598.

Herzman, Ronald B. "Dante and the Apocalypse." In *The Apocalypse in the Middle Ages*, edited by Richard Kenneth Emmerson and Bernard McGinn, 398–413. Ithaca, NY: Cornell University Press, 1992.

Himmelfarb, Martha. *The Apocalypse: A Brief History*. Oxford: Wiley-Blackwell, 2010.

Hitchcock, James. *History of the Catholic Church: From the Apostolic Age to the Third Millennium*. San Francisco: Ignatius, 2012.

Hosler, Dorothy. *The Sounds and Colors of Power: The Sacred Metallurgical Technology of Ancient West Mexico*. Cambridge, MA: MIT Press, 1994.

Hoover, Jesse A. *The Donatist Church in an Apocalyptic Age*. New York: Oxford University Press, 2018.

Hudson, Christopher D. *Heaven and Hell, Are They Real?* Nashville: Thomas Nelson, 2014.

International Theological Commission. "The Hope of Salvation for Infants Who Die without Being Baptised." Created May 8, 2007. http: //www.vatican.va/roman _curia/congregations/cfaith/cti_documents/rc_con_cfaith_doc_20070419_un -baptised-infants_en.html.

Jackson, Robert H. *Conflict and Conversion in Sixteenth Century Central Mexico: The Augustinian War on and Beyond the Chichimeca Frontier*. Leiden, Netherlands: Brill, 2013.

Jenkins, John Major. *The 2012 Story: The Myths, Fallacies, and Truth behind the Most Intriguing Date in History*. New York: Jeremy P. Tarcher/Penguin, 2009.

Jerome. *The Principal Works of St. Jerome*. Translated by W. H. Fremantle, G. Lewis, and W. G. Martley. Grand Rapids, MI: Wm. B. Eerdmans, 1893.

Kagan, Richard L. *Urban Images of the Hispanic World 1493–1793*. New Haven, CT: Yale University Press, 2000.

Kashanipour, Ryan Amir. "A World of Cures: Magic and Medicine in Colonial Yucatan." PhD diss., University of Arizona, 2012.

Keck, David. *Angels and Angelology in the Middle Ages*. New York: Oxford University Press, 1998.

Kelly, Henry Ansgar. "Hell with Purgatory and Two Limbos: The Geography and Theology of the Underworld." In *Hell and Its Afterlife: Historical and Contemporary Perspectives*, edited by Isabel Moreira and Margaret Toscano, 121–36. Burlington, VT: Ashgate, 2010.

Kempis, Thomas À. *The Imitation of Christ*. Translated by Aloysius Croft and Harold Bolton. Milwaukee: Bruce, 1940.

Kerkhove, Ray. "Dark Religion?: Aztec Perspectives on Human Sacrifice." *Sydney Studies in Religion*, (2008): 136–60.

Kirkland-Ives, Mitzi. "Alternate Routes: Variation in Early Modern Stational Devotions." *Viator* 40, no. 1 (2009) 249–70.

Knapp, Alex. "No, the Pope Isn't Tweeting Indulgences to His Followers." *Forbes*, July 18, 2013. https://www.forbes.com/sites/alexknapp/2013/07/18/no-the-pope-isnt-tweeting-indulgences-to-his-followers/#1b6ceb2e1dd6.

Knowlton, Timothy. "Dynamics of Indigenous Language Ideologies in the Colonial Redaction of a Yucatec Maya Cosmological Text." *Anthropological Linguistics* 50, no. 1 (2008): 90–112.

———. "Filth and Healing in Yucatan: Interpreting Ix Hun Ahau, A Maya Goddess." *Ancient Mesoamerica* 27, no. 2 (2016): 319–32.

———. *Maya Creation Myths: Words and Worlds of the Chilam Balam*. Boulder: University Press of Colorado, 2010.

Knowlton, Timothy W., and Gabrielle Vail. "Hybrid Cosmologies in Mesoamerica: A Reevaluation of the *Yax Cheel Cab*, A Maya World Tree." *Ethnohistory* 57, no. 4 (2010): 709–39.

La Piana, George. "The Roman Church at the End of the Second Century." *Harvard Theological Review* 18, no. 3 (1925): 201–77

Ladero Quesada, Miguel Angel. "Spain circa 1492: Social Values and Structures." In *Implicit Understandings: Observing, Reporting, and Reflecting on the Encounters between Europeans and Other Peoples in the Early Modern Era*, edited by Stuart B. Schwartz, 96–133. Studies in Comparative Early Modern History. Cambridge: Cambridge University Press, 1994.

Laird, Andrew. "Classical Letters and Millenarian Madness in Post-Conquest Mexico: The Ecstasis of Fray Cristóbal Cabrera (1548)." *International Journal of the Classical Tradition* 24, no. 1 (2017): 78–108.

———. "The Teaching of Latin to the Native Nobility in Mexico in the Mid–1500s: Contexts, Methods, and Results." In *Learning Latin and Greek from Antiquity to the Present*, edited by Elizabeth Archibald, William Brockliss, and Jonothan Gnoza, 118–37. Cambridge: Cambridge University Press, 2015.

Landa, Diego de. *Relación de las cosas de Yucatán*. Introduction by Angel Maria Garibay K. 8th ed. Mexico City: Editorial Porrúa, 1959.

Lane, Kris, ed. *Defending the Conquest: Bernardo de Vargas Machuca's Defense and Discourse of the Western Conquests*. Translated by Timothy F. Johnson. University Park, PA: Pennsylvania State University Press, 2010.

Lansing, Richard, ed. *The Dante Encyclopedia*. New York: Garland, 2000.

Lara, Jaime. *City, Temple, Stage: Eschatological Architecture and Liturgical Theatrics in New Spain*. Notre Dame: University of Notre Dame Press, 2004.

————. "Francis Alive and Aloft: Franciscan Apocalypticism in the Colonial Andes." *Americas* 70, no. 2 (2013): 139–63.

Larkin, Brian. "Liturgy, Devotion, and Religious Reform in Eighteenth-Century Mexico City." *Americas* 60, no. 4 (2004): 493–518.

Latteri, Natalie E. "Jewish Apocalypticism: An Historiography." In *A Companion to the Premodern Apocalypse*, edited by Michael A. Ryan, 67–102. Leiden, Netherlands: Brill, 2016.

Le Goff, Jacque. *The Birth of Purgatory.* Translated by Arthur Goldhammer. Chicago: University of Chicago Press, 1984.

Leeming, Benjamin H. "Aztec Antichrist: Christianity, Transculturation, and Apocalypse on Stage in Two Sixteenth-Century Nahuatl Dramas." PhD diss., University at Albany, State University of New York, 2017.

————. "'Jade Water, Gunpowder Water': Water Imagery in Nahuatl Descriptions of Heaven and Hell." Paper presented at American Society for Ethnohistory Conference, New Orleans, April 2013.

León, Martín de. *Camino del cielo en lengua mexicana.* Mexico City: Diego López Dávalos, 1611.

————. *Primera parte del sermonario del tiempo de todo el año, duplicado, en lengua mexicana.* Mexico City: Diego López Dávalos, 1614.

León-Portilla, Miguel. *Bernardino de Sahagún: First Anthropologist.* Translated by Mauricio J. Mixco. Norman: University of Oklahoma Press, 2002.

————. *Los franciscanos vistos por el hombre náhuatl: Testimonios indígenas de siglo XVI.* Mexico City: Universidad Nacional Autónoma de México, 1985.

————, ed. *Native Mesoamerican Spirituality: Ancient Myths, Discourses, Stories, Doctrines, Hymns, Poems from the Aztec, Yucatec, Quiche-Maya and Other Sacred Traditions.* Mahwah, N.J.: Paulist, 1980.

Lerner, Robert E. *The Feast of St. Abraham: Medieval Millenarians and the Jews.* Philadelphia: University of Pennsylvania Press, 2001.

————. "The Medieval Return to the Thousand–Year Sabbath." In *Apocalypse in the Middle Ages*, edited by Richard Kenneth Emmerson and Bernard McGinn, 51–71. Ithaca, NY: Cornell University Press, 1992.

Liss, Peggy. *Isabel the Queen: Life and Times.* Philadelphia: University of Pennsylvania Press, 2004.

Lizana, Bernardo de. *Historia de Yucatán: Devocionario de Nuestra Señora de Izamal y conquista espiritual.* 1633. Reprint. 2nd ed. Mexico City: Museo Nacional, 1893.

Lockhart, James. "The Language of the Texts." In *Here in This Year: Seventeenth-Century Nahuatl Annals of the Tlaxcala-Puebla Valley*, edited by Camilla Townsend, 45–65. Stanford: Stanford University Press, 2010.

Logan, F. Donald. *A History of the Church in the Middle Ages.* 2nd ed. New York: Routledge, 2013.

Lomnitz, Claudio. *Death and the Idea of Mexico.* Brooklyn, NY: Zone Books, 2005.

Long, Siobhán Dowling, and John F. A. Sawyer. *The Bible in Music: A Dictionary of Songs, Works, and More.* New York: Rowman and Littlefield, 2015.

López Austin, "El núcleo duro, la cosmovisión y la tradición mesoamericana." In *Cosmovisión, ritual e identidad de los pueblos indígenas de Mexico*, ed. Johanna

Broda y Félix Báez-Jorge, 47–65. Mexico City: Fondo de Cultura Económica, 2001.

López-Lozano, Miguel. *Utopian Dreams, Apocalyptic Nightmares: Globalization in Recent Mexican and Chicano Narrative.* West Lafayette, IN: Purdue University Press, 2008.

Love, Bruce. "¿Qué son los *Libros de Chilam Balam?*" *Arqueología mexicana* 28, no. 166 (2021): 36–43.

Luther, Martin. "A Treatise on Christian Liberty." Introduction and translation by C. M. Jacobs. In *Works of Martin Luther,* edited by Lane Hall, 2:295–348. Philadelphia: S. J. Holman and Castle, 1915.

Lynch, Joseph H., and Phillip C. Adamo. *The Medieval Church: A Brief History.* 2nd ed. New York: Routledge, 2014.

Magaloni-Kerpel, Diana. *Albores de la Conquista: La historia pintada del* Códice Florentino. Mexico City: Artes de México y del Mundo S.A. de C.V., 2016.

———. "Painting a New Era: Conquest, Prophecy, and the World to Come." In *Invasion and Transformation: Interdisciplinary Perspectives on the Conquest of Mexico,* edited by Rebecca P. Brienen and Margaret A. Jackson, 125–49. Boulder: University Press of Colorado, 2008.

———. "Visualizing the Nahua/Christian Dialogue: Images of the Conquest in Sahagún's *Florentine Codex* and their Sources." In *Sahagún at 500: Essays on the Quincentenary of the Birth of Fr. Bernardino de Sahagún,* edited by John F. Schwaller, 193–221. Berkeley: Academy of American Franciscan History, 2003.

Magnier, Grace. *Pedro de Valencia and the Catholic Apologists of the Expulsion of the Moriscos: Visions of Christianity and Kingship.* Leiden, Netherlands: Brill, 2010.

Magnus, Albertus. *Enarrationes in secundam partem evang. Lucae (X–XXIV).* Vol. 23, *Opera omnia,* edited by Augusti Borgnet. Paris: Vivès, 1895.

Marchand, James W. "Gonzalo de Berceo's *De los signos que aparesçerán ante del juiçio.*" *Hispanic Review* 45, no. 3 (Summer 1977): 283–95.

Marthaler, Berard L. *The Creed: The Apostolic Faith in Contemporary Theology.* 3rd ed. New London, CT: Twenty-Third, 2007.

Martínez Gil, Fernando. *Muerte y sociedad en la España de los Austrias.* Cuenca: Ediciones de la Universidad de Castilla-La Mancha, 2000.

Mathes, W. Michael. *The America's First Academic Library: Santa Cruz de Tlatelolco.* Sacramento: California State Library Foundation, 1985.

Matovina, Timothy. *Latino Catholicism: Transformation in America's Largest Church.* Princeton, NJ: Princeton University Press, 2012.

McAndrew, John. *The Open-Air Churches of Sixteenth-Century Mexico: Atrios, Posas, Open Chapels, and Other Studies.* Cambridge, MA: Harvard University Press, 1965.

McClure, Julia. *The Franciscan Invention of the New World.* The New Middle Ages. Cham, Switzerland: Springer International, 2017.

McDannell, Colleen, and Bernhard Lang. *Heaven: A History.* New Haven, CT: Yale University Press, 1988.

McGinn, Bernard. "Introduction: Joachim of Fiore in the History of Western Culture." In *A Companion to Joachim of Fiore,* edited by Matthias Riedl, 1–19. Leiden, Netherlands: Brill, 2018.

————. "Introduction: John's Apocalypse and the Apocalyptic Mentality." In *Apocalypse in the Middle Ages*, edited by Richard K. Emmerson and Bernard McGinn, 3–19. Ithaca, NY: Cornell University Press, 1992.

————. *Visions of the End: Apocalyptic Traditions in the Middle Ages*. New York: Columbia University Press, 1998.

McGuire, Brian Patrick. "Purgatory, the Communion of Saints, and Medieval Change." *Viator* 20 (1989): 61–84.

McKinnie, Ruth L. "Mansion of Death Yields 39 Bodies." *The San Diego Union–Tribune*, March 27, 1997.

Melton-Villanueva, Miriam. *The Aztecs at Independence: Nahua Culture Makers in Central Mexico, 1799–1832*. Tucson: University of Arizona Press, 2016.

Mendieta, Gerónimo de. *Historia eclesiástica indiana: Obra escrita a fines del siglo XVI*. 2nd facsimile ed. Mexico City: Editorial Porrúa, 1971.

Meyer, Ann R, *Medieval Allegory and the Building of the New Jerusalem*. Woodbridge, UK: D. S. Brewer, 2003.

Milton, John. *Paradise Lost*. Introduction by Philip Pullman. New York: Oxford University Press, 2005.

Mitchell, David. *Cloud Atlas: A Novel*. New York: Random House, 2004.

Molina, Alonso de. *Confesionario mayor en la lengua mexicana y castellana (1569)*. With an introduction by Roberto Moreno. Mexico City: Instituto de Investigaiones Filológicas, Instituto de Investigaciones Históricas, Universidad Nacional Autónoma de México, 1984.

Montes de Oca Vega, Mercedes. *Los difrasismos en el náhuatl de los siglos XVI y XVII*. Mexico City: Universidad Nacional Autónoma de México, 2013.

Morales, Francisco. "The Native Encounter with Christianity: Franciscans and Nahuas in Sixteenth–Century Mexico." *Americas* 65, no. 2 (2008): 137–59.

Moreno, Doris, and Ricardo García Cárcel. "Introduction." In *The Complexity of Hispanic Religious Life in the 16th–18th Centuries*, edited by Doris Moreno, translated by Phil Grayston, 1–12. Leiden, Netherlands: Brill, 2020.

Morris, Chris. "Claire's is the Latest Victim of the Retail Apocalypse." *Fortune*, March 9, 2018. https: //fortune.com/2018/03/09/claires-bankruptcy/.

————. "Country's Biggest Mall Owner Warns Retail Apocalypse May Not Be Over." *Fortune*, February 1, 2019. https://fortune.com/2019/02/01/simon-property -malls-retail-apocalypse/.

Morris, Richard, ed. *Cursor Mundi: A Northumbrian Poem of the XIVth Century*. London: N. Trübner, 1874.

Mosquera, Daniel. "Nahuatl Catechistic Drama: New Translations, Old Preoccupations." In *Death and Life in Colonial Nahua Mexico*, edited by Barry D. Sell and Louise M. Burkhart, 55–84. Vol. 1 of *Nahuatl Theater*. Norman: University of Oklahoma Press, 2004.

Motolinía, Toribio de Benavente. *Epistolario (1526–1555)*. Edited by Javier O. Aragón and P. Lino Gómez Canedo. Mexico City: Penta Com., 1986.

————. *Historia de los indios de la Nueva España*, edited by Mercedes Serna Arnaiz and Bernat Castany Prado. Madrid: Real Academia Española, 2014.

Mundy, Barbara E. *The Death of Aztec Tenochtitlan, the Life of Mexico City*. Austin: University of Texas Press, 2015.

Munro, Martin. *Tropical Apocalypse: Haiti and the Caribbean End Times*. Charlottesville: University of Virginia Press, 2015.

Musper, H. TH., ed. *Der Antichrist und die fünfzehn Zeichen: Faksimile-Ausgabe des einzigen erhaltenen chiroxylographischen Blockbuches*. 2 vols. Munich: Prestel-Verlag, 1970.

Nepaulsingh, Colbert I. *Towards a History of Literary Composition in Medieval Spain*. Toronto: University of Toronto Press, 1986.

Nesvig, Martin Austin. *Forgotten Franciscans: Works from an Inquisitional Theorist, a Heretic, and an Inquisitional Deputy*. Latin American Originals. University Park: Pennsylvania State University Press, 2011.

———. *Ideology and Inquisition: The World of Censors in Early Mexico*. New Haven, CT: Yale University Press, 2009.

Nielsen, Jesper, and Toke Sellner Reunert. "Colliding Universes: A Reconsideration of the Structure of the Precolumbian Mesoamerican Cosmos." In *Reshaping the World: Debates on Mesoamerican Cosmologies*, edited by Ana Díaz, 31–68. Louisville: University Press of Colorado, 2020.

———. "Dante's Heritage: Questioning the Multi-layered Model of the Mesoamerican Universe." *Antiquity* 83, no. 320 (2009): 399–413.

O'Collins, Gerald. *Saint Augustine on the Resurrection of Christ: Teaching, Rhetoric, and Reception*. New York: Oxford University Press, 2017.

O'Hear, Natasha, and Anthony O'Hear. *Picturing the Apocalypse: The Book of Revelation in the Arts over Two Millennia*. New York: Oxford University Press, 2015.

O'Malley, John W. *Saints or Devils Incarnate?: Studies in Jesuit History*. Leiden, Netherlands: Brill, 2013.

Onyema, Eke Wilfred. *The Millennial Kingdom of Christ (Rev 20, 1–10): A Critical History of Exegesis with an Interpretative Proposal*. Rome: Editrice Pontificia de Università Gregoriana, 2013.

Oroz, Pedro de. *The Oroz Codex*. Edited and translated by Angélico Chávez. Washington DC: Academy of American Franciscan History, 1972.

Oviedo y Valdés, Gonzalo Fernández de. *Historia general y natural de las Indias, islas y Tierra Firme del mar océano*, 4 vols. Madrid: Imprenta del Real Academia de Historia, 1851–1918.

Palmer, James. *The Apocalypse in the Early Middle Ages*. Cambridge: Cambridge University Press, 2014.

Paredes, Ignacio de. *Promptuario manual mexicano*. Mexico City: Imprenta de la Bibliotheca Mexicana, 1759.

Parshall, Peter, and Rainer Schoch, eds. *Origins of European Printmaking: Fifteenth-Century Woodcuts and Their Public*. Washington, DC: National Gallery of Art, 2005.

Pastore, Stefania. "Mozas Criollas and New Government: Francis Borgia, Prophetism, and the Spiritual Exercises in Spain and Peru." In *Visions, Prophecies, and Divinations: Early Modern Messianism and Millenarianism in Iberian America*,

Spain and Portugal, edited by Ana Paula Torres and Luís Filipe Silvério Lima, 59–73. Leiden, Netherlands: Brill, 2016.

Pasulka, Diana Walsh. *Heaven Can Wait: Purgatory in Catholic Devotional and Popular Culture.* New York: Oxford University Press, 2015.

Patch, Robert. *Maya Revolt and Revolution in the Eighteenth-Century.* New York: Routledge, 2015.

Patrick, James A., ed. *Renaissance and Reformation.* Vol. 1. Tarrytown, NY: Marshall Cavendish, 2007.

Paul IV (pope). "Dogmatic Constitution on the Church: Lumen Gentium." The Holy See. Created October 21, 2021. https://www.vatican.va/archive/hist_councils/ii _vatican_council/documents/vat-ii_const_19641121_lumen-gentium_en.html.

Pérez de Ribas, Andrés. *History of the Triumphs of Our Holy Faith amongst the Most Barbarous and Fierce Peoples of the New World.* Edited and translated by Daniel T. Reff, Maureen Ahern, and Richard K. Danford. Tucson: University of Arizona Press, 1999.

Peterson, Jeanette Favrot. "Creating the Virgin of Guadalupe: The Cloth, the Artist, and Sources in Sixteenth-Century New Spain." *Americas* 61, no. 4 (2005): 571–610.

———. "Images in Translation: A Codex 'Muy Historiado'." In *The Florentine Codex: An Encyclopedia of the Nahua World in Sixteenth-Century Mexico,* edited by Jeanette Farvot Peterson and Kevin Terraciano, 21–36. Austin: University of Texas Press, 2019.

———. *The Paradise Garden Murals of Malinalco: Utopia and Empire in Sixteenth-Century Mexico.* Austin: University of Texas Press, 1993.

———. "Rhetoric as Acculturation: The Anomalous Book 6." In *The Florentine Codex: An Encyclopedia of the Nahua World in Sixteenth-Century Mexico,* edited by Jeanette Farvot Peterson and Kevin Terraciano, 167–83. Austin: University of Texas Press, 2019.

Peterson, Jeanette Favrot and Kevin Terraciano, eds. *The Florentine Codex: An Encyclopedia of the Nahua World in Sixteenth-Century Mexico.* Austin: University of Texas Press, 2019.

Pew Research Group. "Belief in Heaven." Pew Research Center. Created September 9, 2020. https: //www.pewforum.org/religious-landscape-study/belief-in-heaven/.

———. "Belief in Hell." Pew Research Center. Created September 9, 2020. https: // www.pewforum.org/religious-landscape-study/belief-in-hell/.

———. "Belief in Hell by Religious Group." Pew Research Center, 2014. https: //www.pewforum.org/religious-landscape-study/compare/belief-in-hell/by/ religious-tradition/.

———. "Global Christianity: A Report on the Size and Distribution of the World's Christian Population." Pew Research Center. Created December 19, 2011. https://www.pewforum.org/2011/12/19/global-christianity-exec/

———. "Overview: Pentecostalism in Latin America." Pew Research Center. Created October 5, 2006. https: //www.pewforum.org/2006/10/05/overview -pentecostalism-in-latin-america/.

Phelan, John Leddy. *The Millennial Kingdom of the Franciscans in the New World.* 2nd ed. Berkeley: University of California Press, 1970.

Poggioli, Sylvia. "Pope Francis: Even Atheists Can be Redeemed." *NPR*, May 29, 2013. https://www.npr.org/sections/parallels/2013/05/29/187009384/Pope-Francis-Even-Atheists-Can-Be-Redeemed.

Pollnitz, Aysha. "Old Words and the New World: Liberal Education and the Franciscans in New Spain, 1536–1601." *Transactions of the Royal Historical Society* 27 (2017): 123–52.

Poole, Kevin. "The Western Apocalypse Commentary Tradition of the Early Middle Ages." In *A Companion to the Premodern Apocalypse*, edited by Michael A. Ryan, 103–43. Leiden, Netherlands: Brill, 2016.

Poole, Stafford. "Church Law on the Ordination of Indians and Castas in New Spain." *Hispanic American Historical Review* 61, no. 4 (1981): 637–50.

———. *Our Lady of Guadalupe: The Origins and Sources of a Mexican National Symbol, 1531–1797*. Revised edition. Tucson: University of Arizona Press, 2017.

Post, R. R. *The Modern Devotion: Confrontation with Reformation and Humanism*. Leiden, Netherlands: Brill, 1968.

Powell, Susan. *The Advent and Nativity Sermons from a Fifteenth-Century Revision of John Mirk's Festial*. Heidelberg: Carl Winter, 1981.

Prien, Hans–Jürgen. *Christianity in Latin America*. Revised and expanded edition. Translated by Stephen Buckwalter and Brian McNeil. Leiden, Netherlands: Brill, 2013.

Prusak, Bernard P. "Bodily Resurrection in Catholic Perspectives." *Theological Studies* 61 (2000): 64–105.

Quezada, Sergio. *Maya Lords and Lordship: The Formation of Colonial Society in Yucatán, 1350–1600*. Translated by Terry Rugeley. Norman: University of Oklahoma Press, 2014.

Quintana, Augustín de. *Confessionario en lengua mixe*. Puebla: Viuda de Miguel de Ortega, 1733.

Redfield, Robert, and Alfonso Villa Rojas. *Chan Kom: A Maya Village*. Chicago: University of Chicago Press, 1962.

Reese, Thomas. "Commentary: Pope Francis Believes in Hell, a Place God Doesn't Send People—They Choose It." *Salt Lake Tribune*, April 3, 2018. https://www.sltrib.com/religion/2018/04/03/commentary-pope-francis-believes-in-hell-a-place-god-doesnt-send-people-they-choose-it/.

Regan, Patrick. *Advent to Pentecost: Comparing the Seasons in the Ordinary and Extraordinary Forms of the Roman Rite*. Collegeville, MN: Liturgical Press, 2012.

Restall, Matthew. *The Maya World: Yucatec Culture and Society, 1550–1850*. Stanford: Stanford University Press, 1997.

———. *When Montezuma Met Cortés: The True Story of the Meeting That Changed History*. New York: HarperCollins, 2018.

Restall, Matthew, and Amara Solari. *2012 and the End of the World: The Western Roots of the Maya Apocalypse*. Lanham, MD: Rowman and Littlefield, 2011.

———. *The Maya: A Very Short Introduction*. New York: Oxford University Press, 2020.

———. *The Maya Apocalypse and its Western Roots*. Lanham, MD: Rowman and Littlefield, 2021.

"Resurrection did not Happen, Say Quarter of Christians." *BBC News*, April 9, 2017. https: //www.bbc.com/news/uk-england-39153121.

Ricard, Robert. *The Spiritual Conquest of Mexico: An Essay on the Apostolate and the Evangelizing Methods of the Mendicant Orders in New Spain: 1523–1572*. Translated by Lesley Byrd Simpson. Berkeley: University of California Press, 1966.

Ripalda, Gerónimo de. *Catecismo mexicano*. Translated and edited by Ignacio de Paredes. Mexico City: Bibliotheca Mexicana, 1758.

Rodríguez, Alonso. *Exercicio de perfeción i virtudes religiosas*. Sevilla: Matias Clavijo, 1612.

Roest, Bert. "Early Mendicant Mission in the New World: Discourses, Experiments, Realities." *Franciscan Studies* 71 (2013): 197–217.

———. "From *Reconquista* to Mission in the Early Modern World." In *A Companion to Observant Reform in the Late Middle Ages and Beyond*, edited by James D. Mixson and Bert Roest, 331–62. Leiden, Netherlands: Brill, 2015.

Rosica, Rev. Thomas. "Why Is Pope Francis So Obsessed with the Devil?" *CNN*, July 20, 2015. https: //www.cnn.com/2015/07/20/living/pope-francis-devil/index.html.

Rovira, José Carlos, Aníbal Salazar Anglada, Víctor M. Sanchis Amat, eds. *Homero Aridjis: El nuevo Apocalipsis (antología)*. Madrid: Editorial Verbum, 2020.

Roys, Ralph L. *The Book of Chilam Balam of Chumayel*. Washington, DC: Carnegie Institution, 1933.

———. "The Franciscan Contribution to Maya Linguistic Research in Yucatan." *Americas* 8, no. 4 (1952): 417–29.

Ruiz Medrano, Ethelia. *Mexico's Indigenous Communities: Their Lands and Histories, 1500–2010*. Translated by Russ Davidson. Boulder: University Press of Colorado, 2010.

Ruz, Joaquin, trans. *Colección de sermones para los domingos de todo el año, y cuaresma*. Merida: José de Espinosa, 1846.

Ryan, Michael A, ed. *A Companion to the Premodern Apocalypse*. Leiden, Netherlands: Brill, 2016.

Saak, E. L. *Creating Augustine: Interpreting Augustine and Augustinianism in the Later Middle Ages*. Oxford: Oxford University Press, 2012.

Sahagún, Bernardino de. *Coloquios y doctrina cristiana*. Edited and translated by Miguel León-Portilla. Mexico City: Fundación de Investigaciones Sociales, Universidad Nacional Autónoma de México, 1986.

———. *Florentine Codex: General History of the Things of New Spain*. Edited and translated by Arthur J. O. Anderson and Charles E. Dibble. 13 parts. Santa Fe and Salt Lake City: School of American Research and University of Utah Press, 1950–82.

Sahin, Kaya. "Constantinople and the End Time: The Ottoman Conquest as a Portent of the Last Hour." *Journal of Early Modern History* 14, no. 4 (2010): 317–54.

Sánchez de Aguilar, Pedro. *Informe contra idolorum cultores del Obispado de Yucatán*. 3rd ed. Merida: E. G. Triay e Hijos, 1937.

Sánchez de Vercial, Clemente. *The Book of Tales by A. B. C*. Translated and edited by John E. Keller, L. Clark Keating, and Eric M. Furr. New York: Lang, 1992.

Saranyana, Josep I., and Ana de Zaballa. *Joaquín de Fiore y América*. 2nd ed. Pamplona: Ediciones Eunate, 1995.

Scandar, Florencia. "Juan Pío Pérez Bermón y los *Libros del Chilam Balam*." *Arqueología mexicana* 28, no. 166 (2021): 44–47.

Schilling, Heinz. *Early Modern European Civilization and its Political and Cultural Dynamism*. Lebanon, NH: University Press of New England, 2008.

Schmidt, Stephanie. "Conceiving of the End of the World: Christian Doctrine and Nahua Perspectives in the Sermonary of Juan Bautista Viseo." *Ethnohistory* 68 no. 1 (2021): 125–45.

Scholes, France V., Carlos Menéndez, J. Rubio Mañé, and Eleanor B. Adams. *La iglesia en Yucatán*. Vol. 2 of *Documentos para la historia de Yucatán*. Merida: Compañía Tipográfica Yucateca, 1938.

Scholes, France V., and Ralph L. Roys. "Fray Diego de Landa and the Problem of Idolatry in Yucatan." In *Cooperation in Research*, 585–620. Washington, DC: Carnegie Institution, 1938.

Schuessler, Michael K. *Foundational Arts: Mural Paining and Missionary Theater in New Spain*. Tucson: University of Arizona Press, 2013.

Schwaller, John F. *The Fifteenth Month: Aztec History in the Rituals of Panquetzalitztli*. Norman: University of Oklahoma Press, 2019.

———. "The Ilhuica of the Nahua: Is Heaven Just a Place?" *Americas* 62 no. 3 (2006): 391–412.

———. "The Pre-Hispanic Poetics of Sahagún's *Psalmodia christiana*." In *Psalms in the Early Modern World*, edited by Linda Phyllis Austern, Kari Boyd McBride, and David L. Orvis, 315–32. Surrey, UK: Ashgate, 2011.

———, ed. *Sahagún at 500: Essays on the Quincentenary of the Birth of Fr. Bernardino de Sahagún*. Berkeley, CA: Academy of American Franciscan History, 2003.

Schwaller, Robert C. "A Language of Empire, a Quotidian Tongue: The Uses of Nahuatl in Colonial New Spain." *Ethnohistory* 59, no 4 (2012).

Segneri, Paolo. *El infierno abierto* [. . .]. Valencia: Diego de Vega, 1701.

Segundo Guzmán, Miguel Ángel. "El horizonte escatológico de la evangelización franciscana en el nuevo mundo, siglo XVI." In *Evangelization and Cultural Conflict in Colonial Mexico*, edited by Robert H. Jackson, 30–57. Newcastle upon Tyne: Cambridge Scholars, 2014.

Sell, Barry D. "The Classical Age of Nahuatl Publications and Don Bartolomé de Alva's *Confessionario* of 1634." In *A Guide to Confession Large and Small in the Mexican Language, 1634*, edited by Barry D. Sell and John Frederick Schwaller with Lu Ann Homza, 17–32. Norman: University of Oklahoma Press, 1999.

———. "Friars, Nahuas, and Books: Language and Expression in Colonial Nahuatl Publications." PhD diss., University of California, Los Angeles, 1993.

———. "Nahuatl Theater, Nahua Theater." In *Nahua Christianity in Performance*, edited by Barry D. Sell and Louise M. Burkhart, 51–70. Vol. 4 of *Nahuatl Theater*. Norman: University of Oklahoma Press, 2009.

Sell, Barry D., and Louise M. Burkhart, eds. *Nahua Christianity in Performance*. Vol. 4 of *Nahuatl Theater*. Norman: University of Oklahoma Press, 2009.

————, eds. *Nahuatl Theater*. 4 vols. Norman: University of Oklahoma Press, 2004–9.

Seymour, Charles. *A Theodicy of Hell*. Dordrecht: Kluwer Academic Publishers, 2000.

Shakespeare, William. *Hamlet*. Edited by Barbara A. Mowat and Paul Werstine. Folger Shakespeare Library. New York: Simon and Schuster, 2012.

Shore, Paul. "Theology and the Development of the European Confessional State." In *The Oxford Handbook of Early Modern Theology, 1600–1800*, edited by Ulrich L. Lehner, Richard A. Muller, and A. G. Roeber, 43–57. New York: Oxford University Press, 2016.

Sigal, Pete. *The Flower and the Scorpion: Sexuality and Ritual in Early Nahua Culture*. Durham: Duke University Press, 2011.

SilverMoon. "The Imperial College of Tlatelolco and the Emergence of a New Nahua Intellectual Elite in New Spain (1500–1760)." PhD diss., Duke University, 2007.

Silverstein, H. Theodore. "Dante and the *Visio Pauli*." *Modern Language Notes* 47, no. 6 (1932): 397–99.

————. *Visio Sancti Pauli: The History of the Apocalypse in Latin Together with Nine Texts*. London: Christophers, 1935.

Smoller, Laura Ackerman. *The Saint and the Chopped-Up Baby: The Cult of Vincent Ferrer in Medieval and Early Modern Europe*. Ithaca, NY: Cornell University Press, 2014.

Solórzano Pereira, Juan de. *Politíca indiana*. Madrid: Diego Diaz de la Carrera, 1648.

Sousa, Lisa. "Flowers and Speech in Discourses on Deviance in Book 10." In *The Florentine Codex: An Encyclopedia of the Nahua World in Sixteenth-Century Mexico*, edited by Jeanette Favrot Peterson and Kevin Terraciano, 184–99. Austin: University of Texas Press, 2019.

————. *The Woman Who Turned into a Jaguar, and Other Narratives of Native Women in Archives of Colonial Mexico*. Stanford: Stanford University Press, 2017.

Sparks, Garry G, ed. and trans. *The Americas' First Theologies: Early Sources of Post-Contact Indigenous Religion*. New York: Oxford University Press, 2017.

————. *Rewriting Maya Religion: Domingo de Vico, K'iche' Maya Intellectuals, and the Theologia Indorum*. Louisville, CO: University Press of Colorado, 2019.

Stafford Poole, C. M. "Church Law on the Ordination of Indians and Castas in New Spain." *Hispanic American Historical Review* 61, no. 4 (1981): 637–50.

Strathern, Alan. "Catholic Missions and Local Rulers in Sub–Saharan Africa." In *A Companion to Early Modern Catholic Global Missions*, edited by Ronnie Po–Chia Hsia, 151–78. Leiden, Netherlands: Brill, 2018.

Stuart, David. *The Order of Days: The Maya World and the Truth about 2012*. New York: Harmony Books, 2011.

Suárez Castro, María de Guadalupe. "El *Chilam Balam de Na* y sus firmantes." *Arqueología mexicana* 28, no. 166 (2021): 48–51.

Sullivan, Paul. *Unfinished Conversations: Mayas and Foreigners Between Two Wars*. New York: Knopf, 1989.

Sylvest, Edwin Edward, Jr. *Motifs of Franciscan Mission Theory in Sixteenth Century New Spain Province of the Holy Gospel*. Washington, DC: Academy of American Franciscan History, 1975.

Tavárez, David. "Aristotelian Politics among the Aztecs: A Nahuatl Adaptation of a Treatise by Denys the Carthusian." In *Transnational Perspectives on the Conquest and Colonization of Latin America*, edited by Jenny Mander, David Midgely, and Christine D. Beaule, 141–55. New York: Routledge, 2020.

———. *The Invisible War: Indigenous Devotions, Discipline, and Dissent in Colonial Mexico*. Stanford: Stanford University Press, 2011.

———. "Nahua Intellectuals, Franciscan Scholars, and the *Devotio Moderna* in Colonial Mexico." *Americas* 70, no. 2 (2013): 203–35.

———. "Naming the Trinity: From Ideologies of Translation to Dialectics of Reception in Colonial Nahua Texts, 1554–1771." *Colonial Latin American Review* 9, no. 1 (2000): 21–47.

———. "Performing the Zaachila Word: The Dominican Invention of Zapotec Christianity." In *Words and Worlds Turned Around: Indigenous Christianities in Colonial Latin America*, edited by David Tavárez, 29–62. Boulder: University Press of Colorado, 2017.

———. "Reframing Idolatry in Zapotec: Dominican Translations of the Christian Doctrine in Sixteenth-Century Oaxaca." In *Trust and Proof: Translators in Renaissance Print Culture*, edited by Andrea Rizzi, 164–81. Leiden, Netherlands: Brill, 2018.

Thayer, Anne T. *Penitence, Preaching and the Coming of the Reformation*. New York: Routledge, 2017.

Tillard, Jean-Marie-Roger. *Church of Churches: The Ecclesiology of Communion*. Translated by R. C. De Peaux. Collegeville, MN: Liturgical Press, 1992.

Timmer, David E. "Providence and Perdition: Fray Diego de Landa Justifies His Inquisition against the Yucatecan Maya." *Church History* 66, no. 3 (1997): 477–88.

Townsend, Camilla, ed. and trans. *Fifth Sun: A New History of the Aztecs*. New York: Oxford University Press, 2019.

———. *Here in This Year: Seventeenth-Century Nahuatl Annals of the Tlaxcala-Puebla Valley*. Stanford: Stanford University Press, 2010.

Townshend, Henry H. "The Grove Street Cemetery." *New Haven Colonial Historical Society Papers* 10 (1951): 119–46.

Truitt, Jonathan. *Sustaining the Divine in Mexico Tenochtitlan: Nahuas and Catholicism, 1523–1700*. Norman: University of Oklahoma Press, 2018.

Tubach, Frederic C. *Index Exemplorum: A Handbook of Medieval Religious Tales*. Helsinki: Suomalainen Tiedeakatemia, 1969.

Turley, Steven E. *Franciscan Spirituality and Mission in New Spain, 1524–1599: Conflict Beneath the Sycamore Tree (Luke 19:1–10)*. Surrey, UK: Ashgate, 2014.

Twain, Mark. *Mark Twain's Notebooks & Journals*. Vol. 3, *1883–1891*, edited by Robert Pack Browning, Michael B. Frank, and Lin Salamo. Berkeley: University of California Press, 1979.

Tyconius of Carthage. *Exposition of the Apocalypse*. Translated by Francis X. Gumer-lock. Introduction and notes by David C. Robinson. The Fathers of the Church: A New Translation. Vol. 134. Washington, DC: Catholic University of America Press, 2017.

Ucerler, M. Antoni J., "The Christian Missions in Japan in the Early Modern Period." In *A Companion to Early Modern Catholic Global Missions*, edited by Ronnie Po-Chia Hsia, 303–43. Leiden, Netherlands: Brill, 2018.

Underwood, Grant. *The Millenarian World of Early Mormonism*. Urbana: University of Illinois, 1993.

United States Department of Energy. "Historical Gas Prices." Vehicle Technologies Office. Published August 31, 2015. https://www.energy.gov/eere/vehicles/fact -888-august-31-2015-historical-gas-prices.

Valadés, Diego. *Retórica cristiana*. Edited by Esteban J. Palomera. Translated by Tarcicio Herrera Zapién. Mexico City: Fondo de Cultura Económica, 2013.

Van Deusen, Nancy E, ed. and trans. *The Souls of Purgatory: The Spiritual Diary of a Seventeenth-Century Afro-Peruvian Mystic, Ursula de Jesús*. Albuquerque: University of New Mexico Press, 2004.

Van Dyke, Christina, "Aquinas's Shiny Happy People: Perfect Happiness and the Limits of Human Nature." In *Oxford Studies in Philosophy of Religion*, edited by Jonathan L. Kvanvig, vol. 6, 269–91. New York: Oxford University Press, 2015.

Velázquez de Cárdenas y León, Carlos Celedonio. *Breve práctica, y régimen del confessonario de indios, en mexicano y castellano*. Mexico City: Imprenta de la Bibliotheca Mexicana, 1761.

Vidal y Micó, Francisco. *Historia de la portentosa vida, y milagros del valenciano apostol de Europa S. Vincente Ferrer*. Valencia: Joseph Estevan Dolz, 1735.

Villela, Khristaan D., and Mary Ellen Miller, eds. *The Aztec Calendar Stone*. Los Angeles: Getty Research Institute, 2010.

Virgil. *Aeneid*. Translated with an Introduction by W.F. Jackson Knight. Middlesex, England: Penguin Books, 1987.

Vitry, Jacques de. *The Exempla or Illustrative Stories from the Sermones Vulgares of Jacques de Vitry*. Edited by Thomas Frederick Crane. London: David Nutt, 1890.

Von Cochem, Martin. *The Four Last Things: Death, Judgment, Hell and Heaven*. New York: Benziger Brothers, 1899.

Von Ehrenkrook, Jason. "The Afterlife in Philo and Josephus." In *End Time and Afterlife in Judaism*, edited by J. Harold Ellens, 97–118. Vol. 1 of *Heaven, Hell, and the Afterlife: Eternity in Judaism, Christianity, and Islam*. Santa Barbara, CA: Praeger, 2013.

Wainwright, Arthur W. *Mysterious Apocalypse: Interpreting the Book of Revelation*. Eugene, OR: Wipf and Stock, 2001.

Warner, Marina. *Alone of All Her Sex: The Myth and the Cult of the Virgin Mary*. London: Weidenfeld and Nicolson, 1976.

Webster, Susan Verdi. "Art, Ritual, and Confraternities in Sixteenth-Century New Spain: Penitential Imagery at the Monastery of San Miguel, Huejotzingo." *Anales del Instituto de Investigaciones Estéticas* 70 (1997): 5–43.

Weckmann, Luis. "Las esperanzas milenaristas de los franciscanos de la Nueva España." *Historia Mexicana* 32, no. 1 (1982): 89–105.

———. *The Medieval Heritage of Mexico.* Translated by Frances M. López-Morillas. New York: Fordham University Press, 1992.

Weeks, John M. "Karl Hermann Berendt: Colección de manuscritos lingüísticos de Centroamérica y Mesoamérica," *Mesoamérica: Revista del Centro de Investigaciones Regionales de Mesoamérica* 36 (1998): 619–93.

———. *The Library of Daniel Garrison Brinton.* Philadelphia: University of Pennsylvania Museum of Archaeology and Anthropology, 2002.

West, Delno C. "Medieval Ideas of Apocalyptic Mission and the Early Franciscans in Mexico." *Americas* 45, no. 3 (1989): 293–313.

Whalen, Brett Edward. *Dominion of God: Christendom and Apocalypse in the Middle Ages.* Cambridge, MA: Harvard University Press, 2009.

———. "Joachim the Theorist of History and Society." In *A Companion to Joachim of Fiore,* edited by Matthias Riedl, 88–108. Leiden, Netherlands: Brill, 2018.

Whalen, Gretchen. "An Annotated Translation of a Colonial Yucatec Manuscript: On Religious and Cosmological Topics by a Native Author." Foundation for the Advancement of Mesoamerican Studies, 2002. http://www.famsi.org/reports/01017.

White, Thomas Joseph. *The Light of Christ: An Introduction to Catholicism.* Washington, DC: Catholic University of America Press, 2017.

White, Richard. *The Middle Ground: Indians, Empires, and Republics in the Great Lakes Region, 1650–1815.* New York: Cambridge University Press, 1991.

Williams, John. "Purpose and Imagery in the Apocalypse Commentary of Beatus of Liébana." In *The Apocalypse in the Middle Ages,* edited by Richard K. Emmerson and Bernard McGinn, 217–33. Ithaca, NY: Cornell University Press, 1992.

Woolf, Steven H., and Heidi Schoomaker. "Life Expectancy and Mortality Rates in the United States, 1959–2017." *Journal of the American Medical Association* 322, no. 20 (2019): 1996–2016

Wooden, Cindy. "The World Will End with Peace, not Annihilation, Pope Francis says." *National Catholic Reporter,* November 26, 2014. https://www.ncronline.org/blogs/francis-chronicles/world-will-end-peace-not-annihilation-pope-francis-says.

Yáñez Rosales, Rosa H. "De 'Dios,' 'pecados,' 'demonios' y otros vocablos en dos confesionarios en lengua náhuatl del siglo XVII." *Indiana* 35, no. 2 (2018): 119–49.

Zeller, Benjamin E. *Prophets and Protons: New Religious Movements and Science in Late Twentieth-Century America.* New York: New York University Press, 2010.

Zulaica Gárate, Román. *Los franciscanos y la imprenta en México en el siglo XVI.* Mexico City: Universidad Nacional Autónoma de México, 1991.

Index

CPSIA information can be obtained
at www.ICGtesting.com
Printed in the USA
LVHW111722250722
724360LV00002B/76